The Definitive
Digital Art Collection

prime

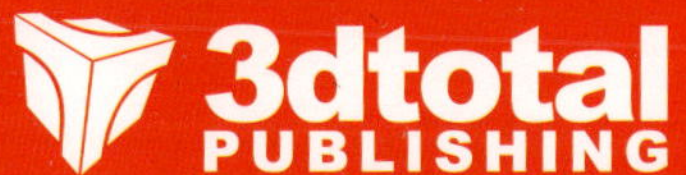

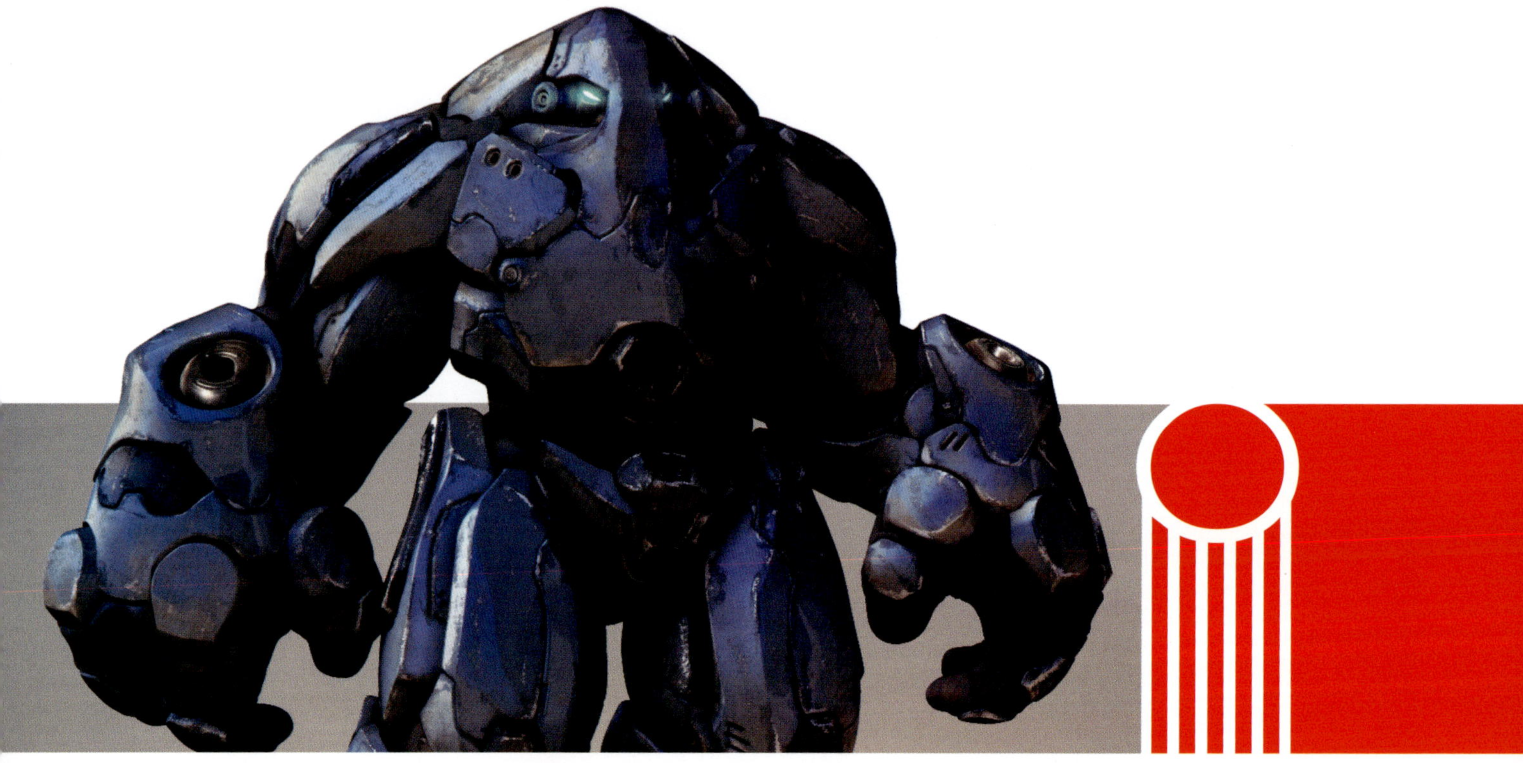

Prime Sci-fi

Whether in literature, movies or art, sci-fi has a huge following. So many of you reading this will remember the first time that you saw *Star Wars*, and the huge impact and influence that it had on your imagination. Artist creating sci-fi art can enjoy the fact that there are no limitations on their creativity as they design alien races, futuristic space transports and epic landscapes that can defy all of the rules of science. The art in this book demonstrates this vast creativity and will take you on the most amazing tour of the minds of the most inventive artists on this or any other planet!

The Definitive
Digital Art Collection

1

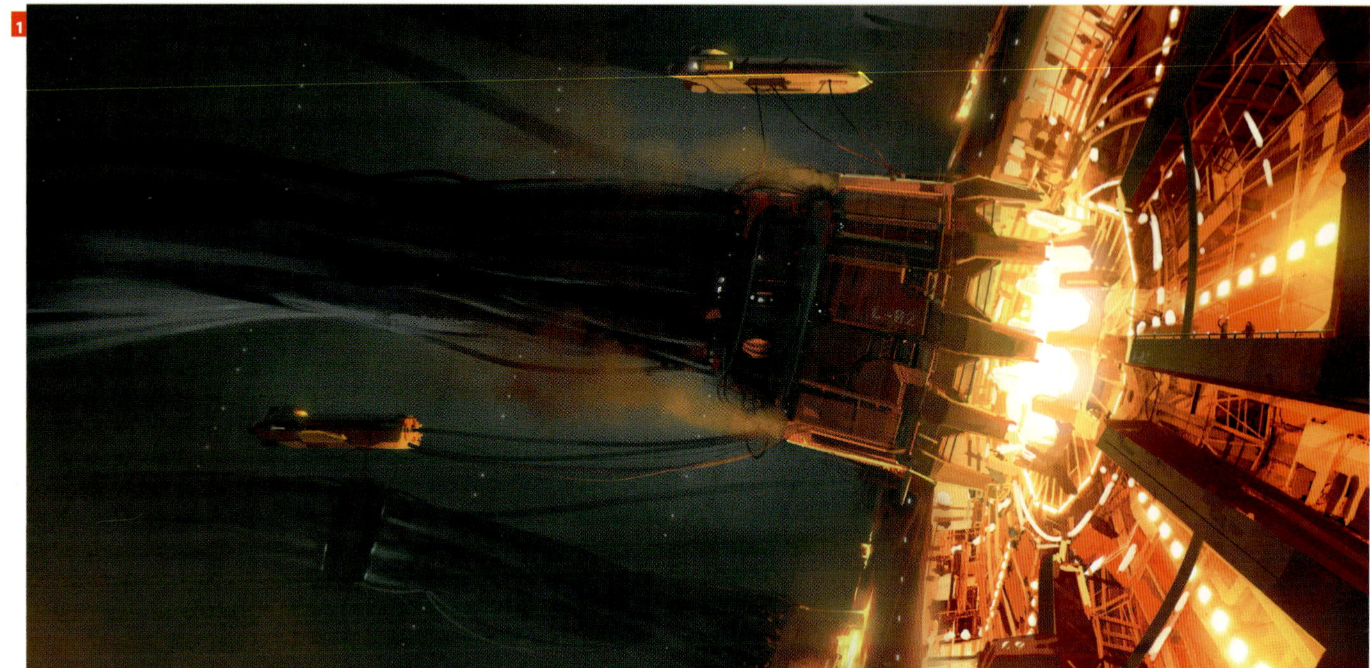

2

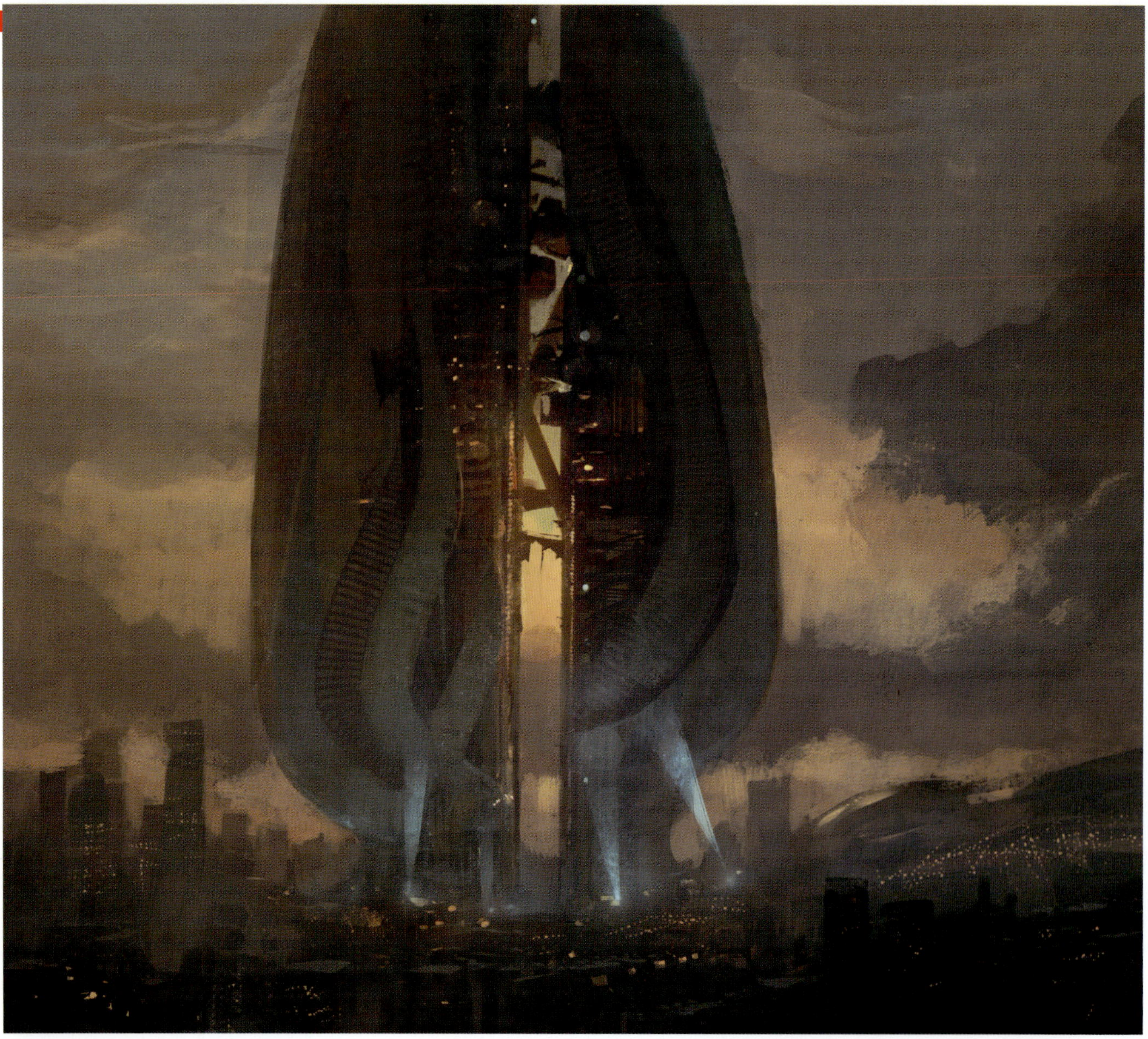

Connection 1.0 by Fabio Barretta Zungrone [1]
Photoshop CS5 | © Fabio Barretta Zungrone

Alpha by Vukasin Bagic [2]
Photoshop CS2 | © Vukasin Bagic

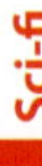

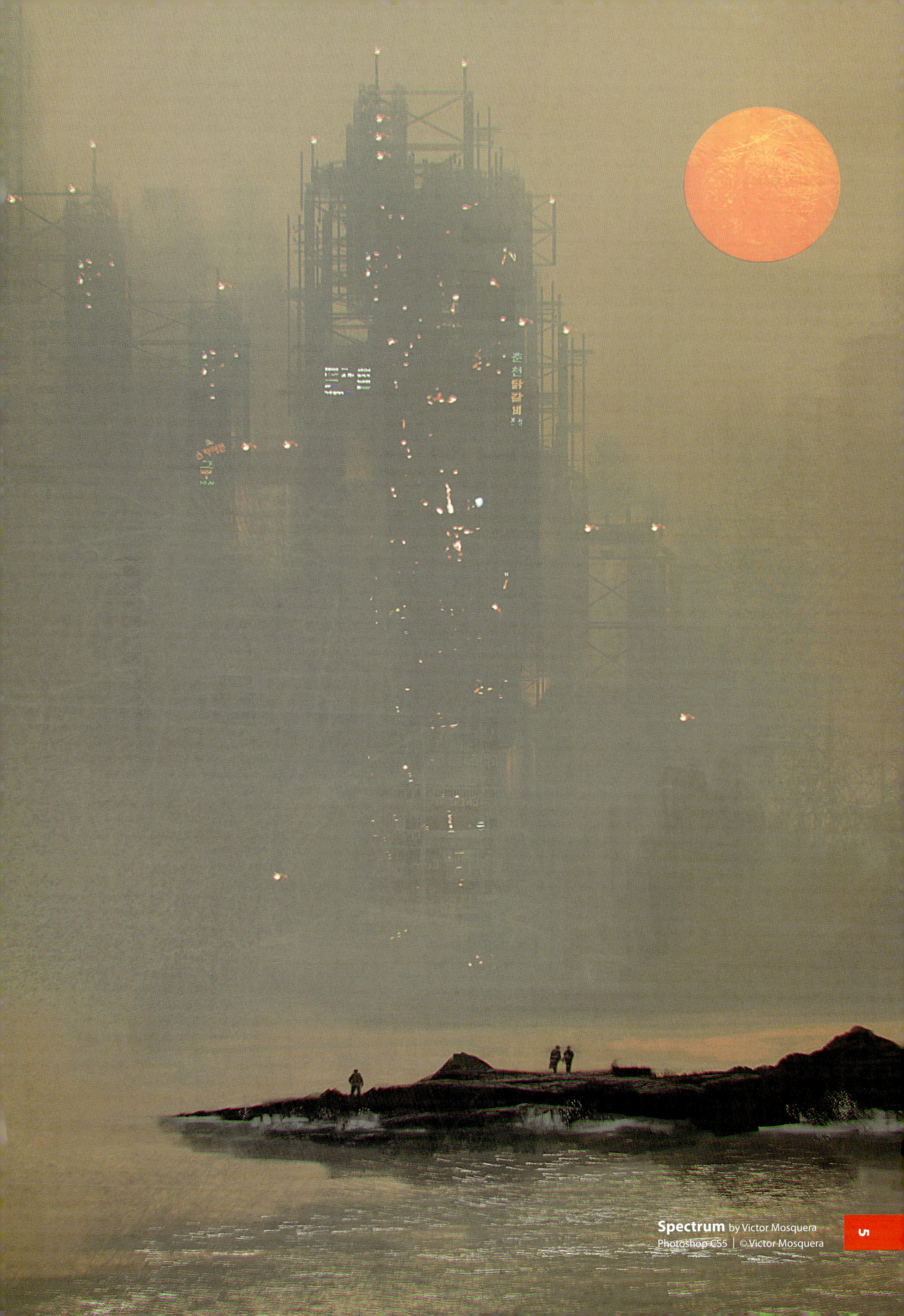

Spectrum by Victor Mosquera
Photoshop CS5 | © Victor Mosquera

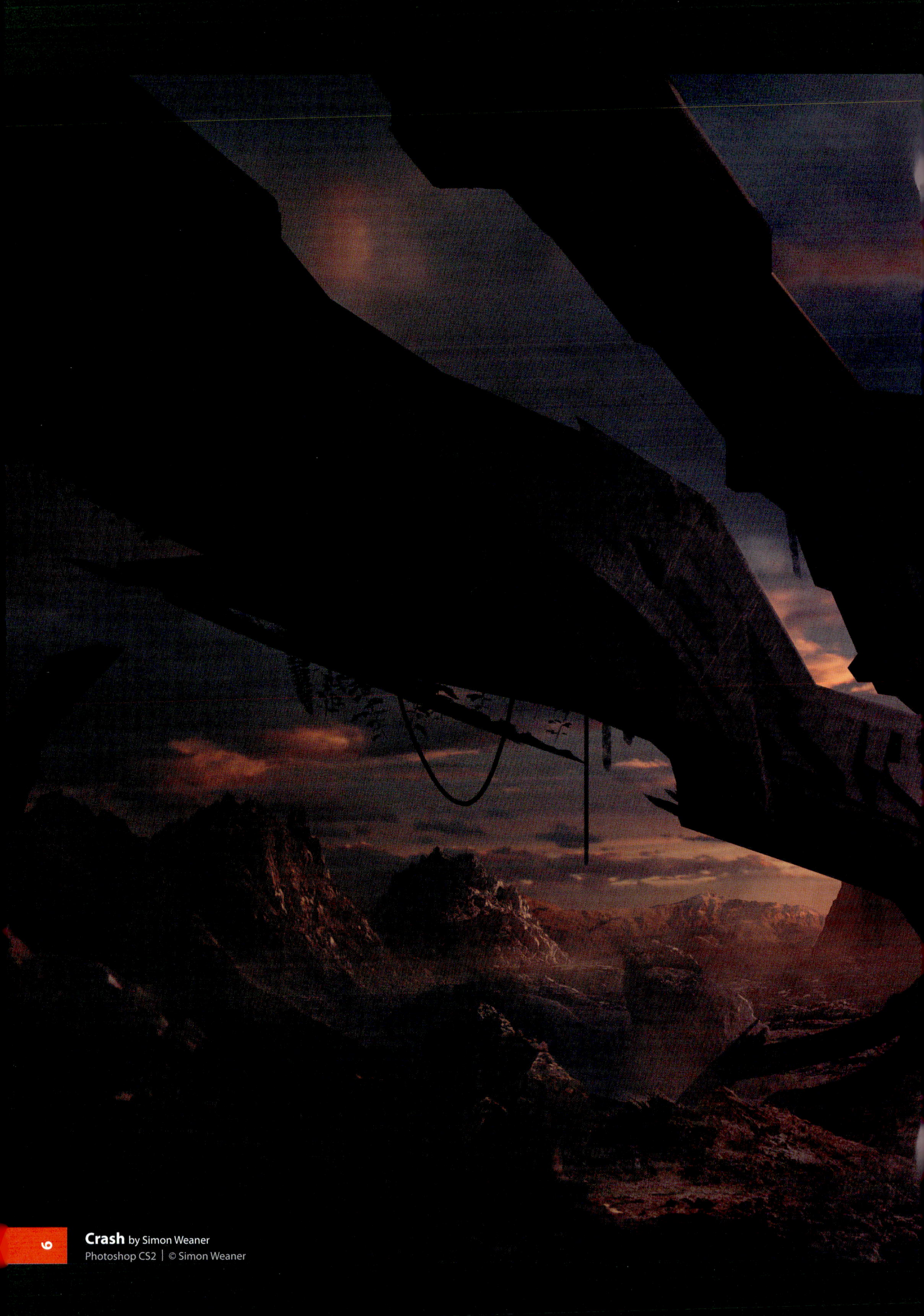

Crash by Simon Weaner
Photoshop CS2 | © Simon Weaner

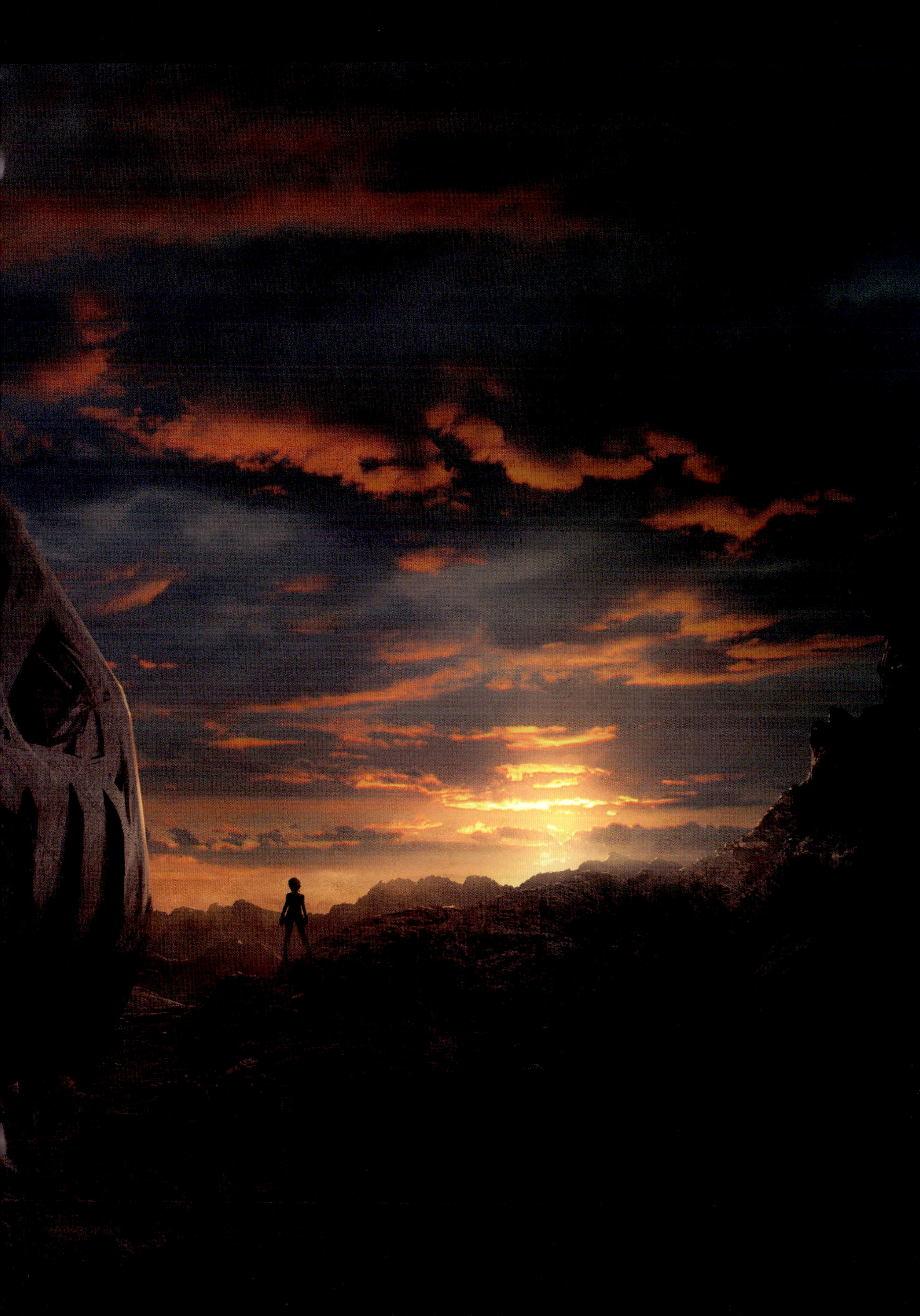

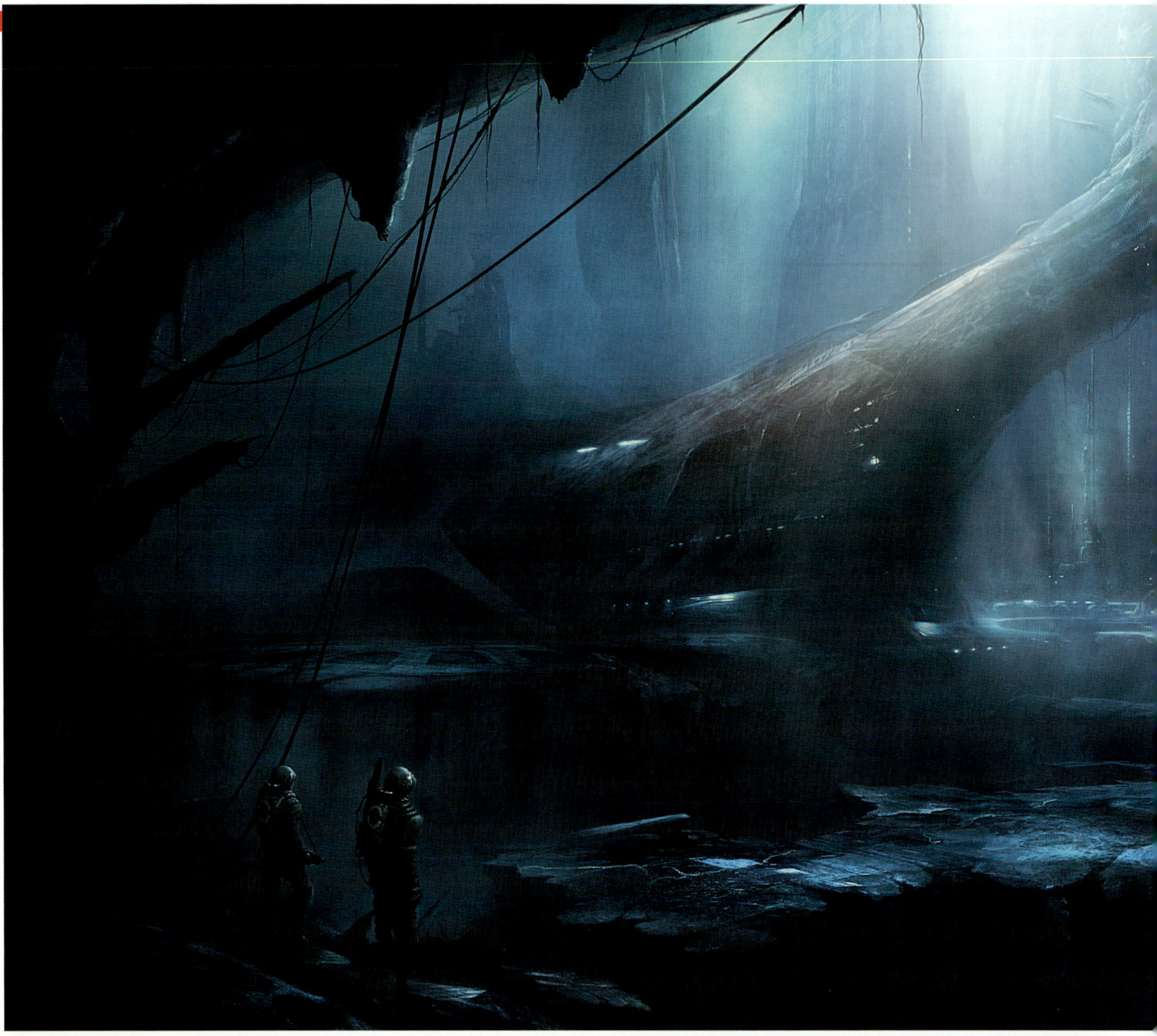

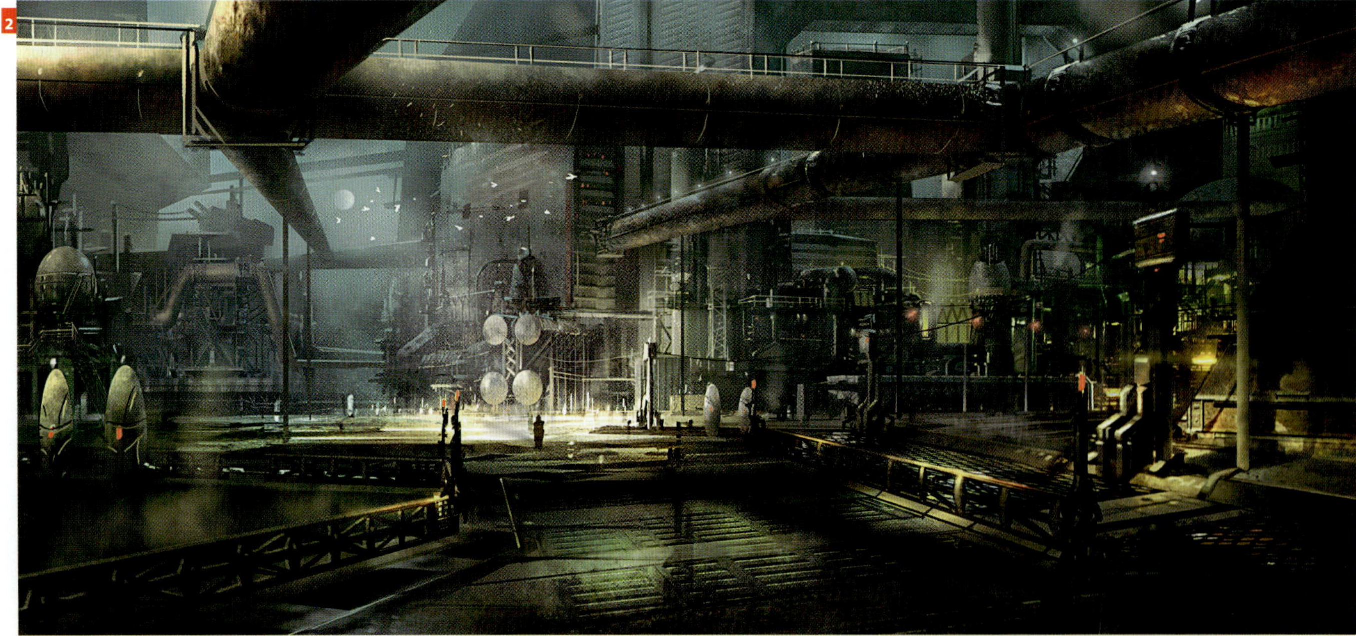

Breathe by Kentaro Kanamoto [1]
Photoshop CS2 | © Kentaro Kanamoto

Industrial Site by Gia Nguyen Hoang [2]
Photoshop CS5 | © GiaNguyen

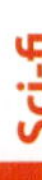

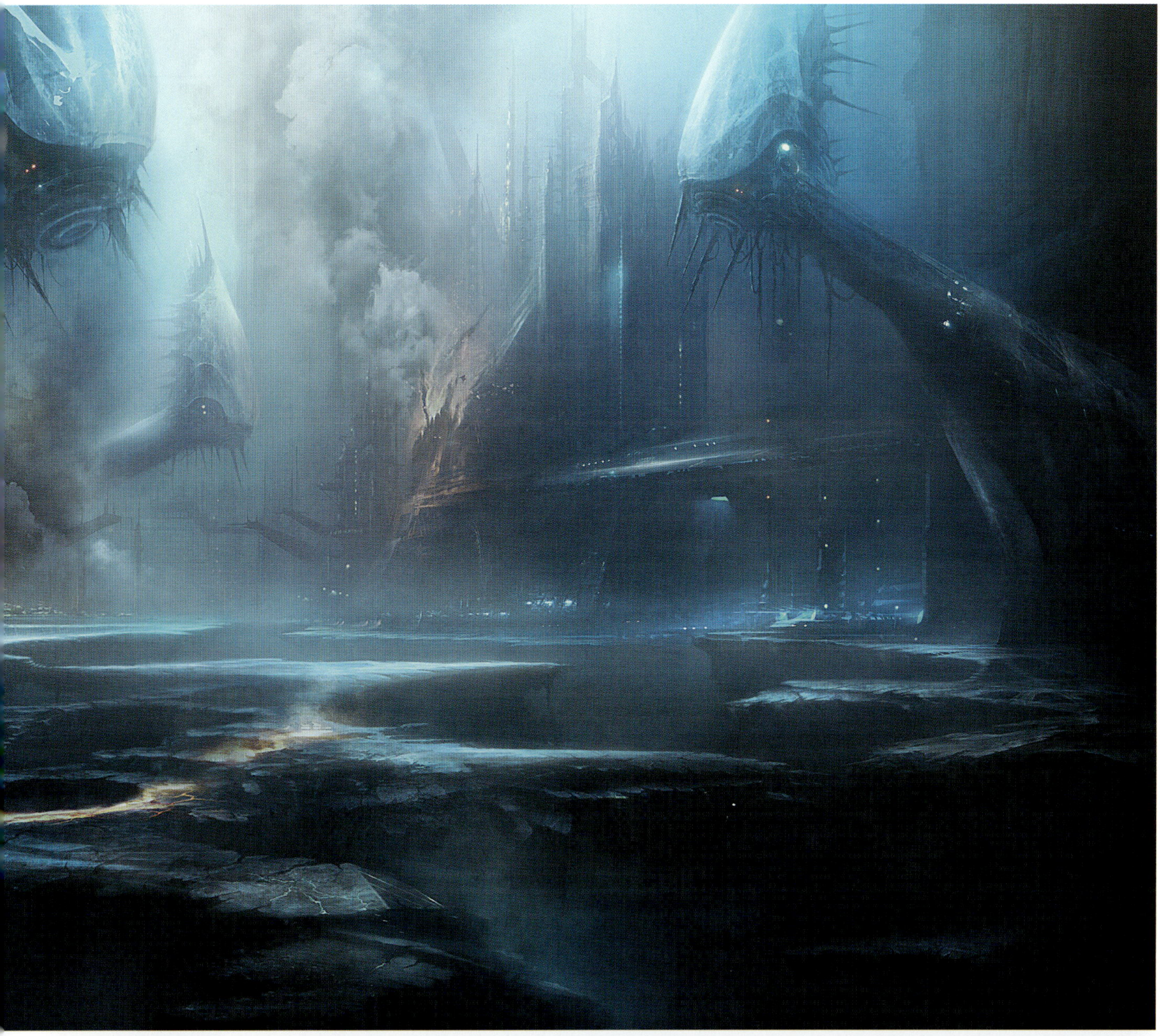

3

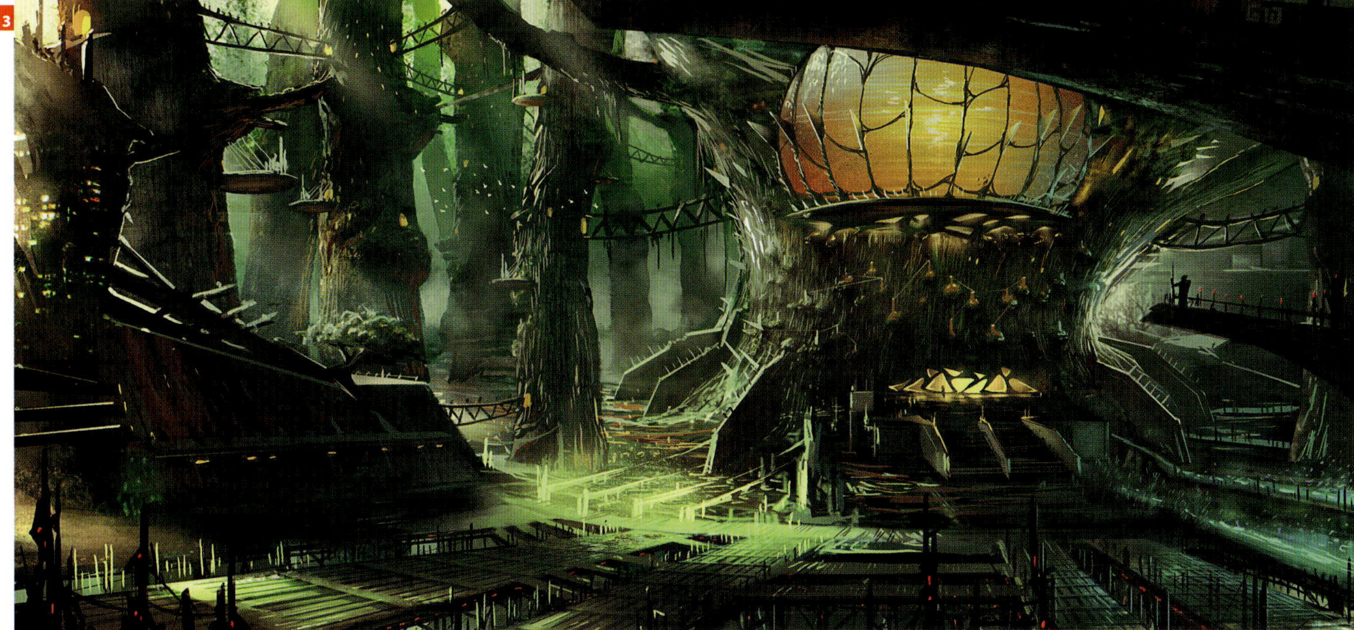

Tree House by Gia Nguyen Hoang [3]
Photoshop CS5 | © GiaNguyen

1

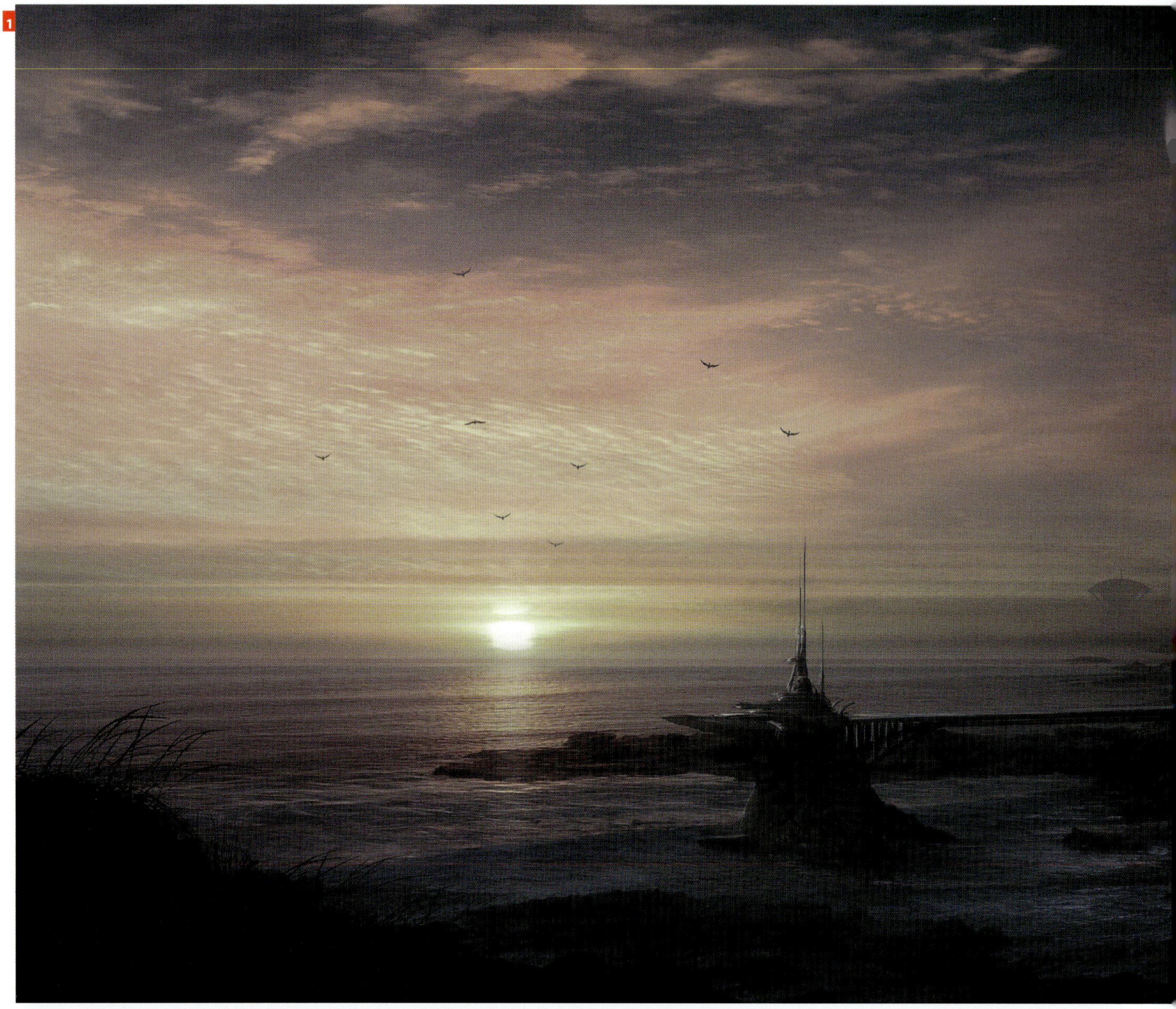

2

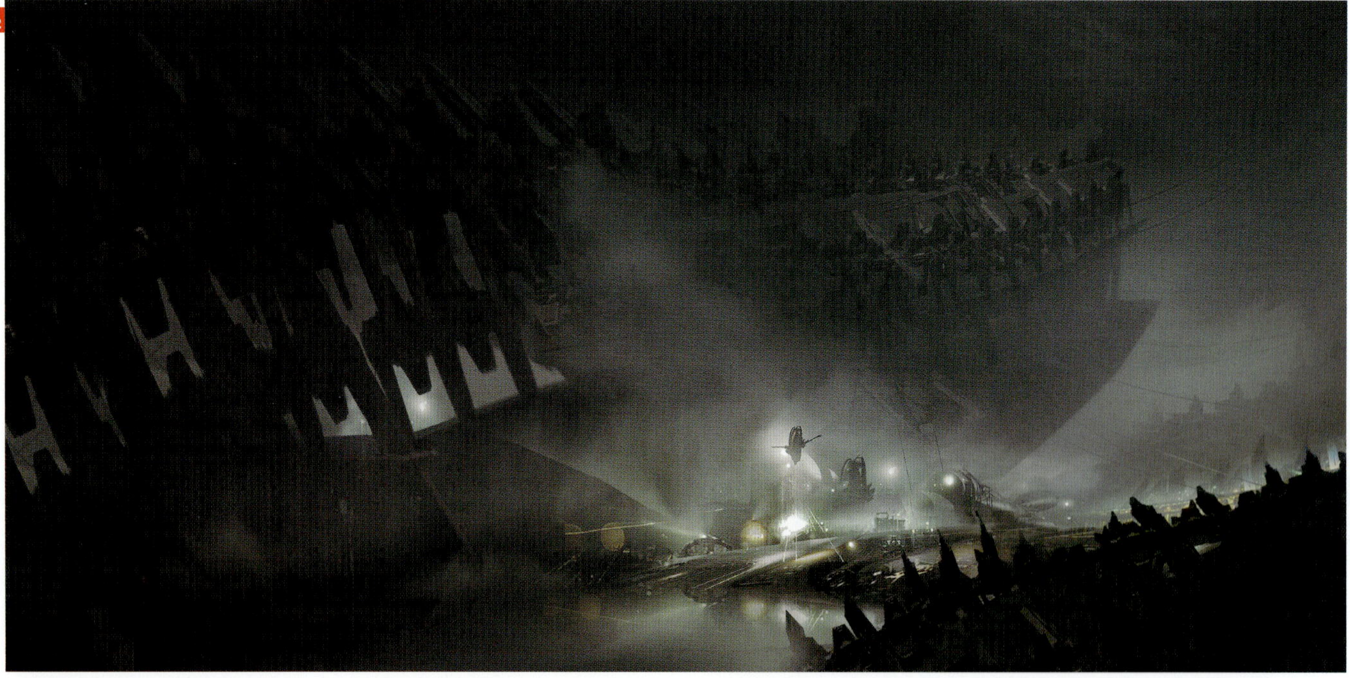

Guardians by Rudolf Herczog [1]
Cinema 4D R11 | © Rudolf Herczog

Salvaged by Levi Hopkins [2]
Photoshop CS5 | © Levi Hopkins

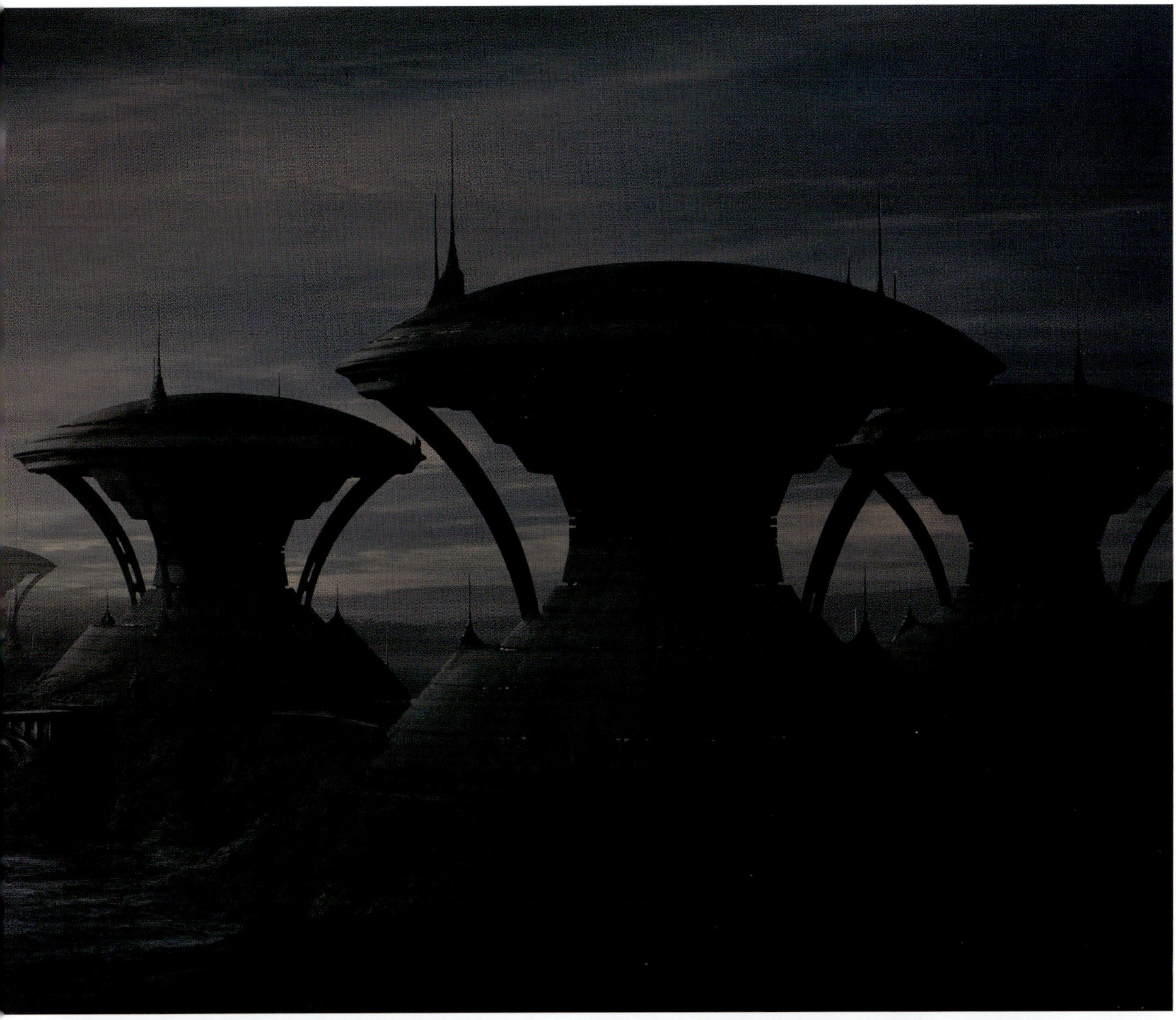

3

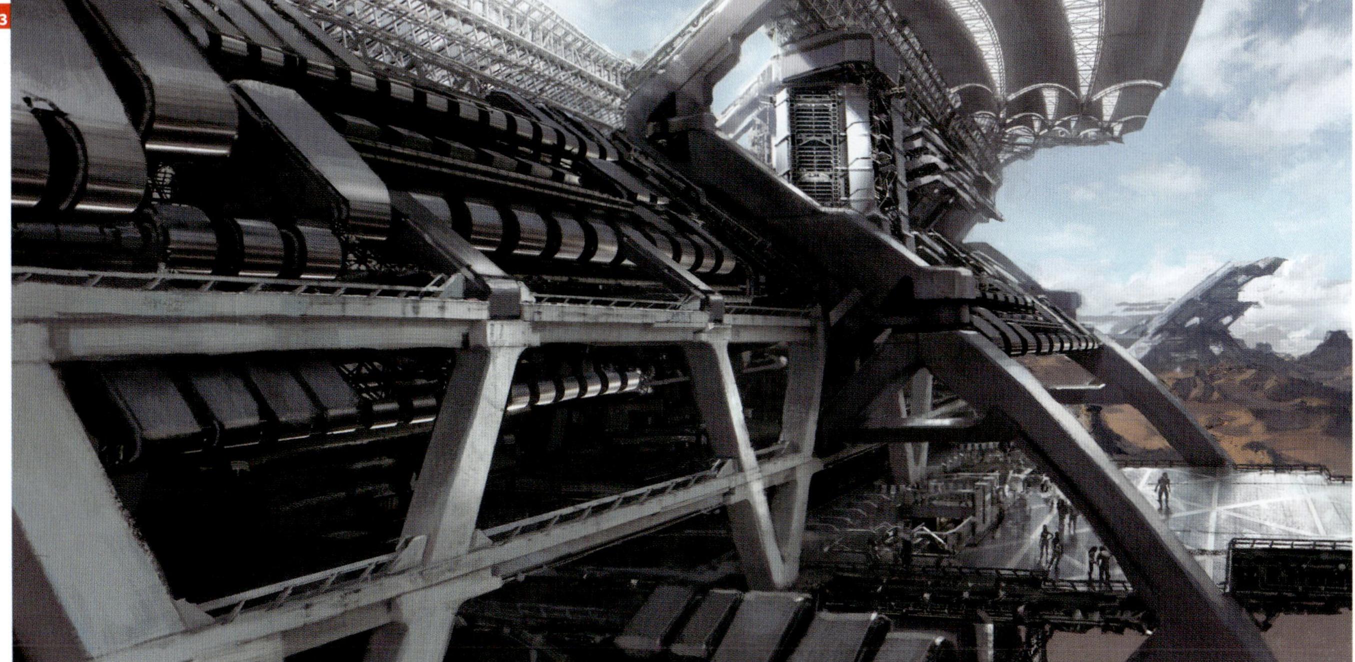

Rannoch by Brian Sum [3]

Photoshop CS3 |

1

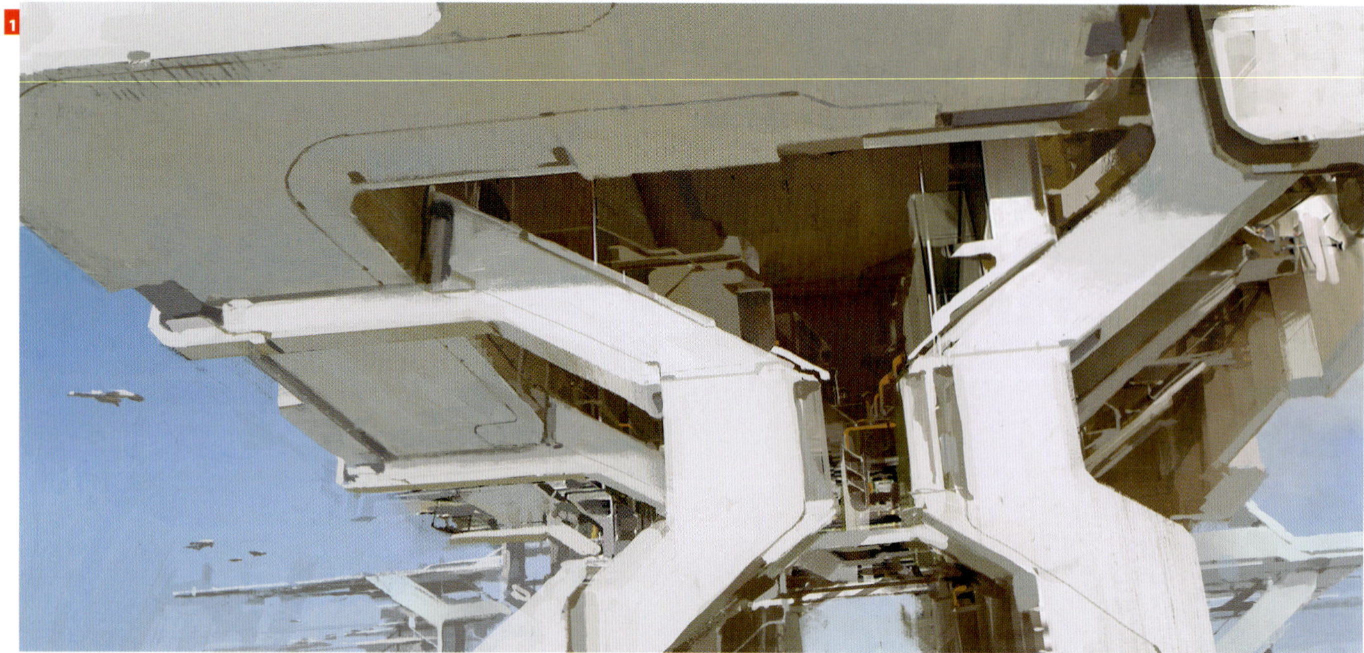

2

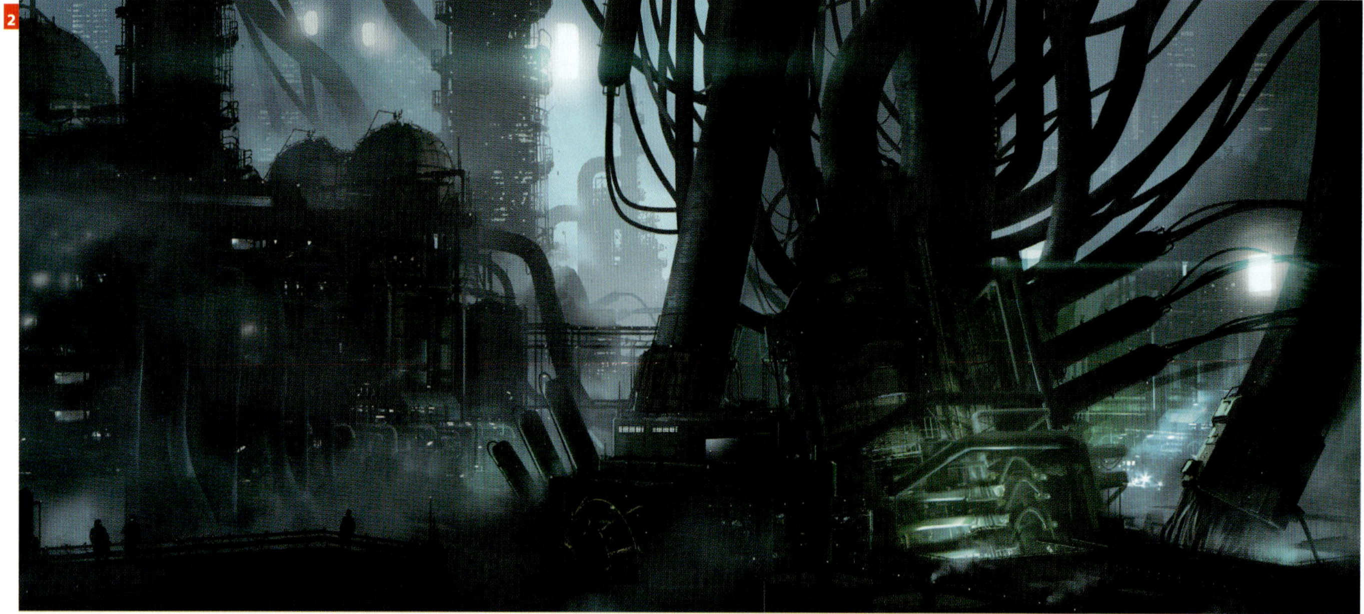

3

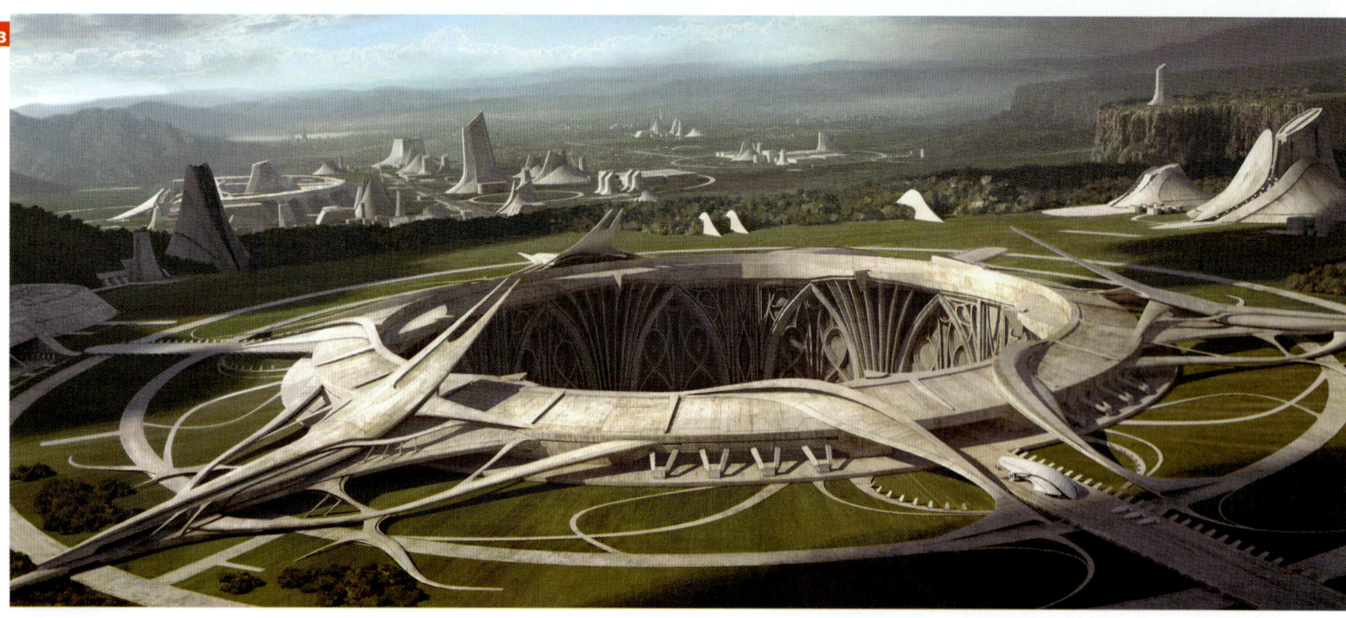

Sky City by Brian Sum [1]
Photoshop CS3 | © Brian Sum

City's Heart by Fabio Barretta Zungrone [2]
Photoshop CS5 | © Fabio Barretta Zungrone

Temple by Joon Hyung Ahn [3]
Photoshop CS3 | © JoonAhn

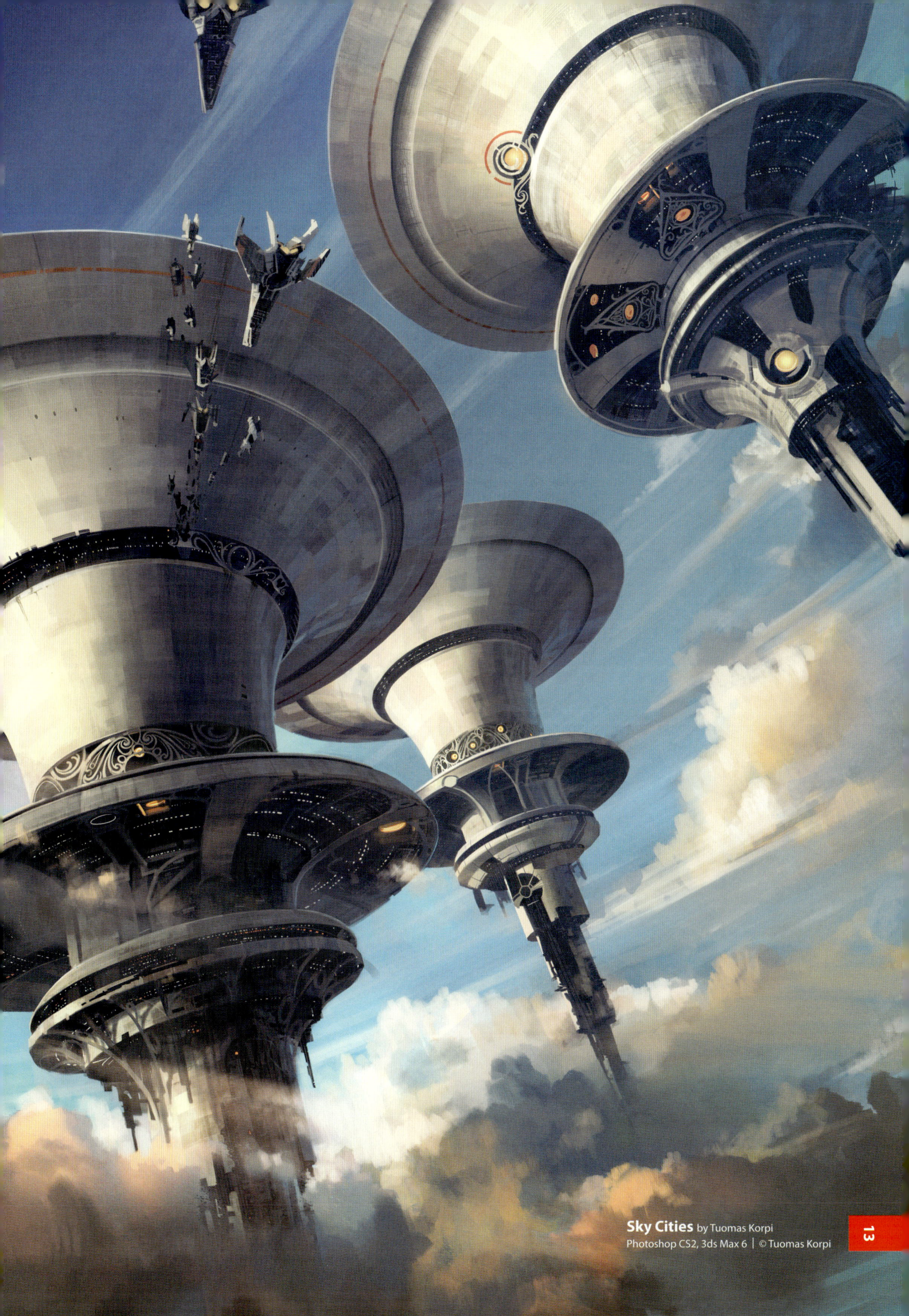

Sky Cities by Tuomas Korpi
Photoshop CS2, 3ds Max 6 | © Tuomas Korpi

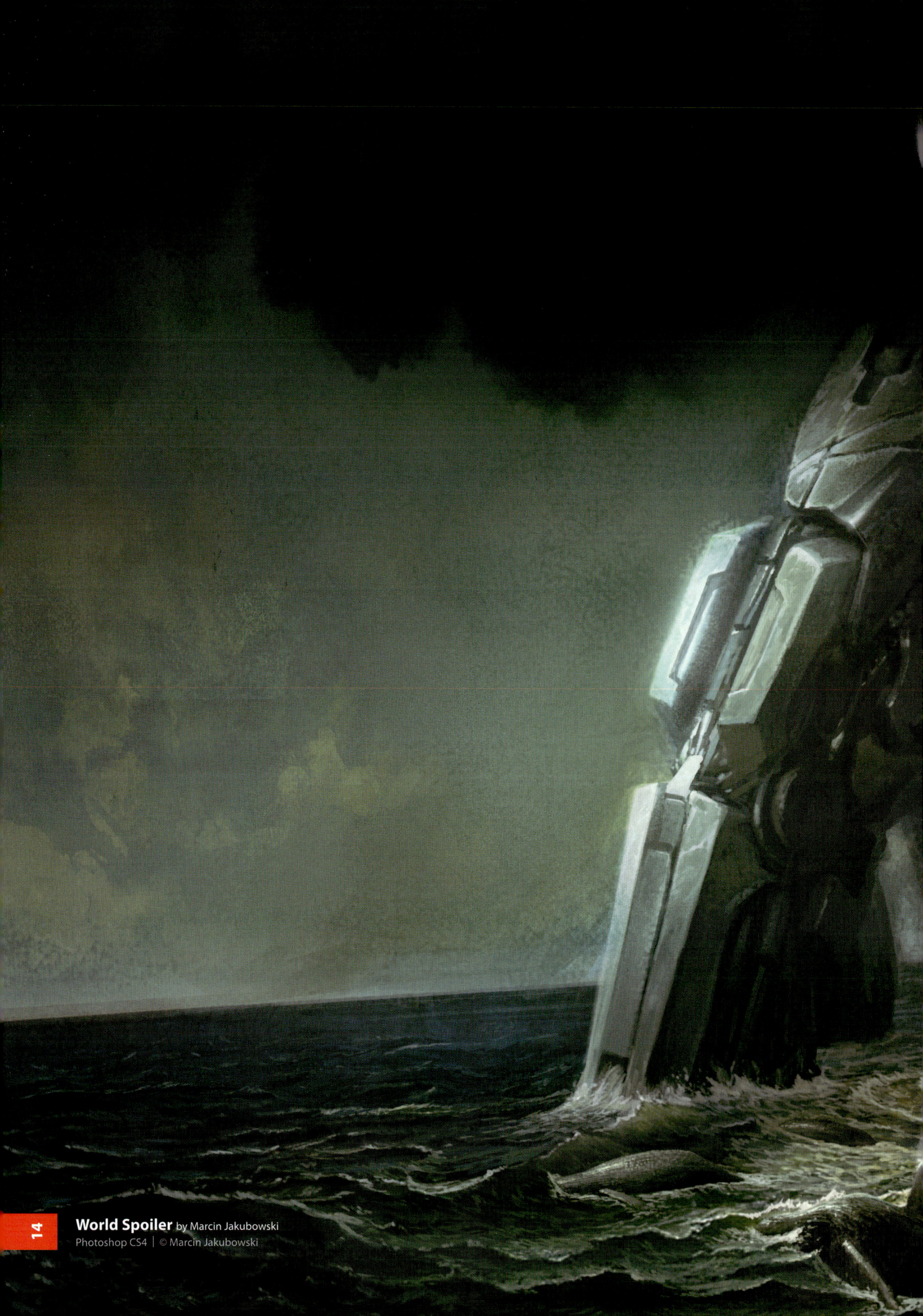

World Spoiler by Marcin Jakubowski
Photoshop CS4 |

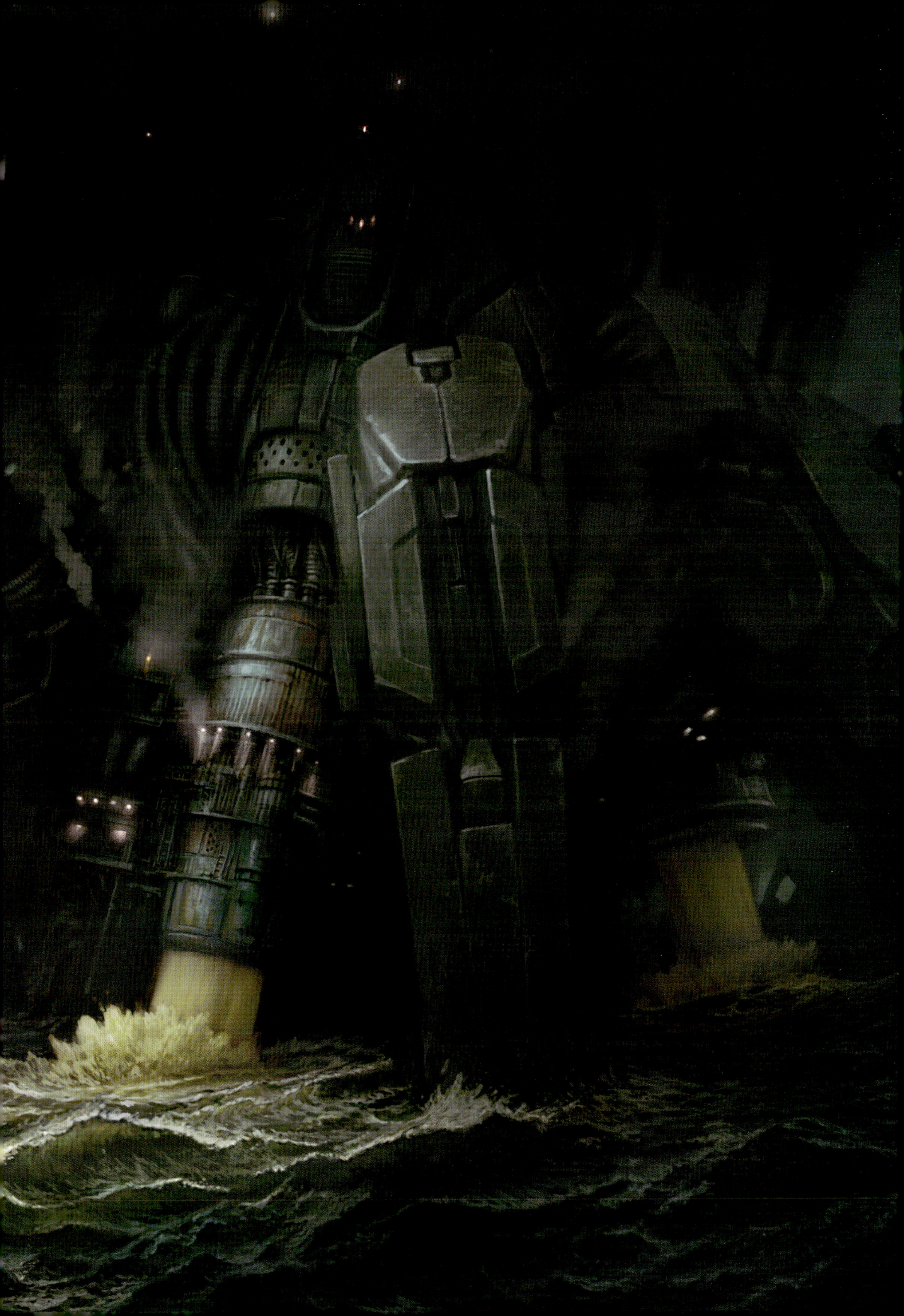

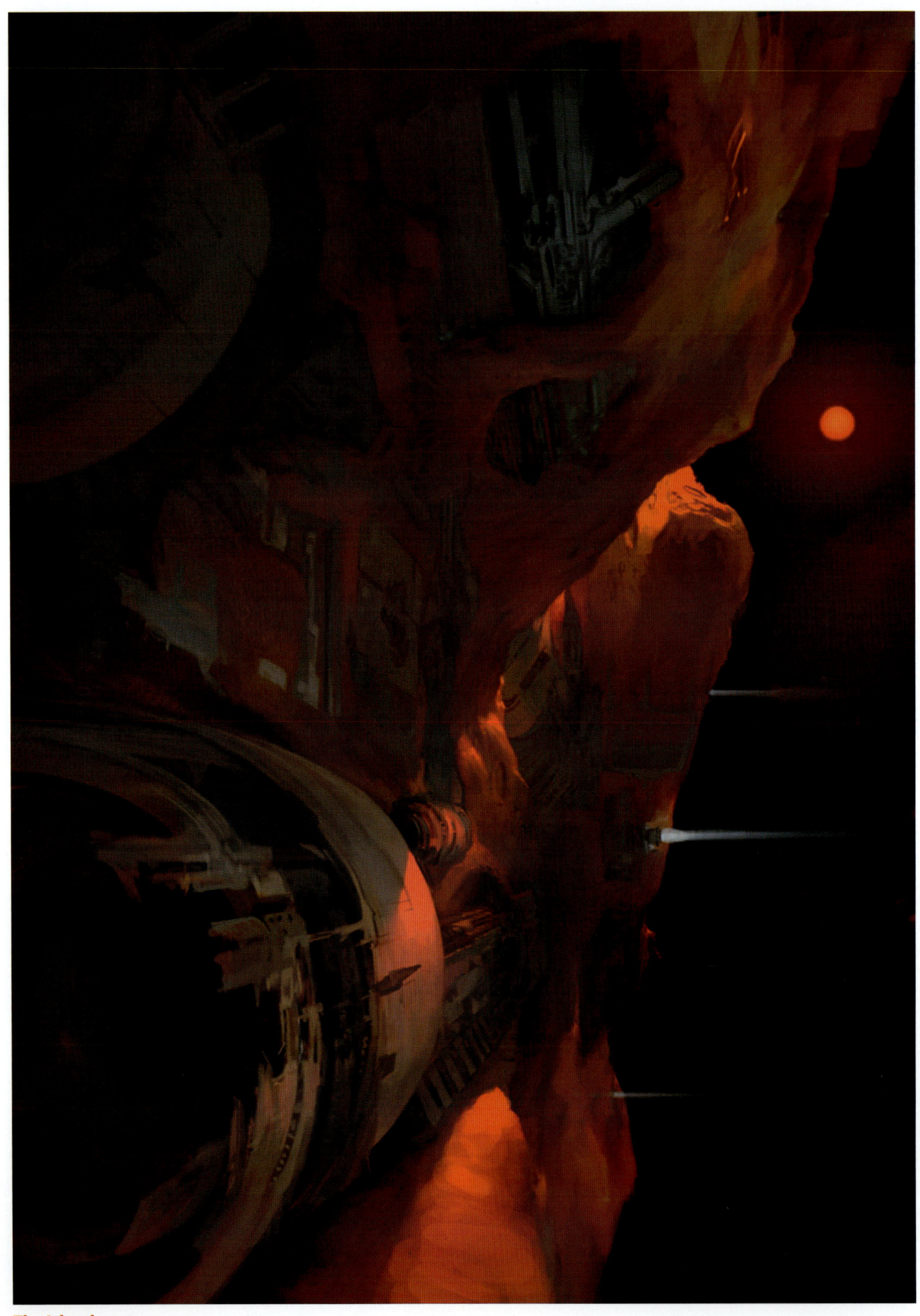

The Island by Dan Ghiordanescu
Photoshop CS3 | © danghiordanescu

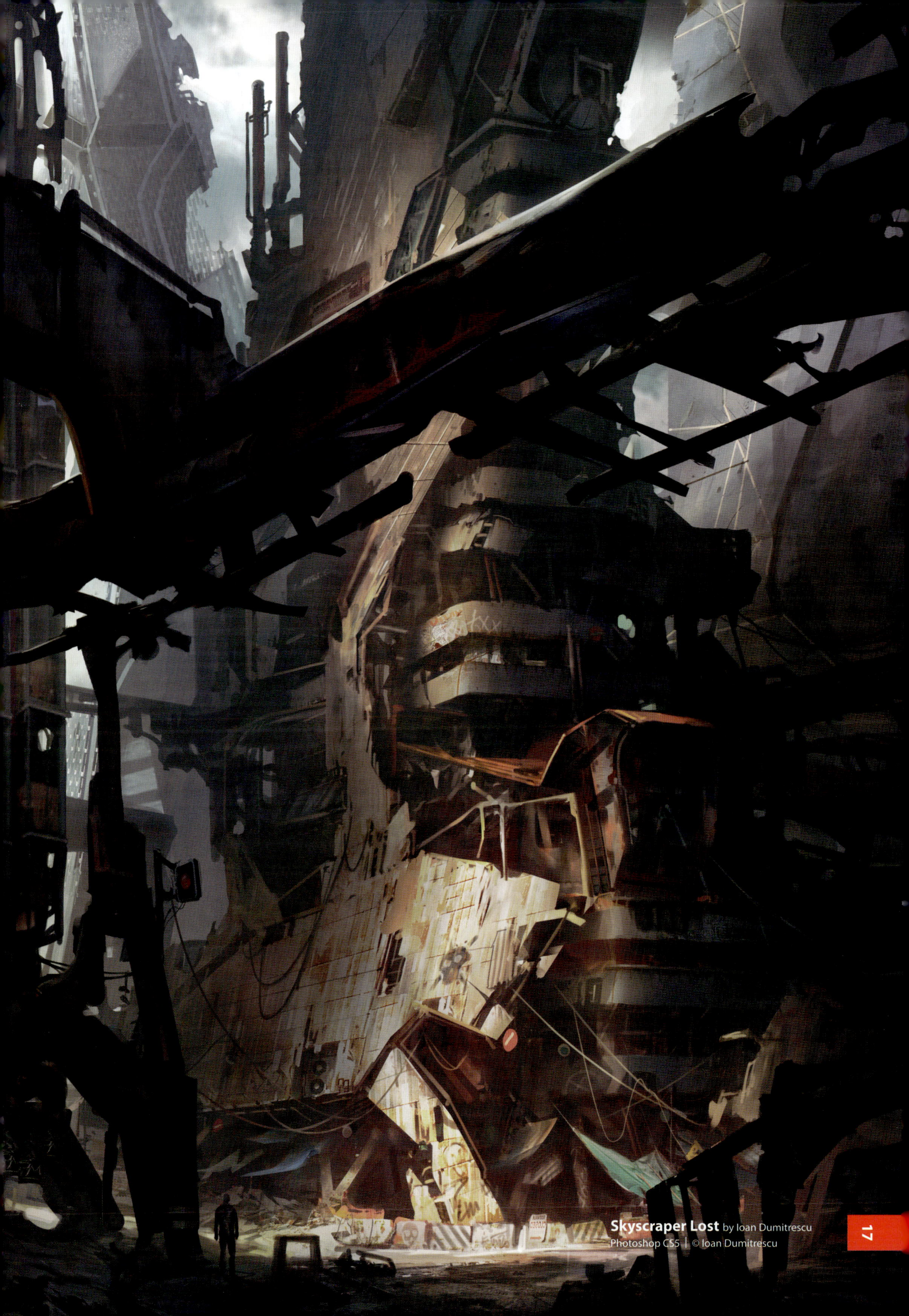

Skyscraper Lost by Ioan Dumitrescu
Photoshop CS5 | © Ioan Dumitrescu

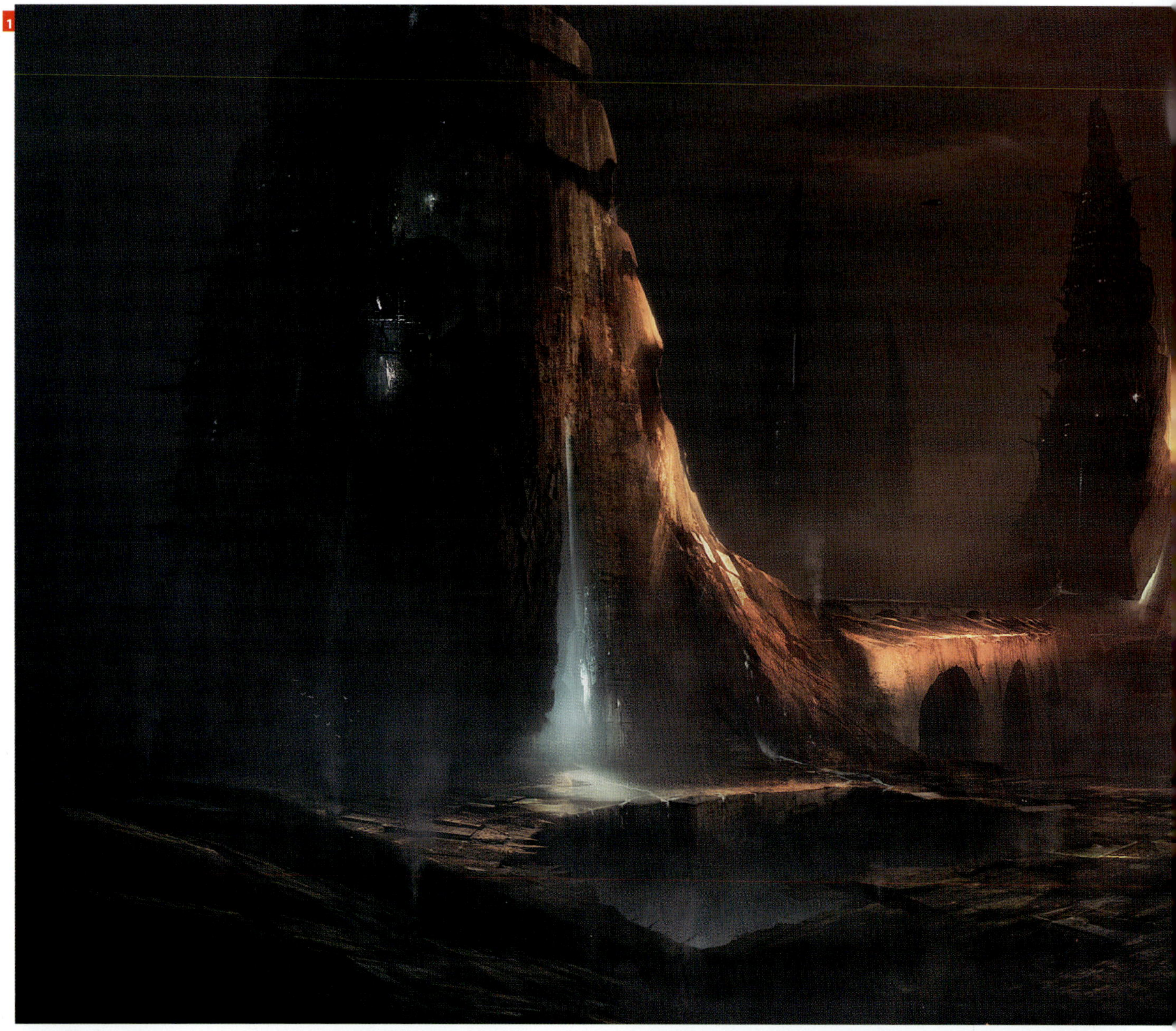

1

2

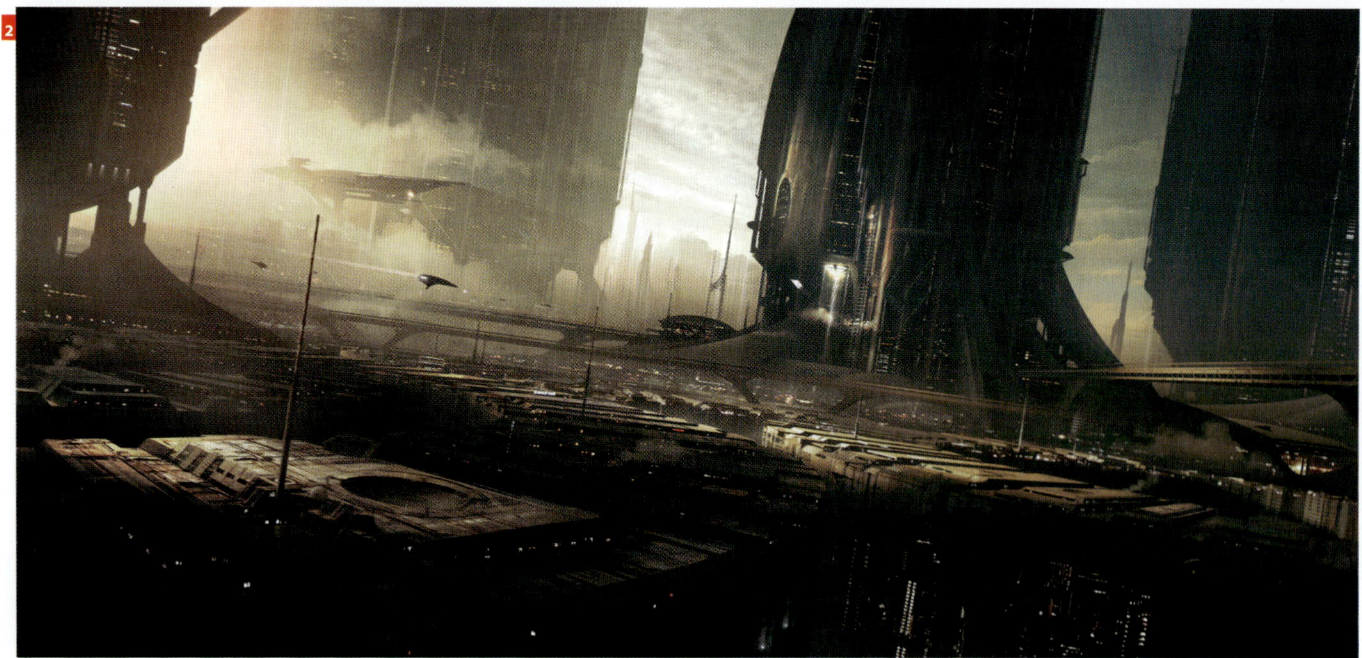

Distant Amber by Kentaro Kanamoto [1]
Photoshop CS2 | © Kentaro Kanamoto

Downtown by Andrée Wallin [2]
Photoshop CS3 | © Andrée Wallin

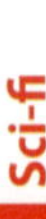

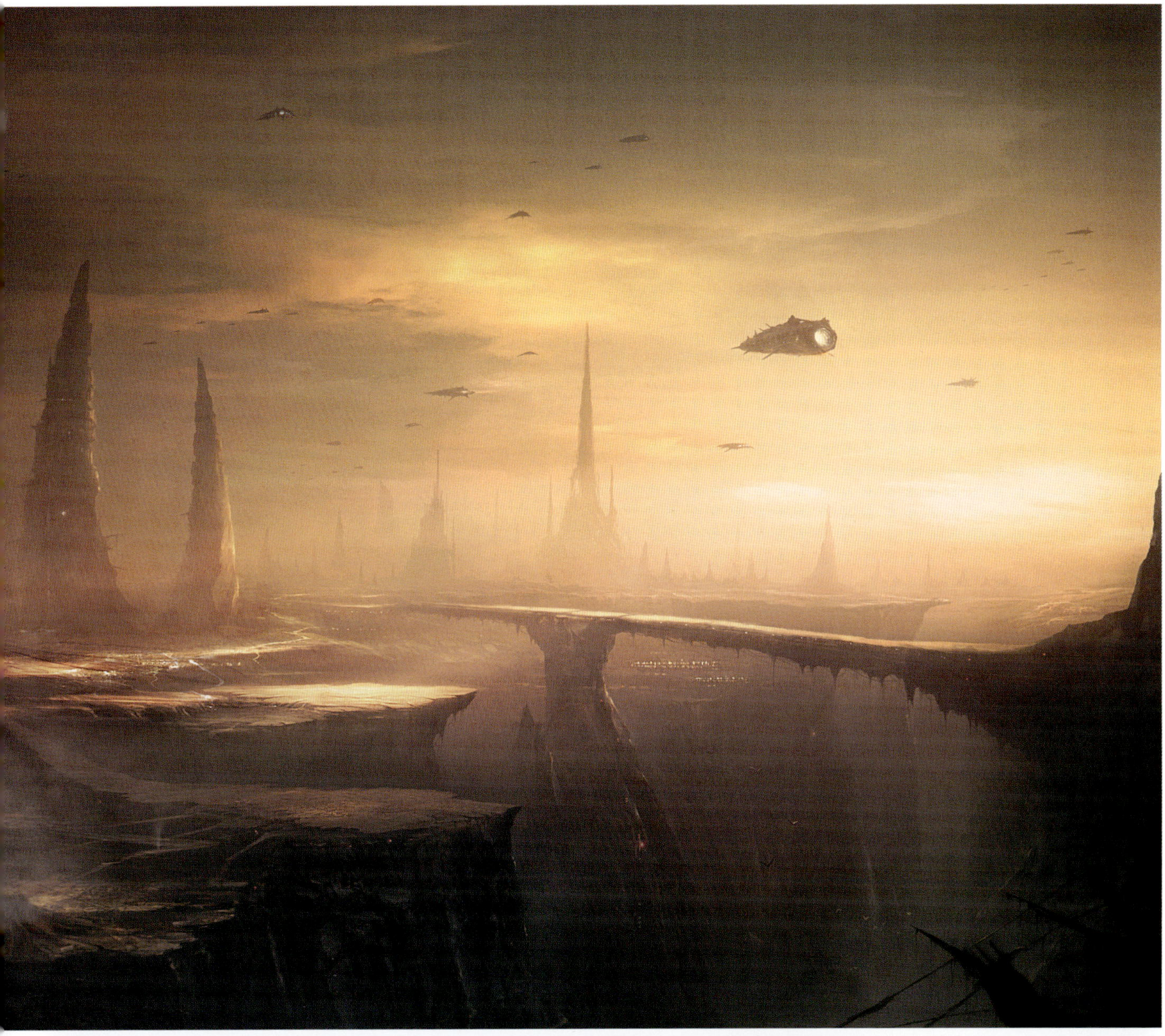

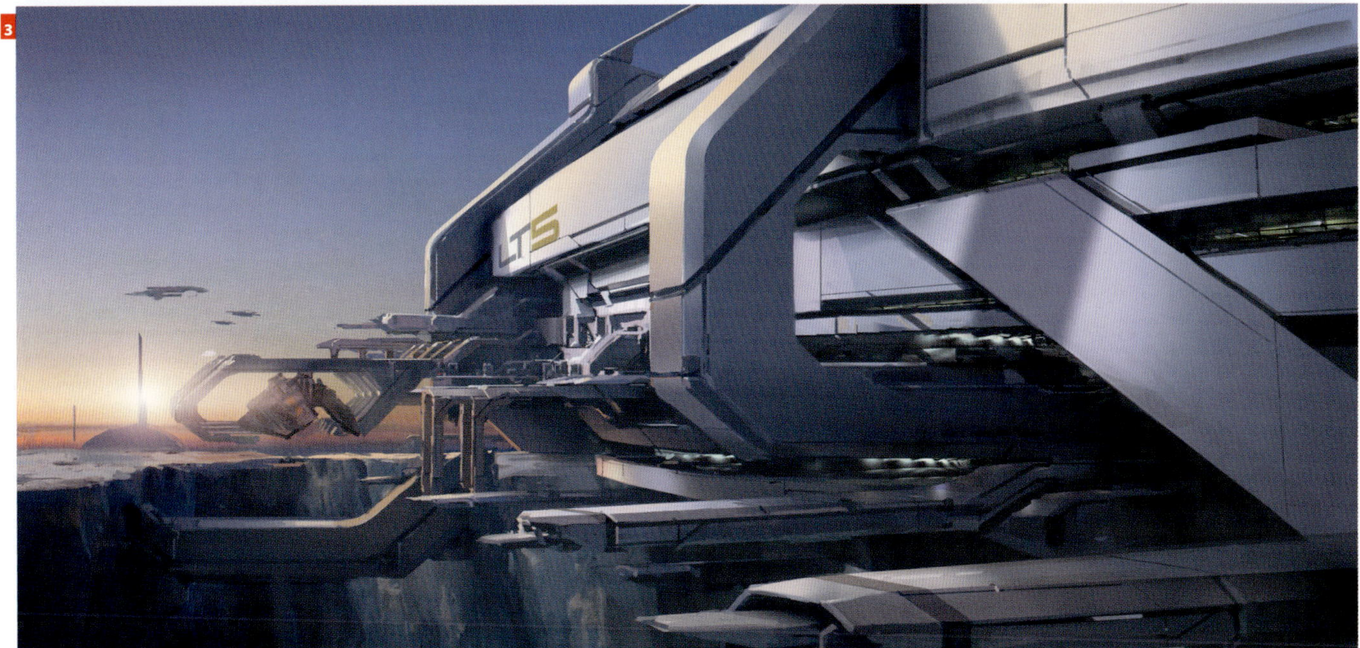

Cerberus Base by Brian Sum [3]

Photoshop CS3 | © 2012 EA International (Studio and Publishing) Ltd. *Mass Effect*, the *Mass Effect* logo, BioWare and the BioWare logo are trademarks of EA International (Studio and Publishing) Ltd. EA and the EA logo are trademarks of Electronic Arts Inc. All other trademarks are the property of their respective owners.

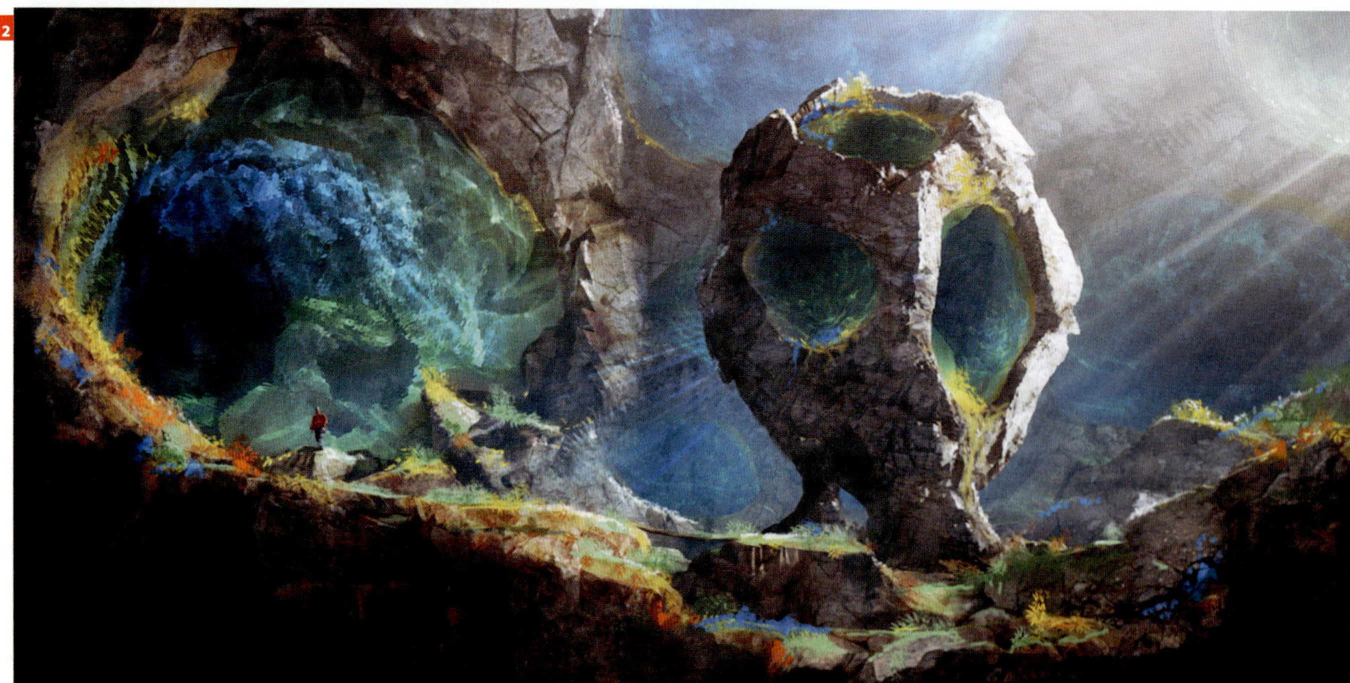

Cove Village by Theo Prins [1]
Photoshop CS3 | © Theo Prins

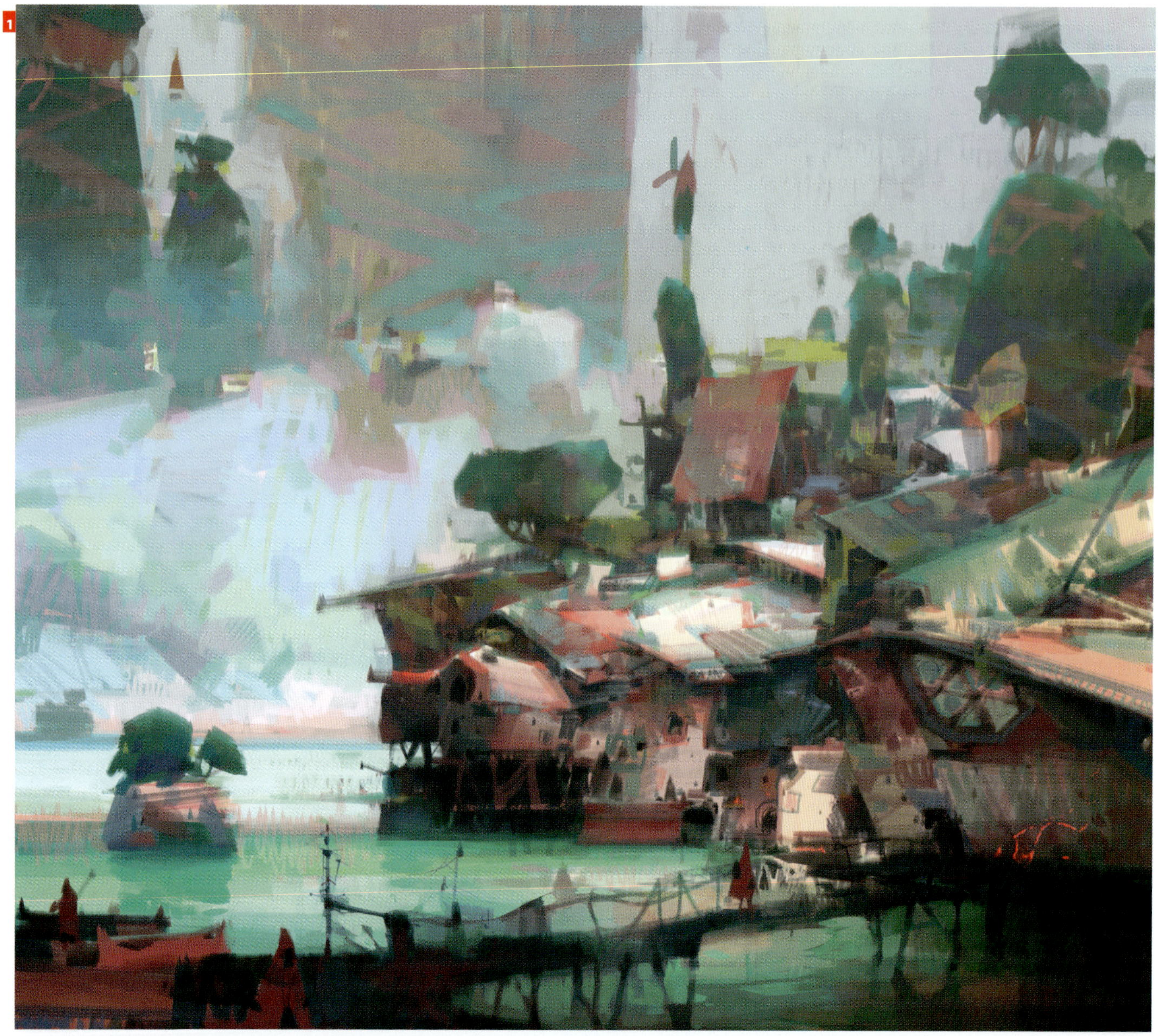

The Hub by Andrzej Sykut [2]
3ds Max 2011, Photoshop CS5 | © Andrzej Sykut

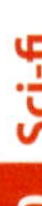
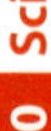

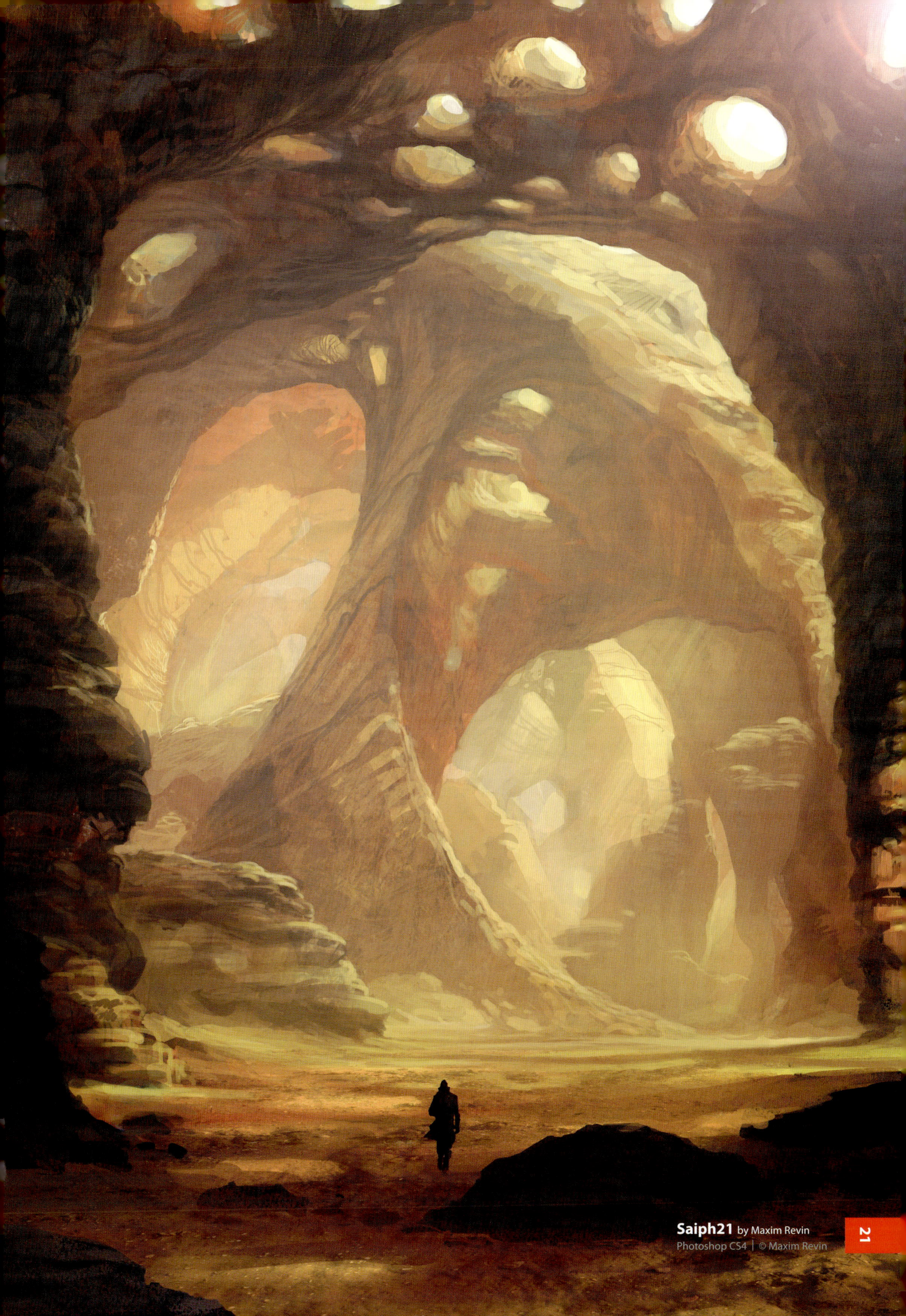

Saiph21 by Maxim Revin
Photoshop CS4 | © Maxim Revin

1

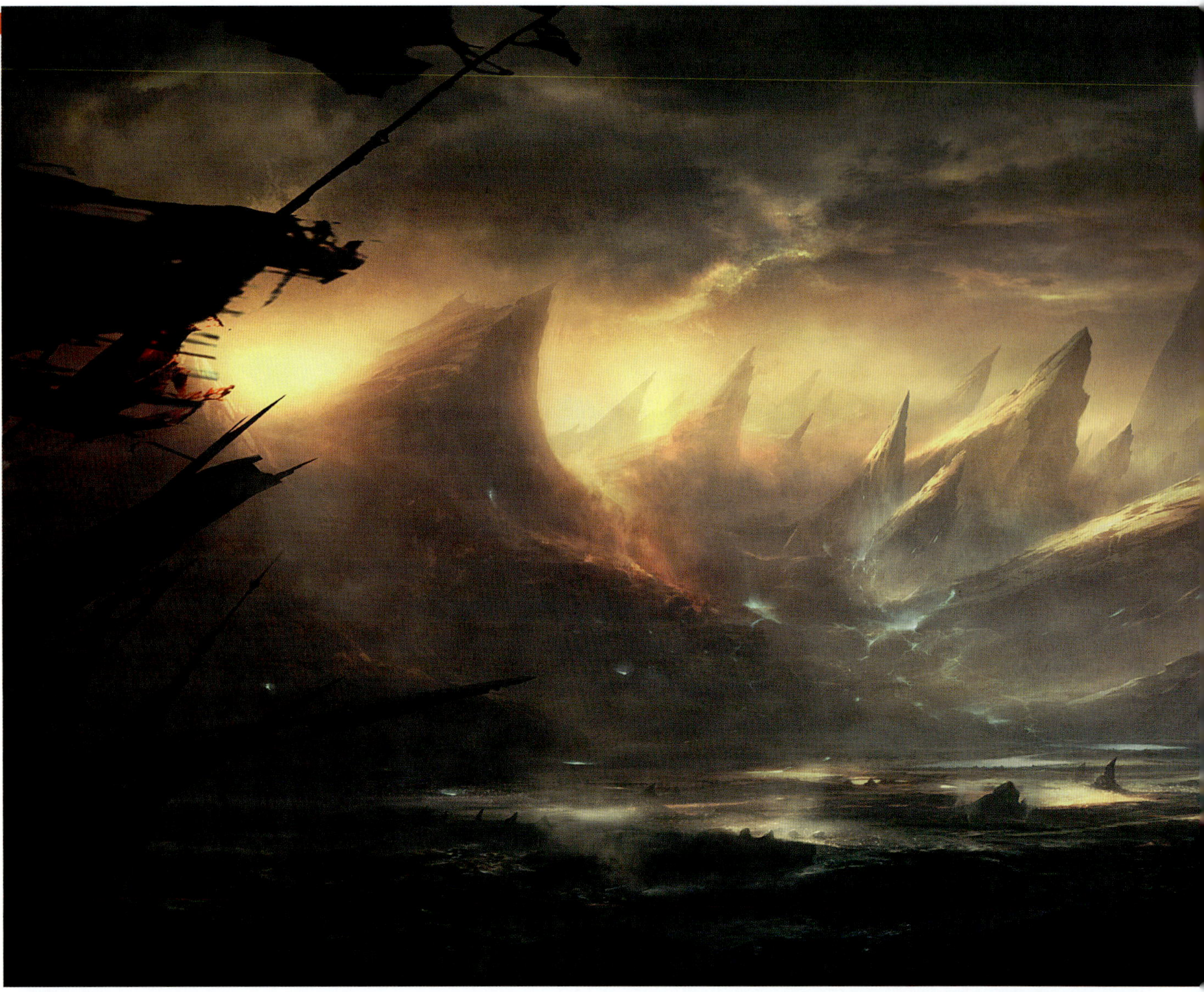

2

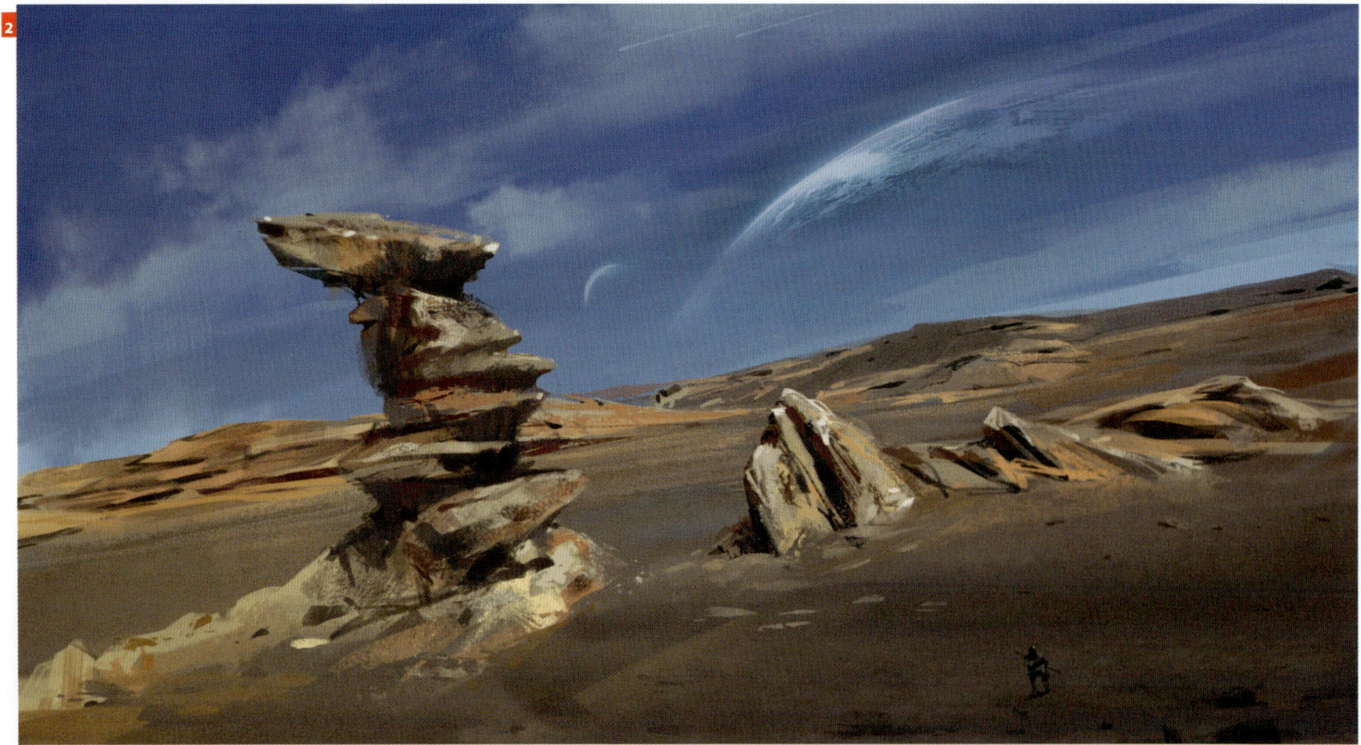

Evolvo by Kentaro Kanamoto [1]
Photoshop CS2 | © Kentaro Kanamoto

Journey by Ray Jin [2]
Photoshop CS5 | © Ray Jin

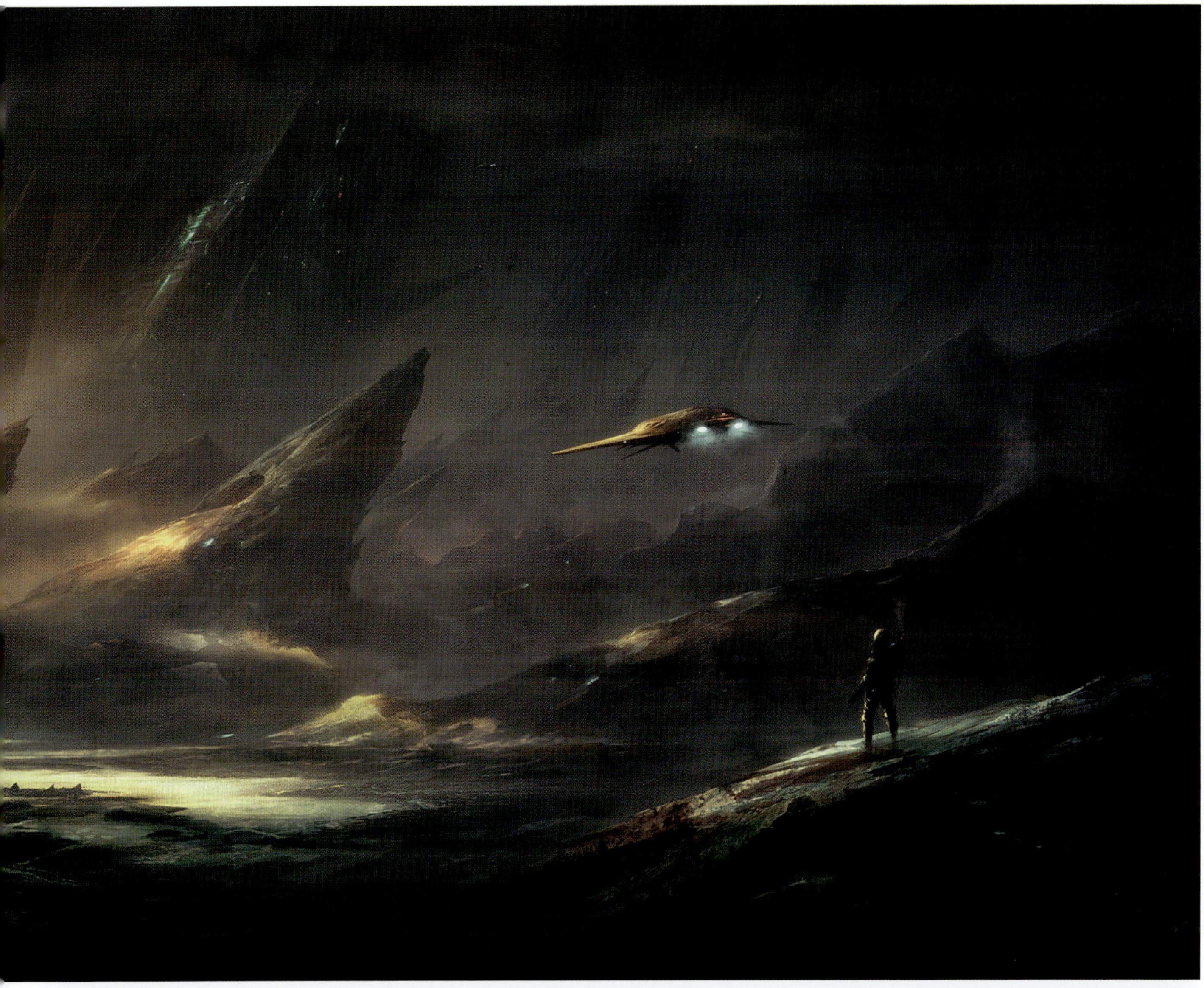

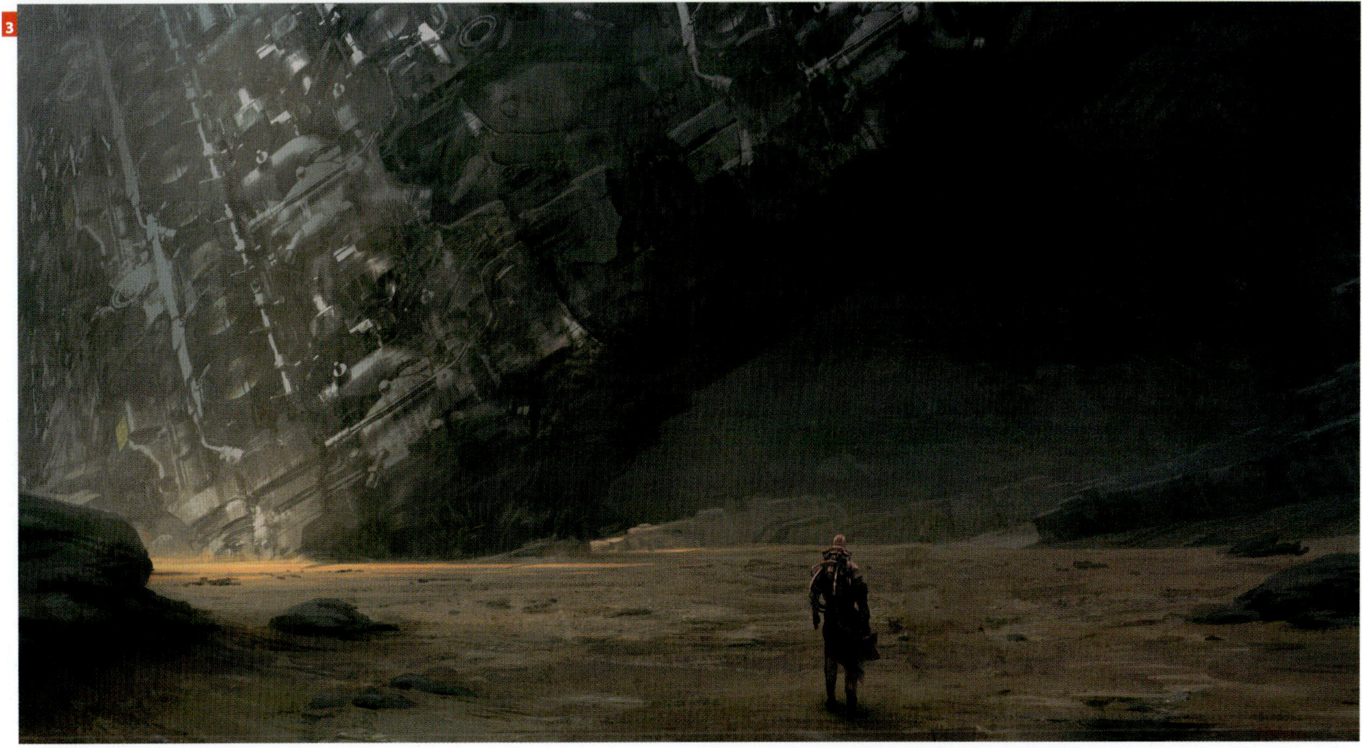

103 by Maxim Revin [3]
Photoshop CS4 | © Maxim Revin

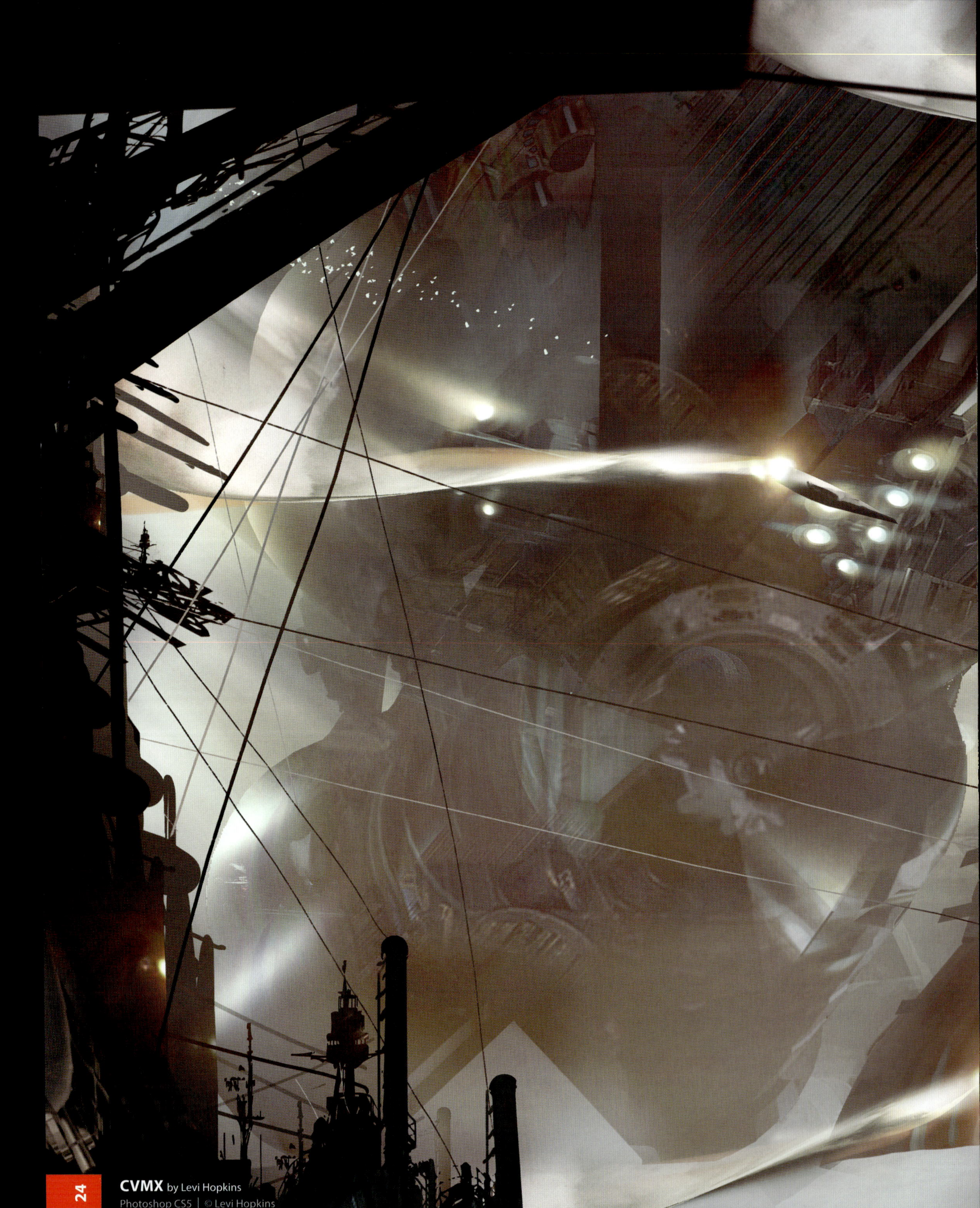

CVMX by Levi Hopkins
Photoshop CS5 | © Levi Hopkins

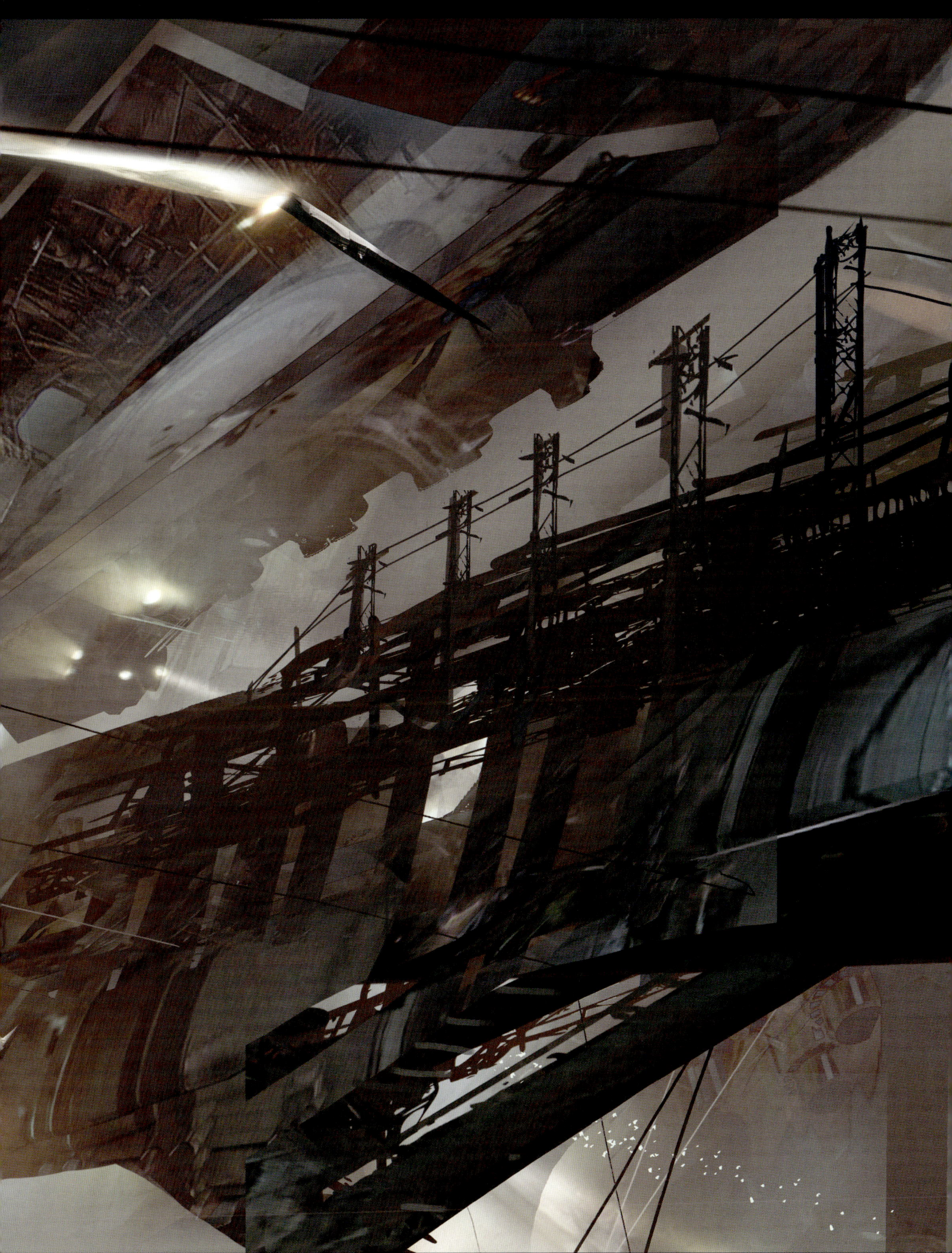

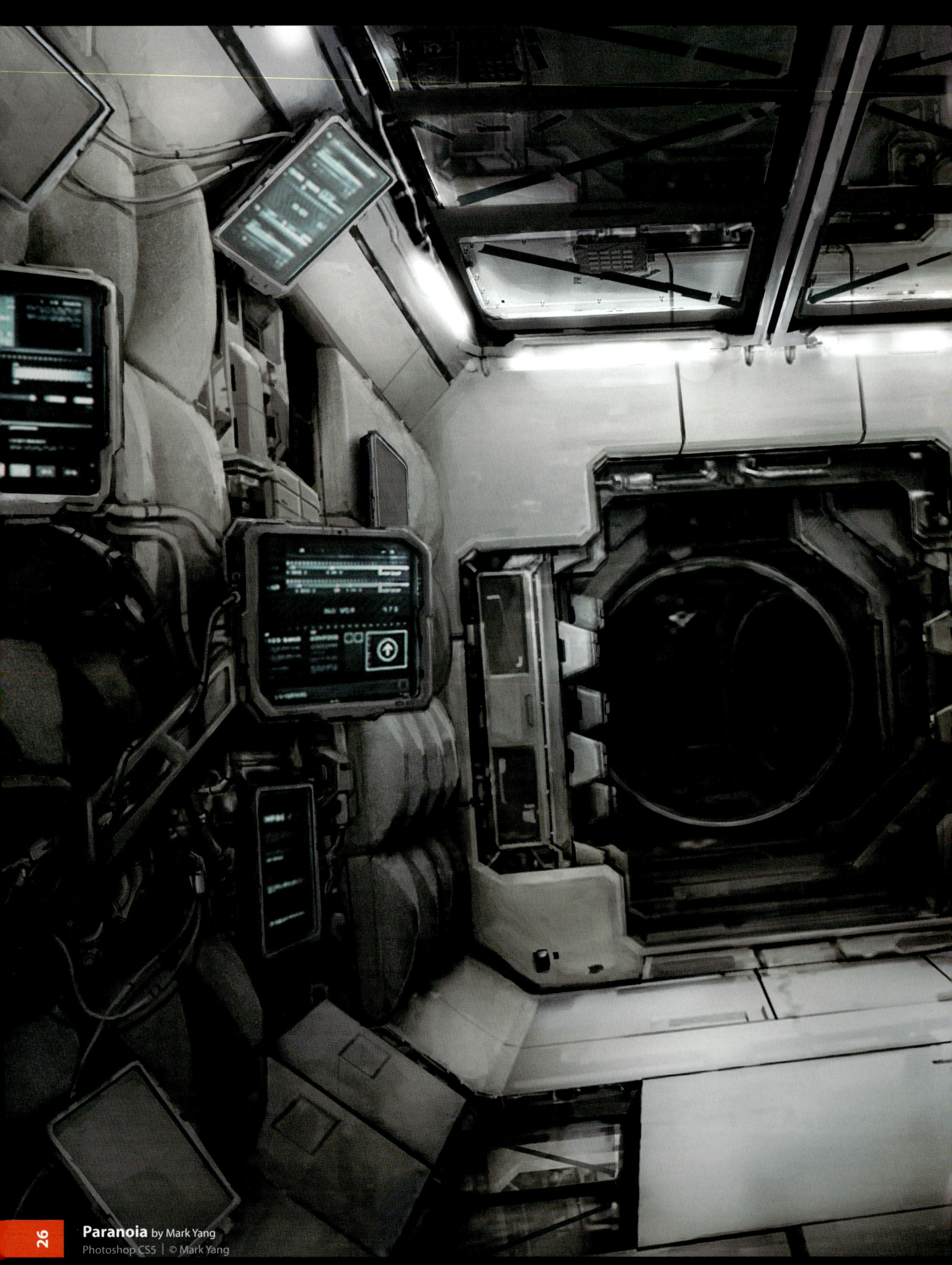

Paranoia by Mark Yang
Photoshop CS5 | © Mark Yang

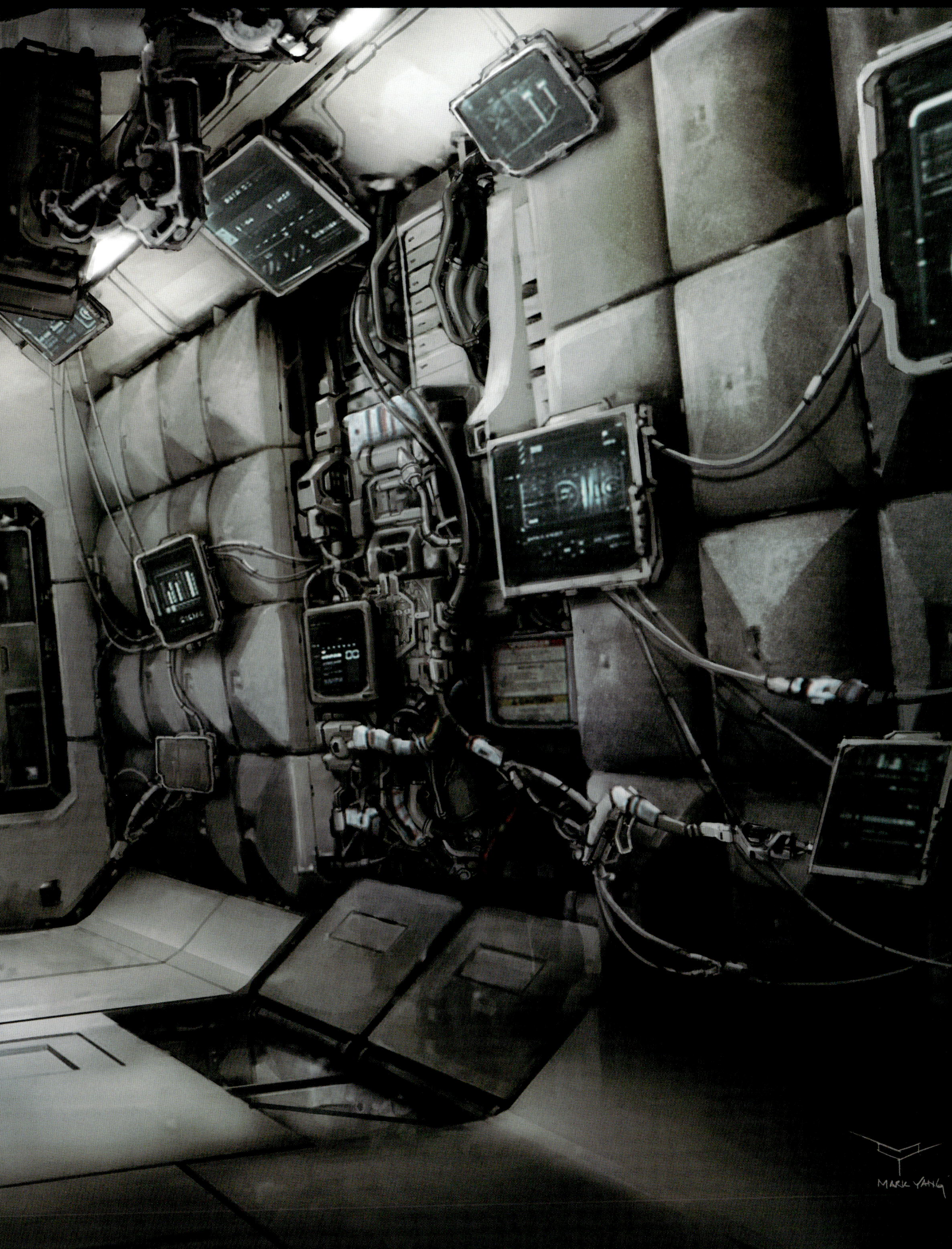
MARK YANG

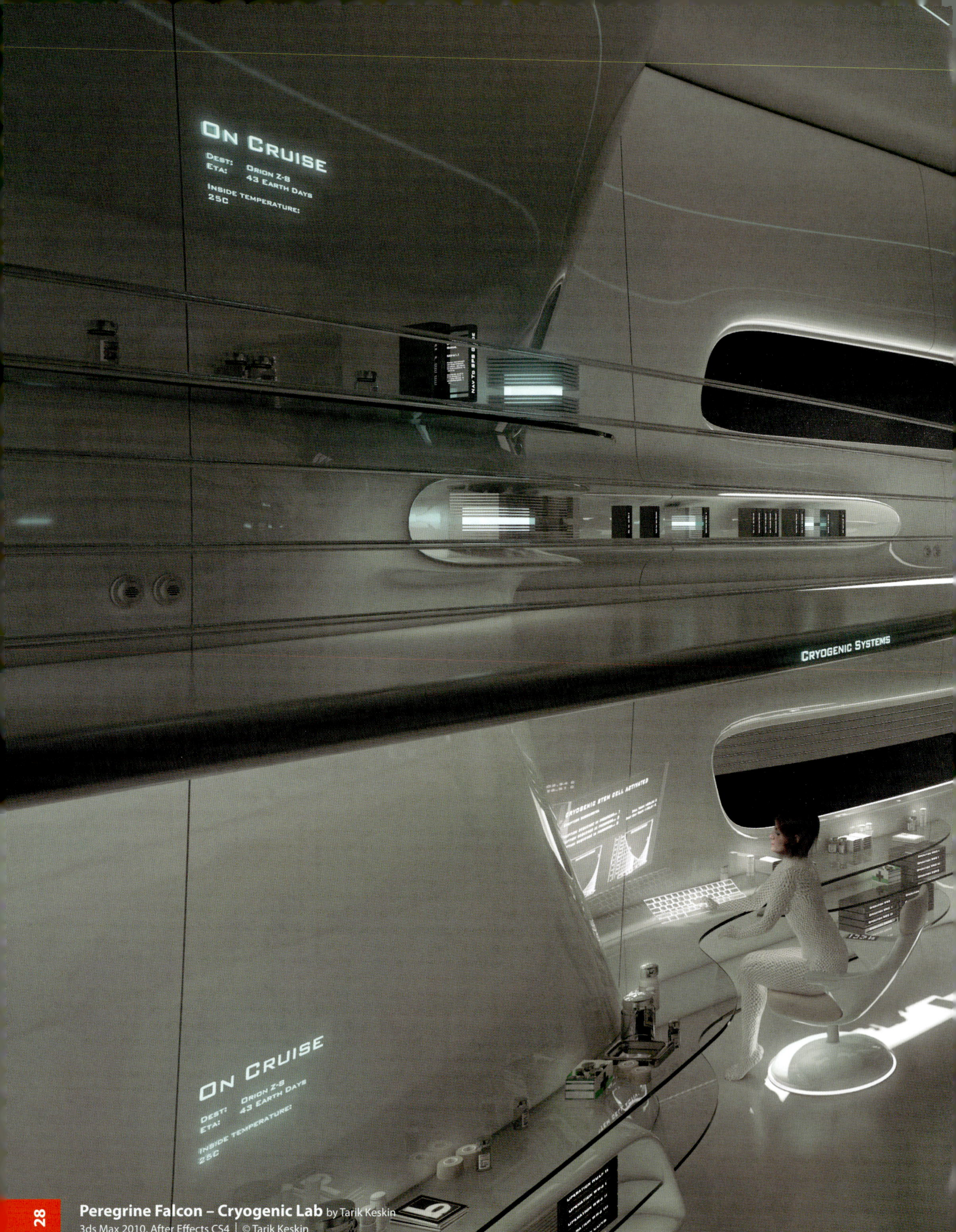

Peregrine Falcon – Cryogenic Lab by Tarik Keskin
3ds Max 2010, After Effects CS4 | © Tarik Keskin

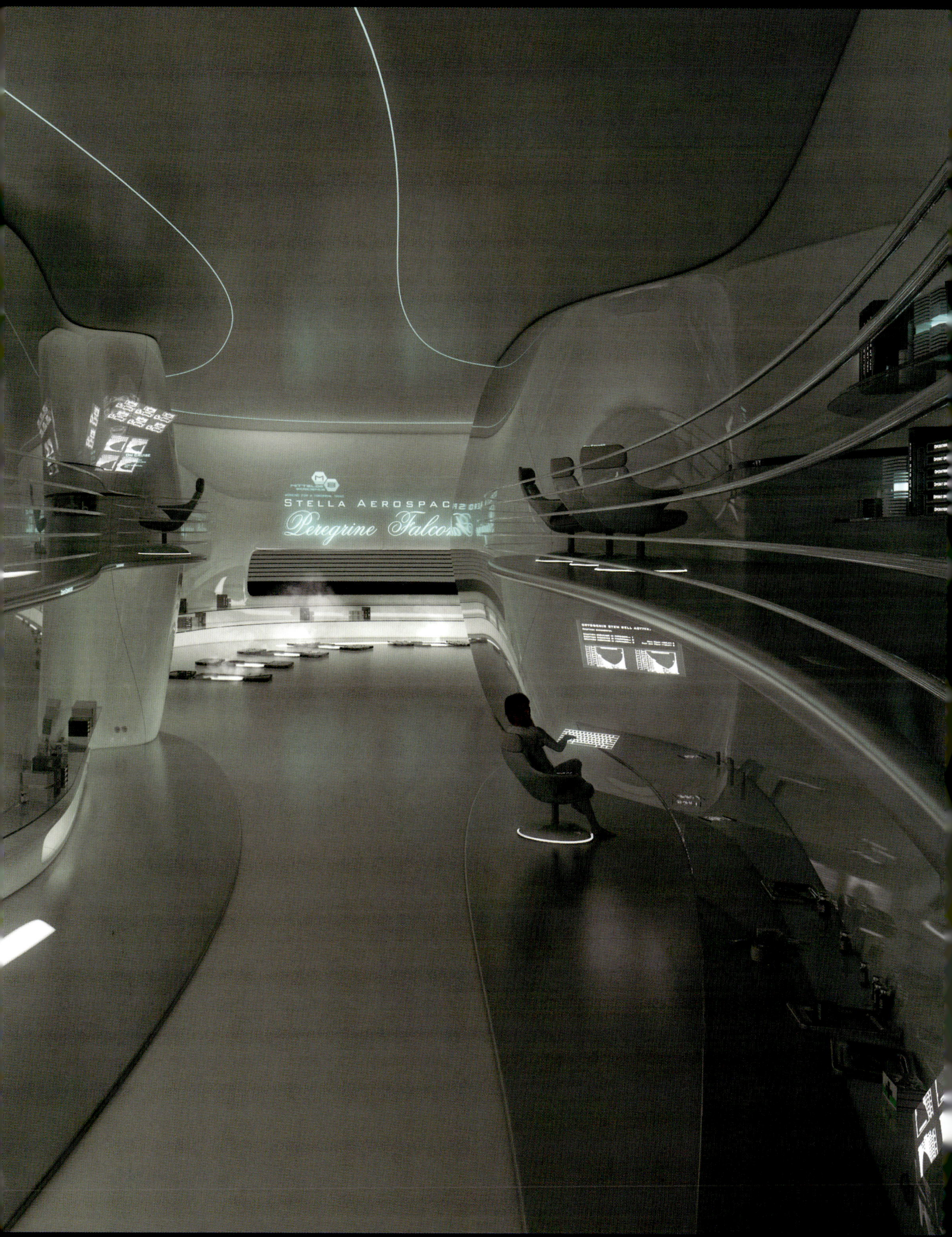
STELLA AEROSPAC
Peregrine Falco

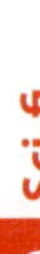

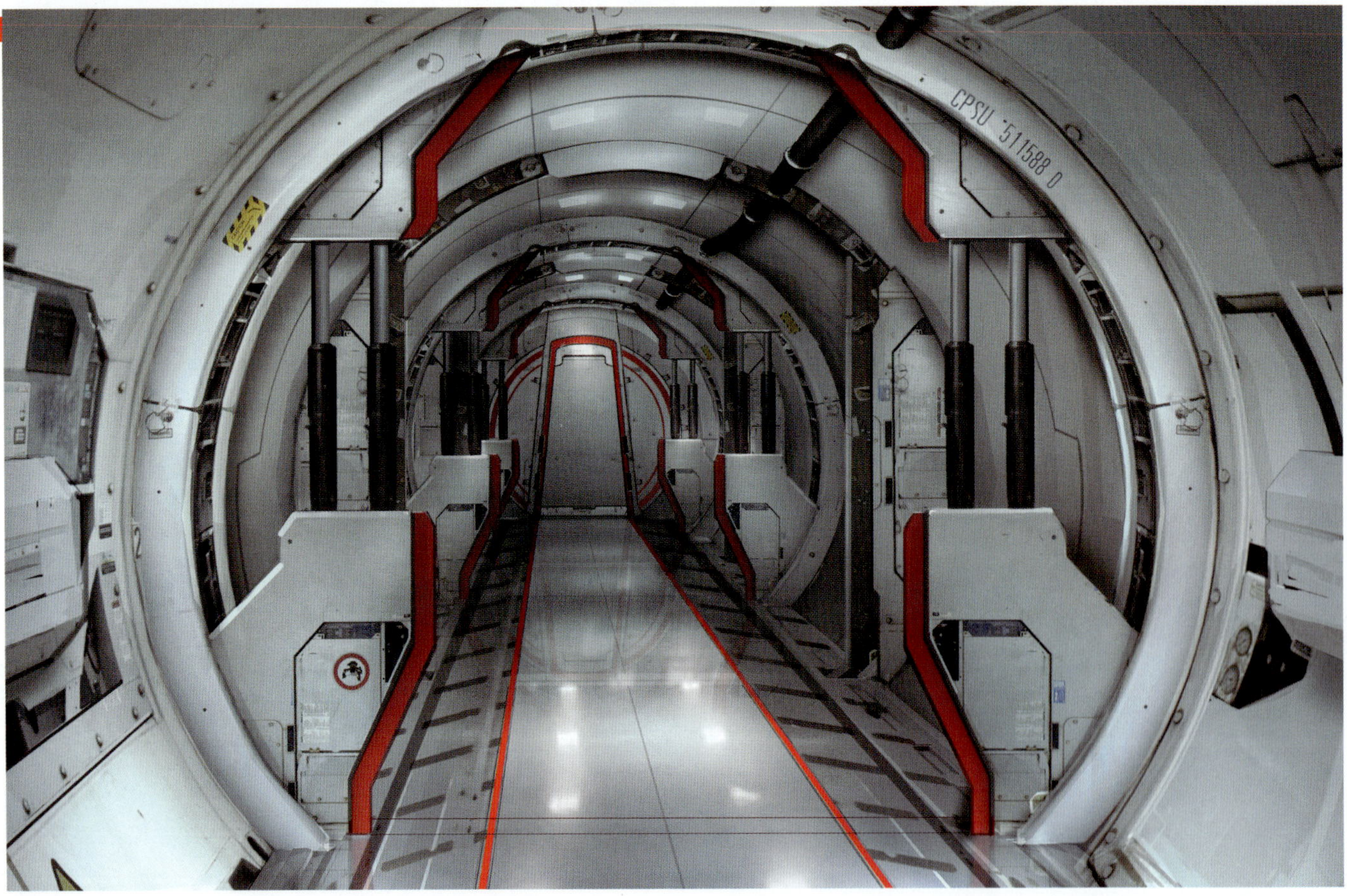

Landing by Jon McCoy [1]
Photoshop CS5 | © Jon McCoy

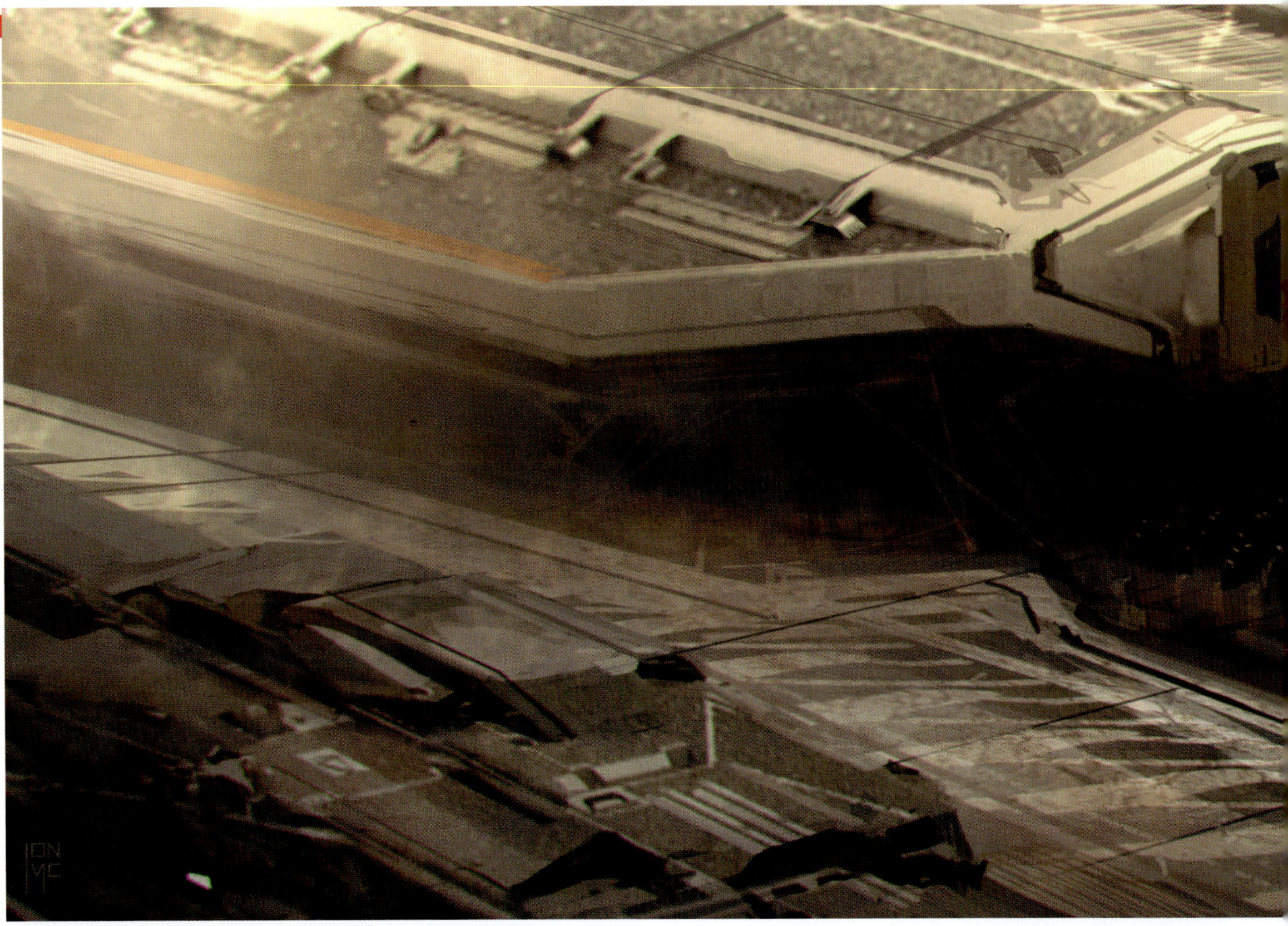

Space Station Hallway 01 by Sam Brown [2]
Photoshop CS2, Google SketchUp | © Sam Brown

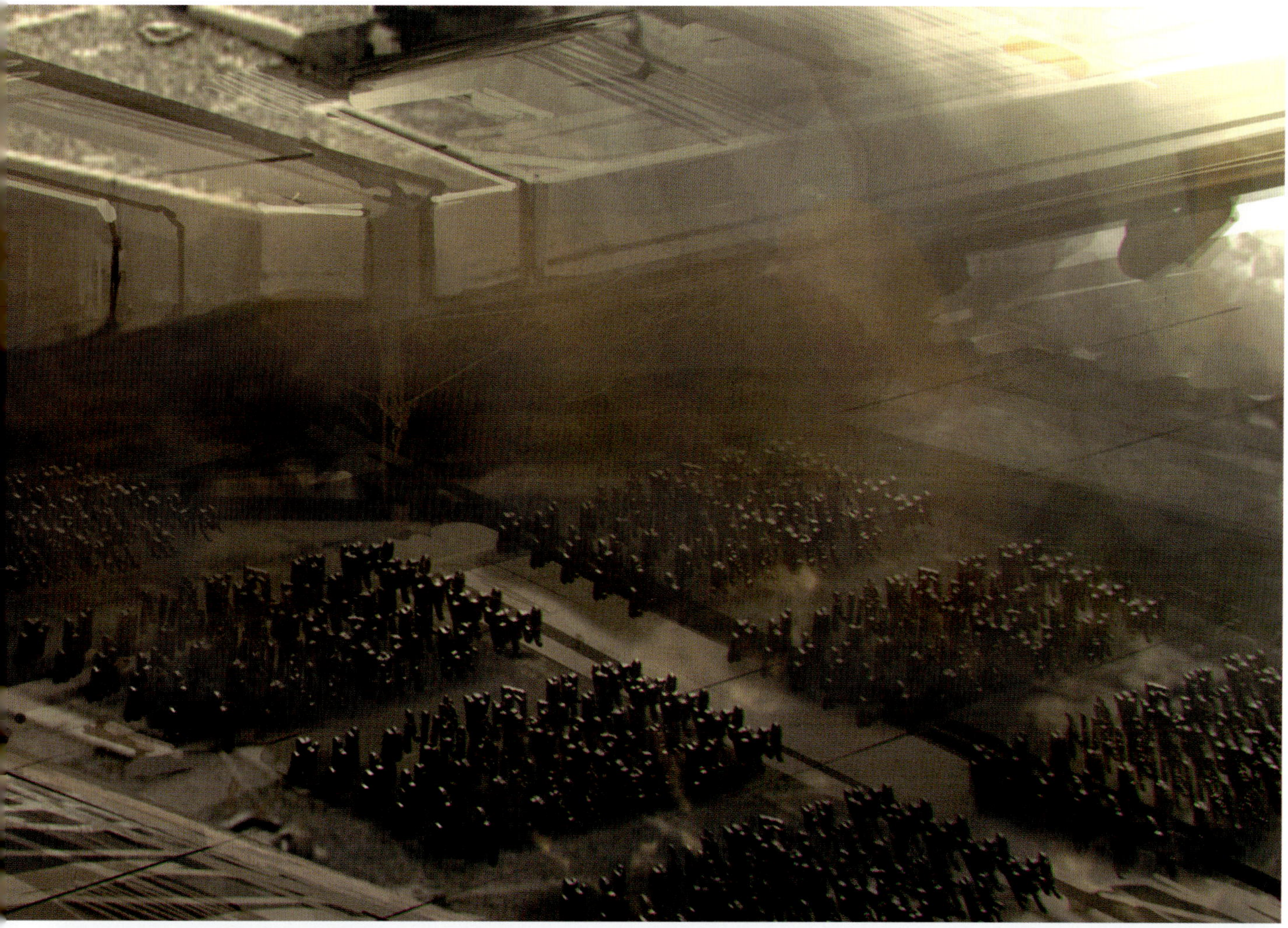

3

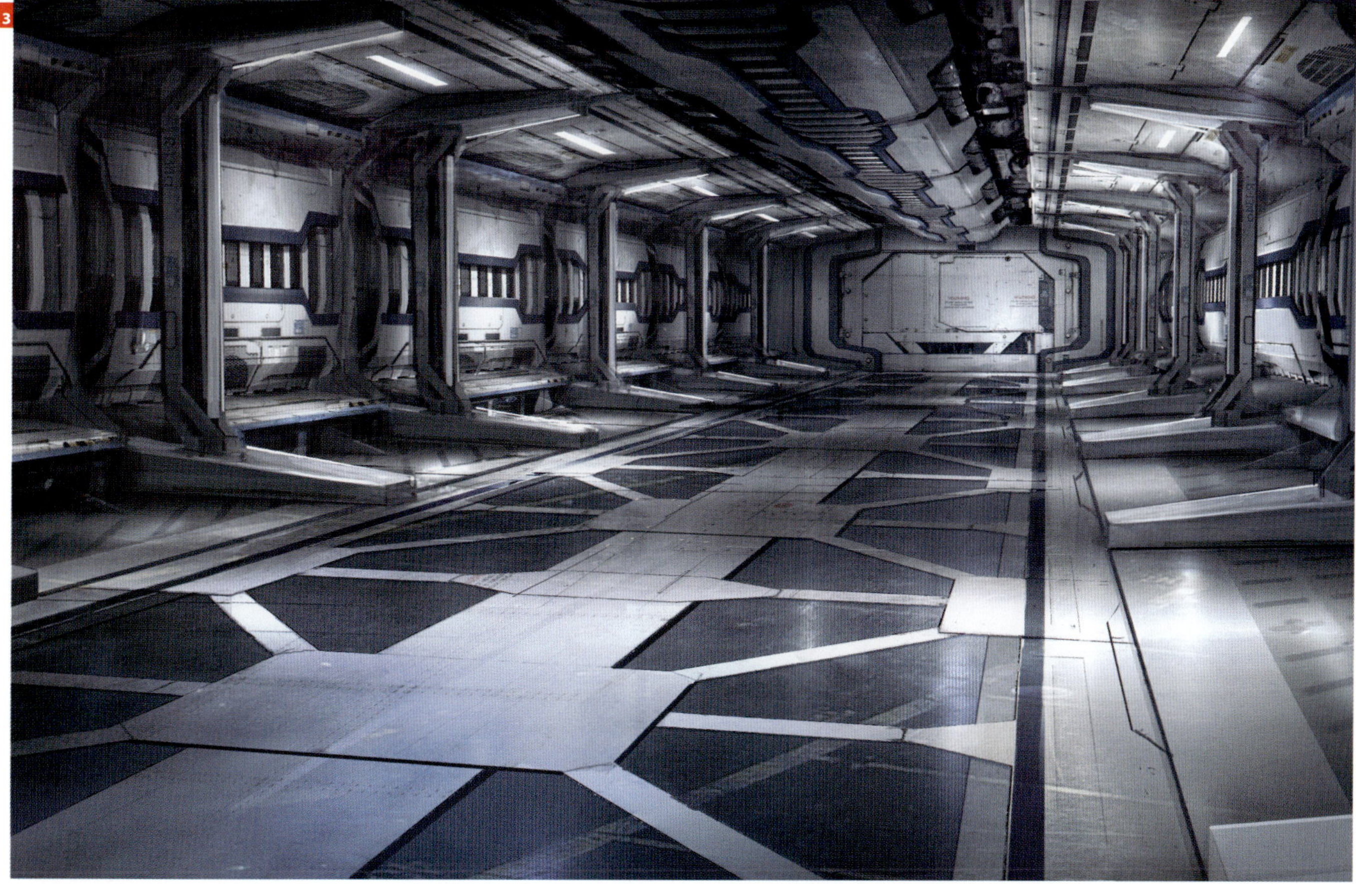

Space Station Hallway 02 by Sam Brown [3]
Photoshop CS2, Google SketchUp | © Sam Brown

1

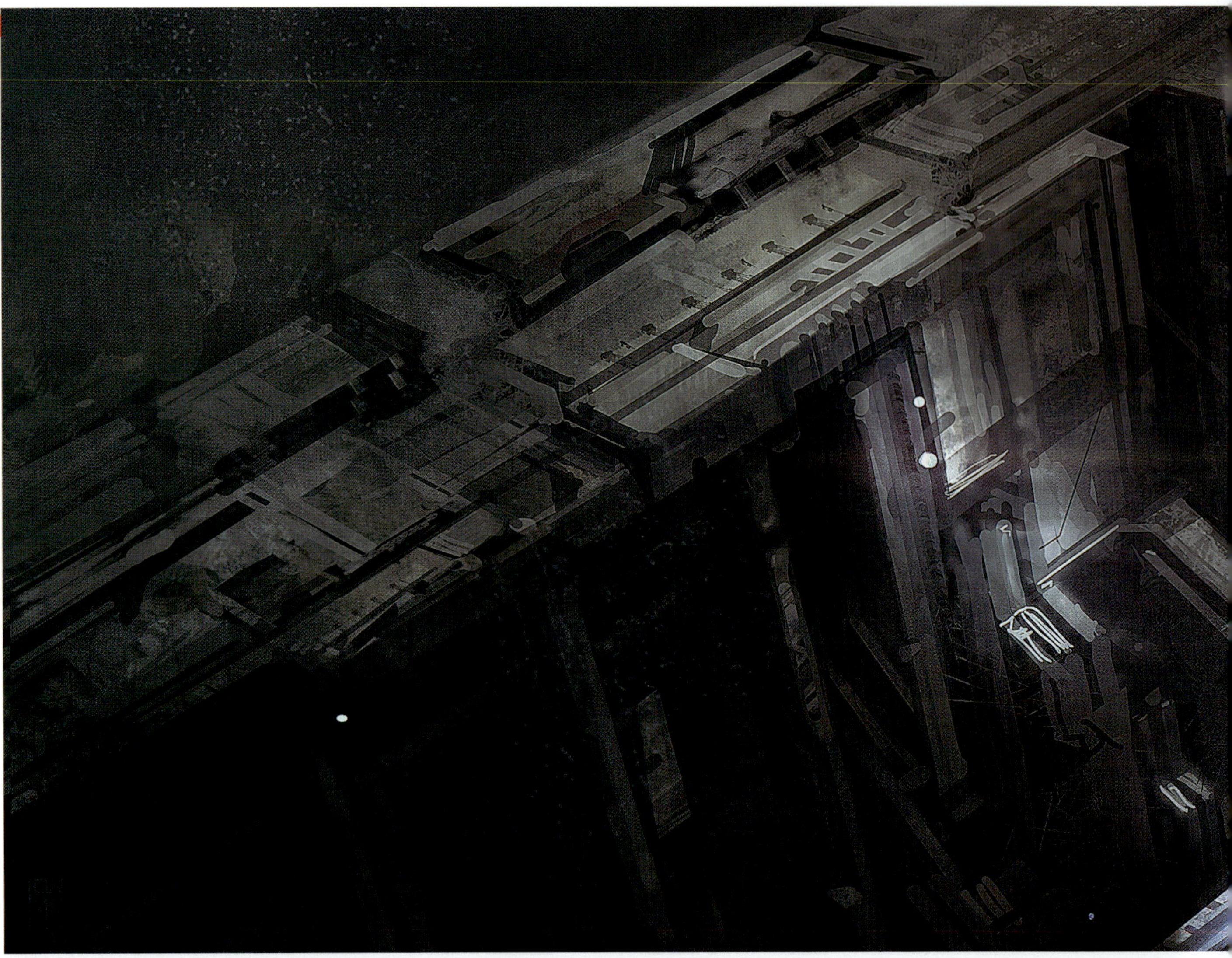

2

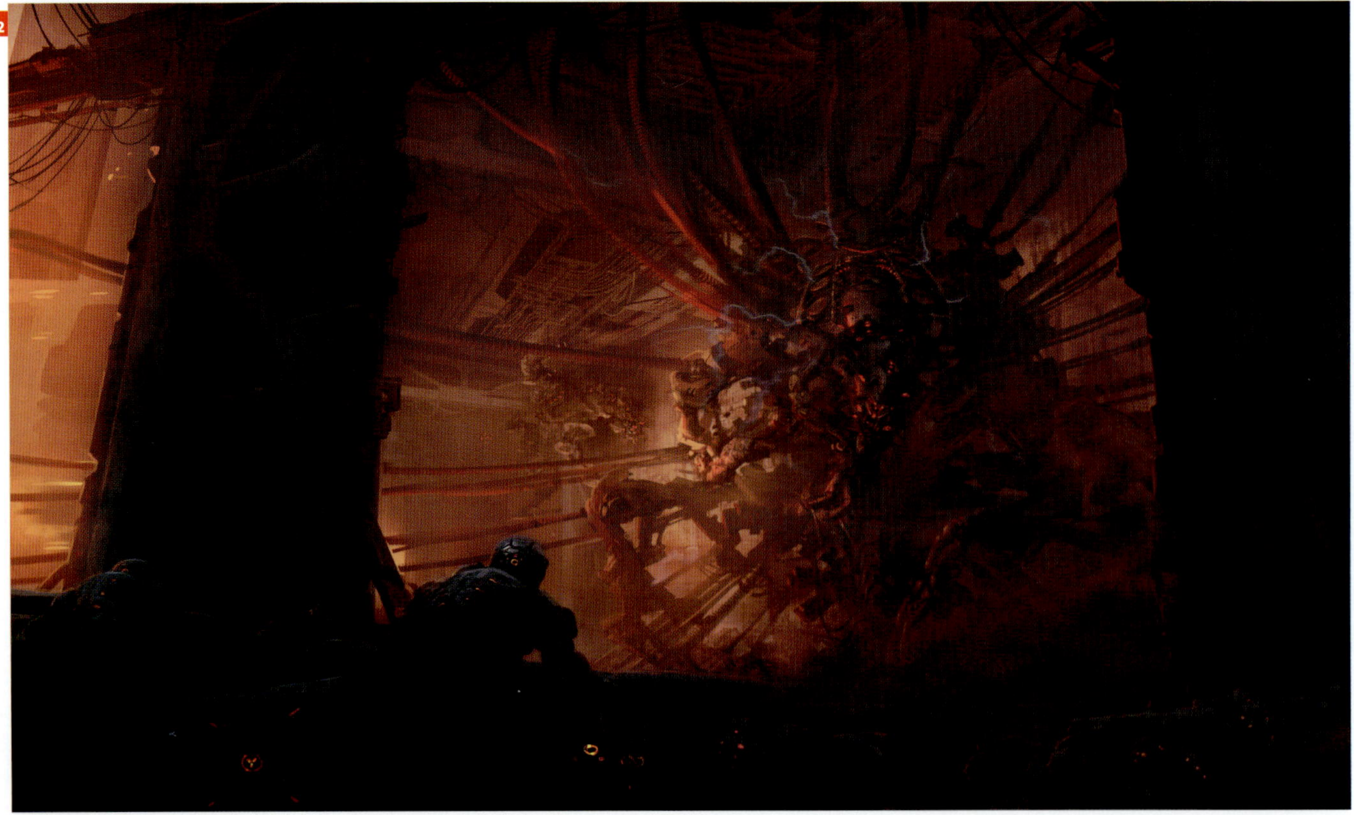

DarkSci 01 by Jon McCoy [1]
Photoshop CS5 | © Jon McCoy

Virus Detected by Maxim Revin [2]
Photoshop CS4 | © Maxim Revin

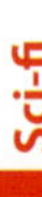

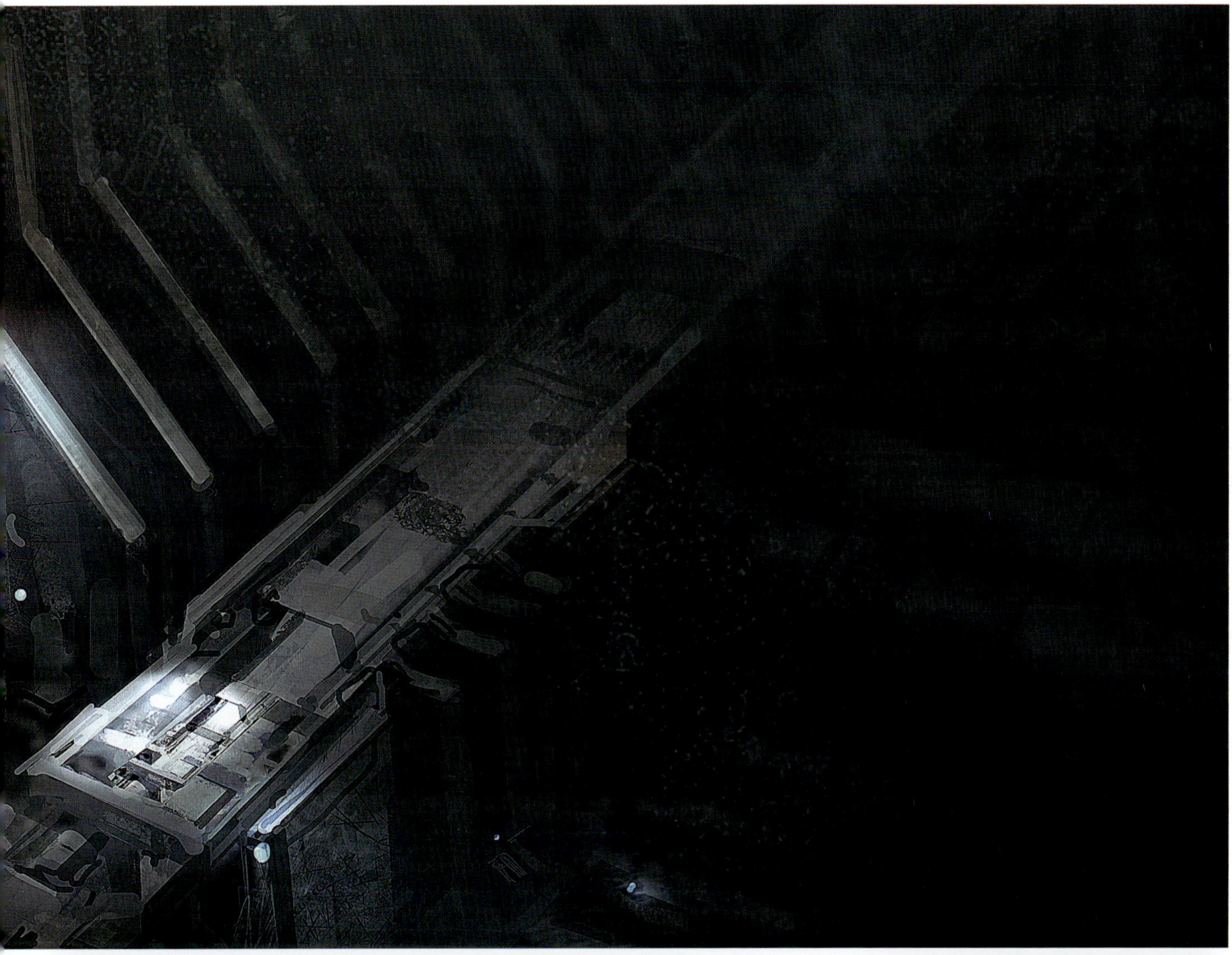

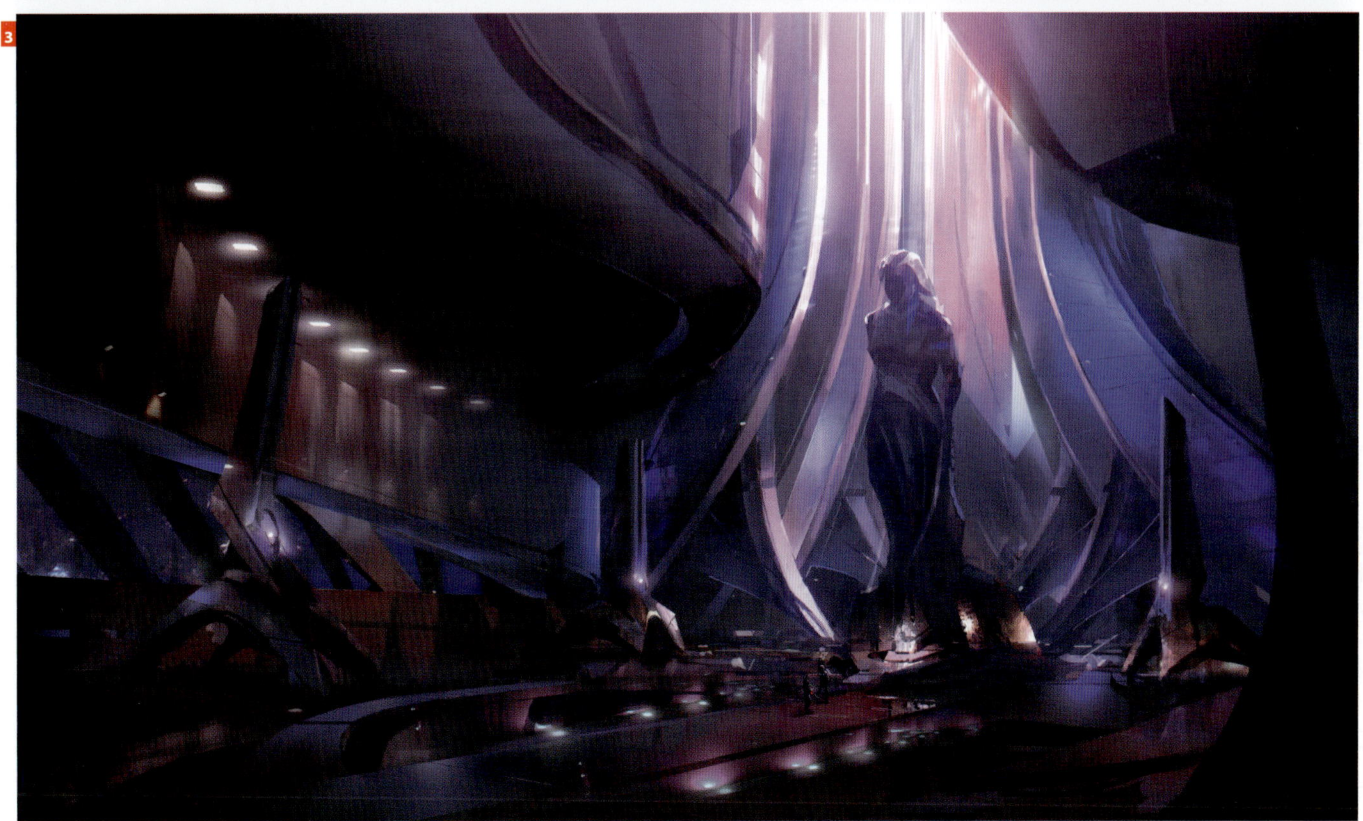

Thessia Temple by Brian Sum [3]

Photoshop CS3 |

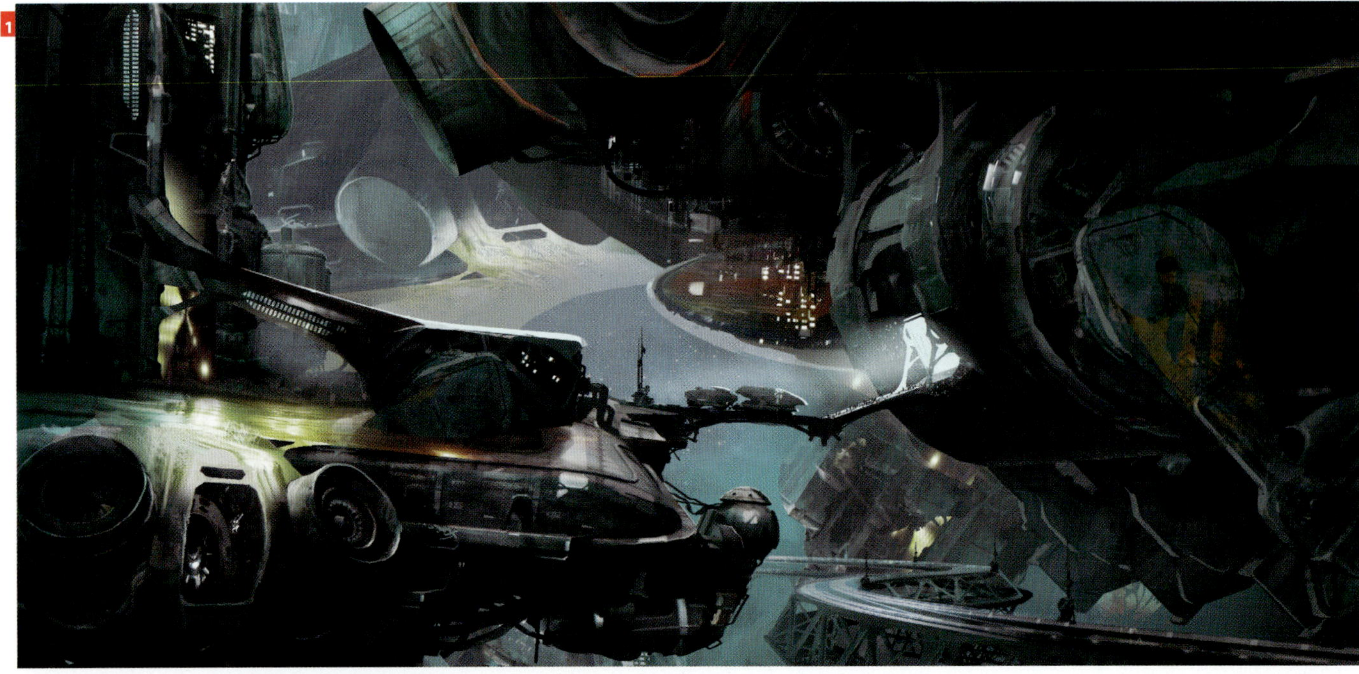

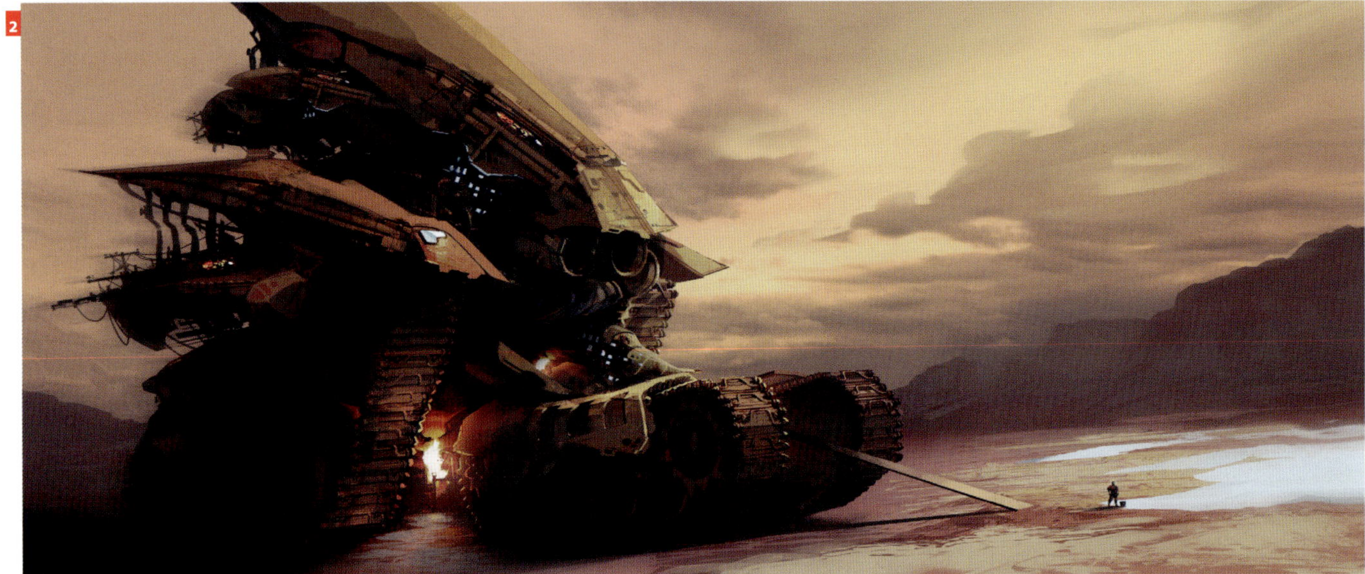

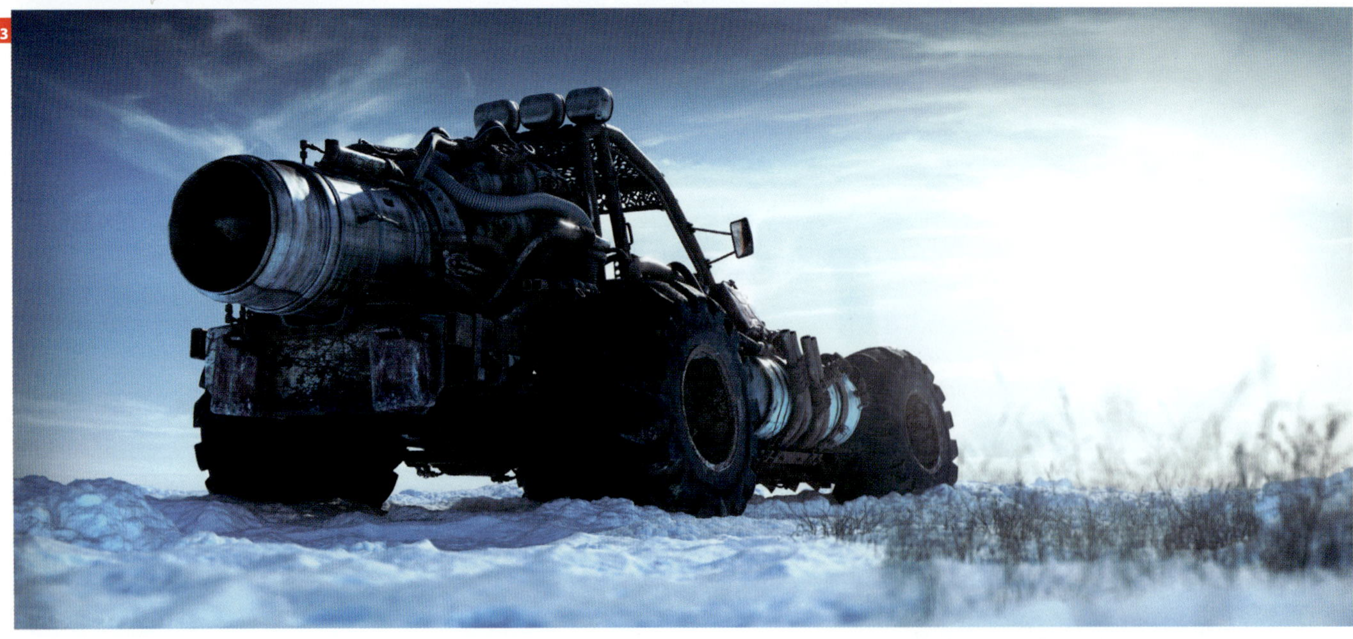

Bucket Dock by Jason Stokes [1]
Photoshop CS3, 3ds Max 2010 | © Jason Stokes

Thirsty Tank by Jason Stokes [2]
Photoshop CS3, 3ds Max 2010 | © Jason Stokes

Buggy Nuclear Winter by Marek Denko [3]
3ds Max 2009, V-Ray 1.5 | © Marek Denko

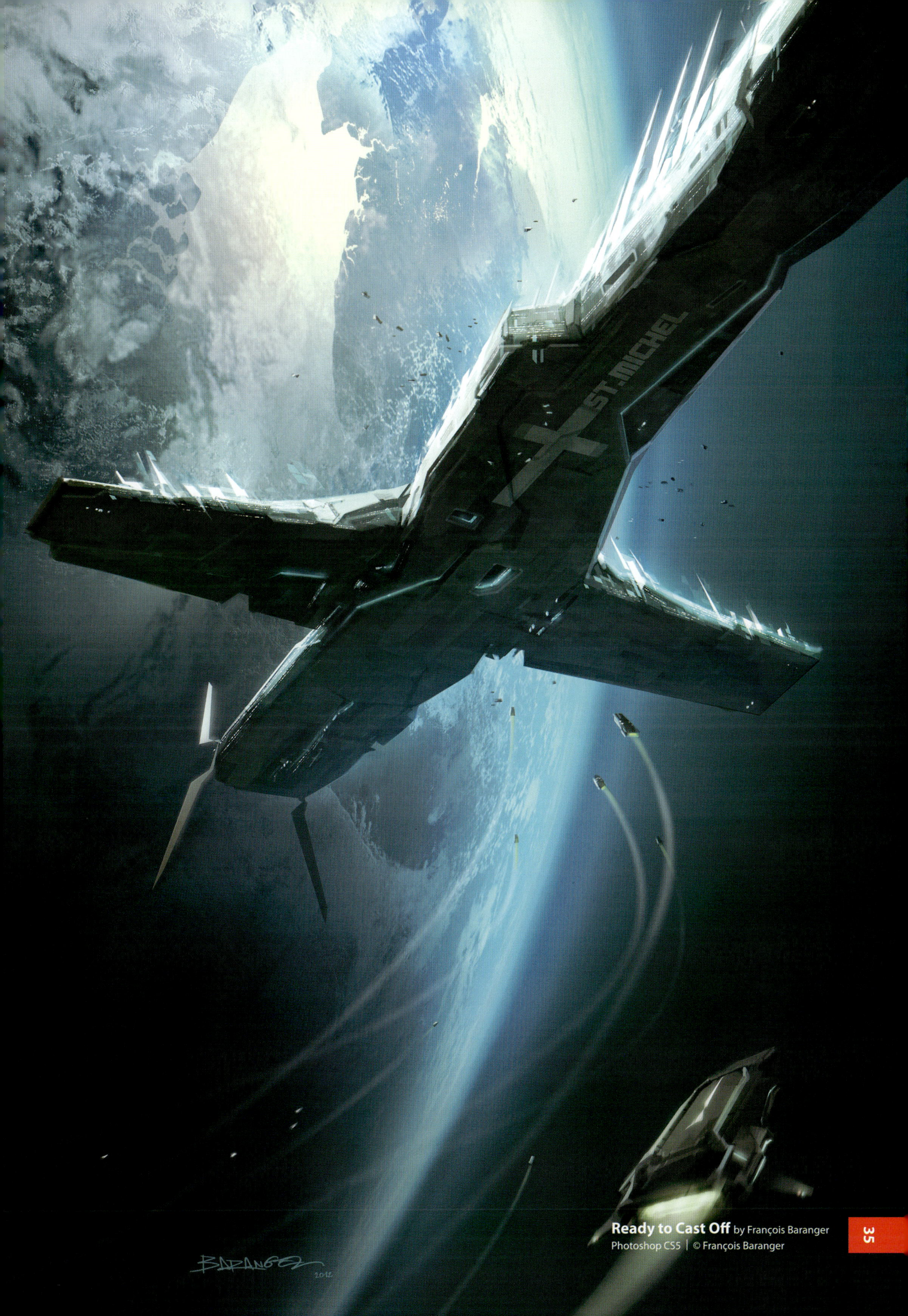

Ready to Cast Off by François Baranger
Photoshop CS5 | © François Baranger

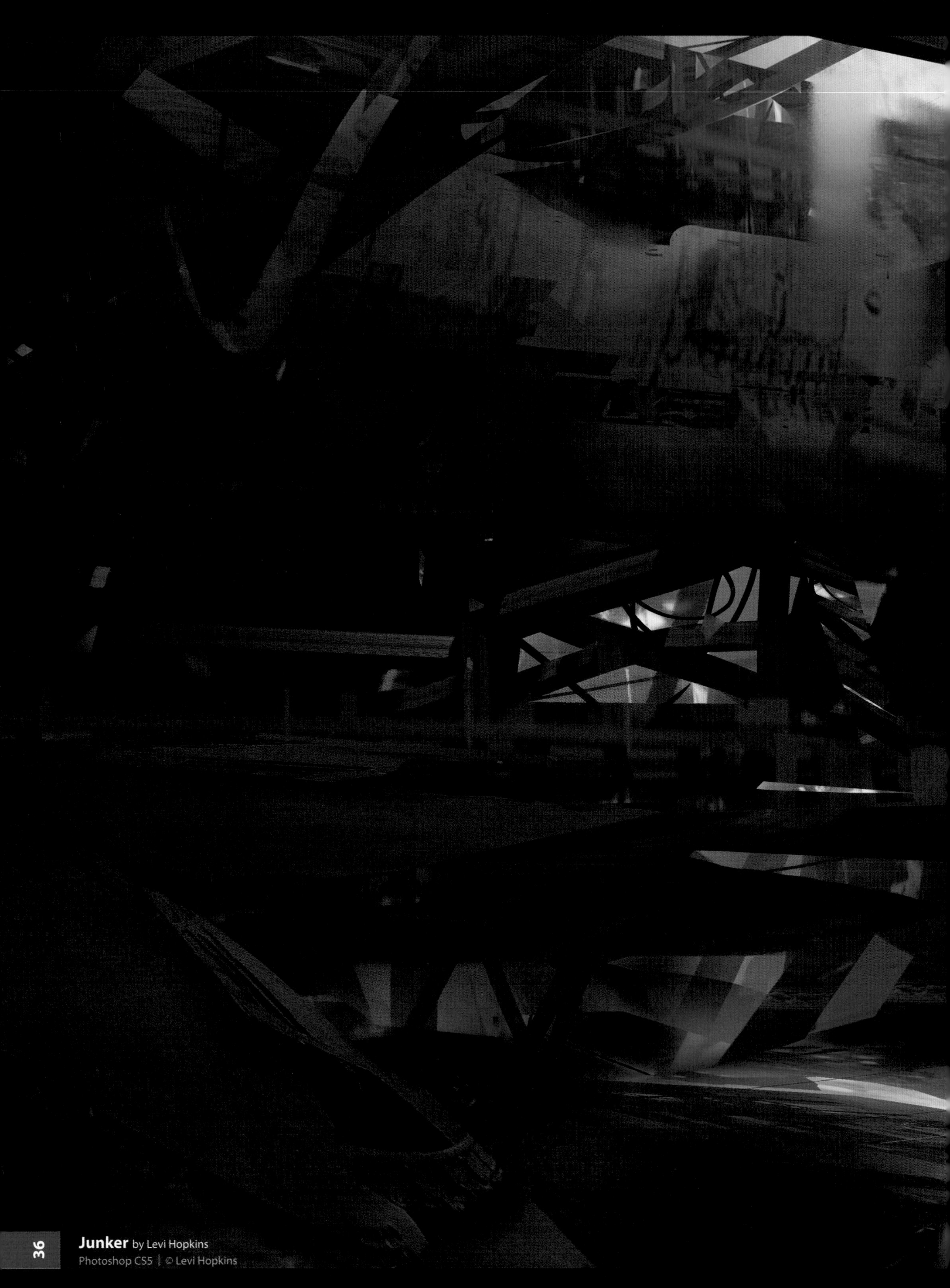

Junker by Levi Hopkins
Photoshop CS5 |

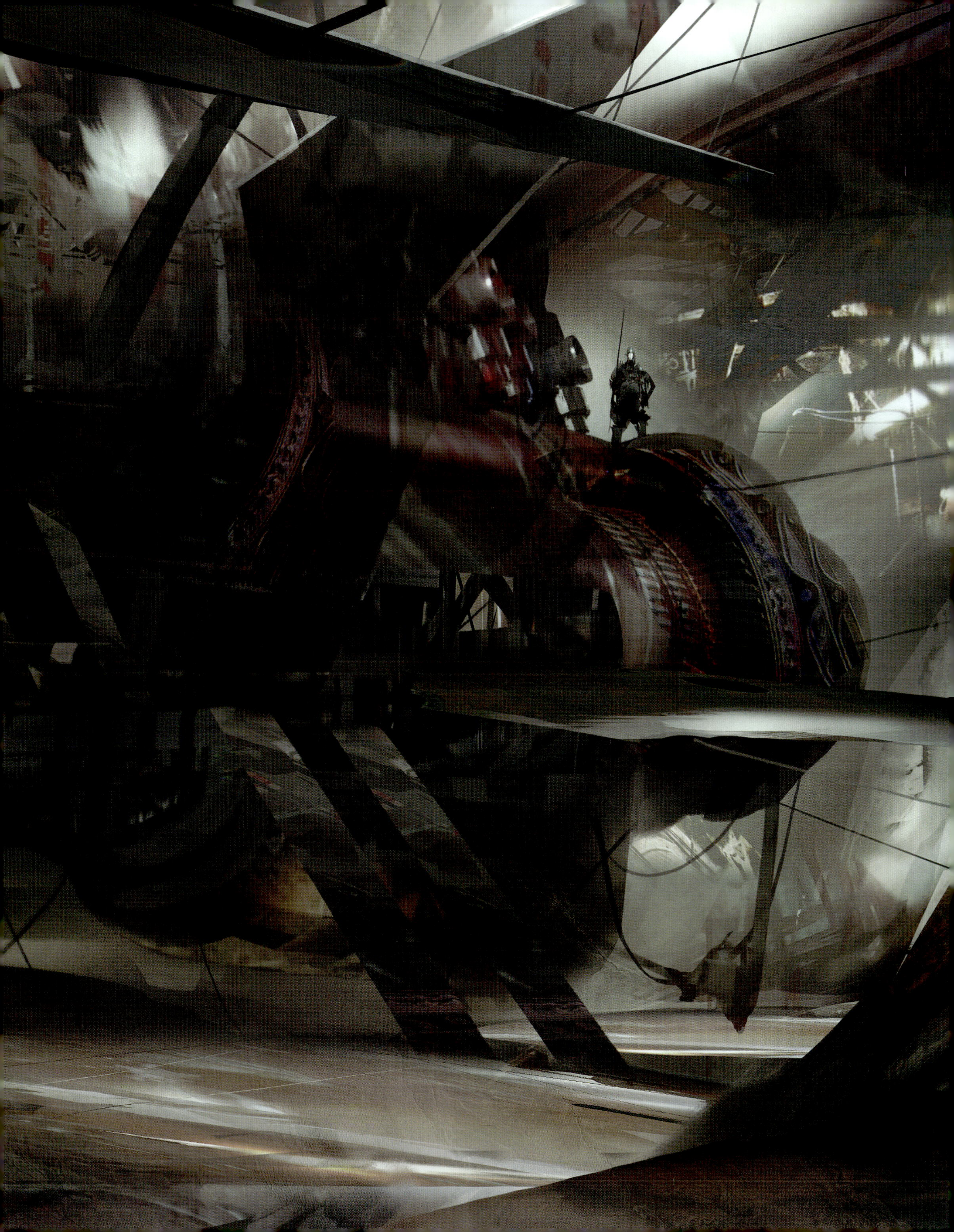

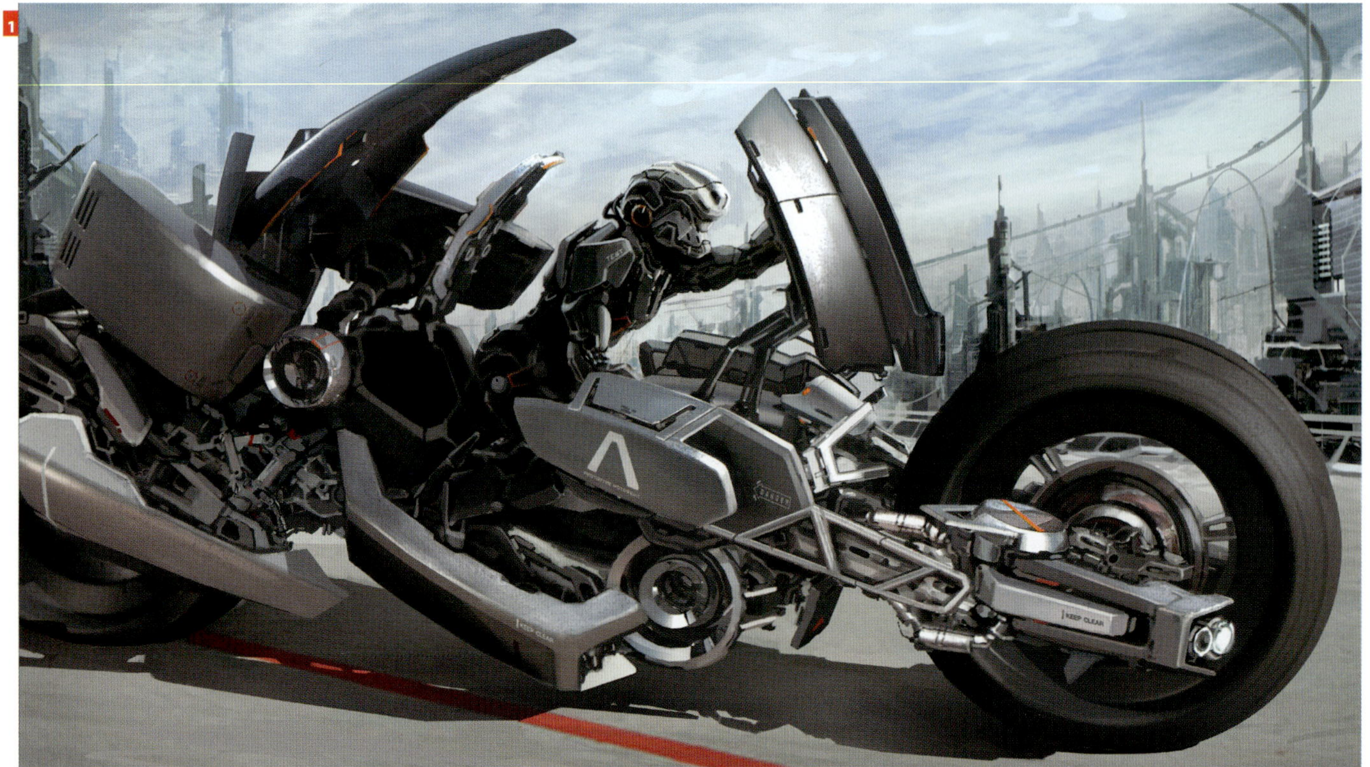

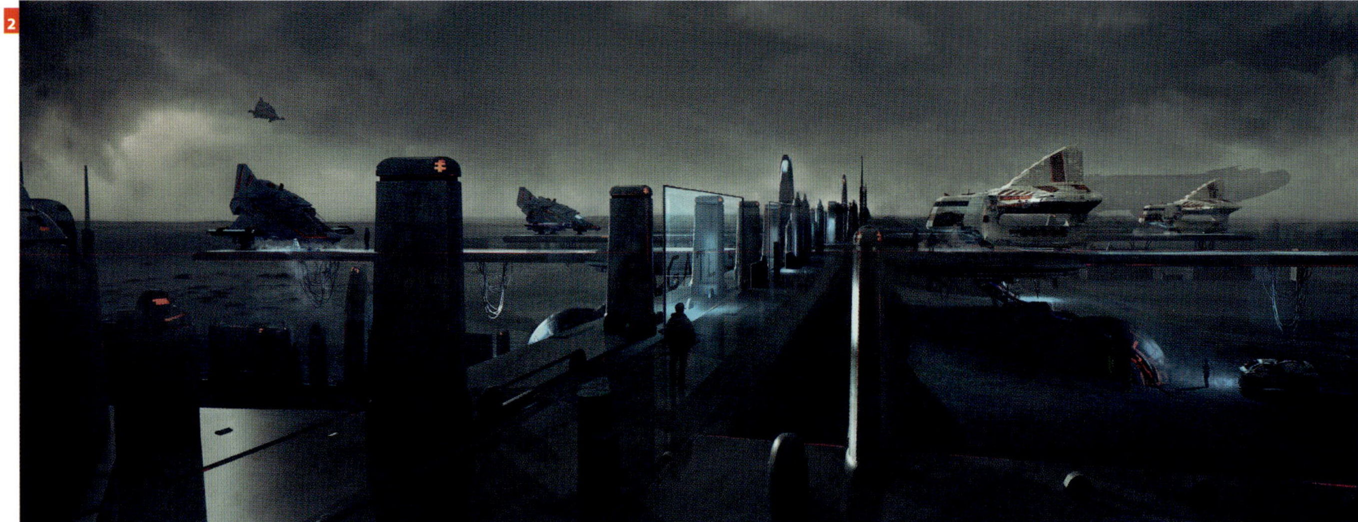

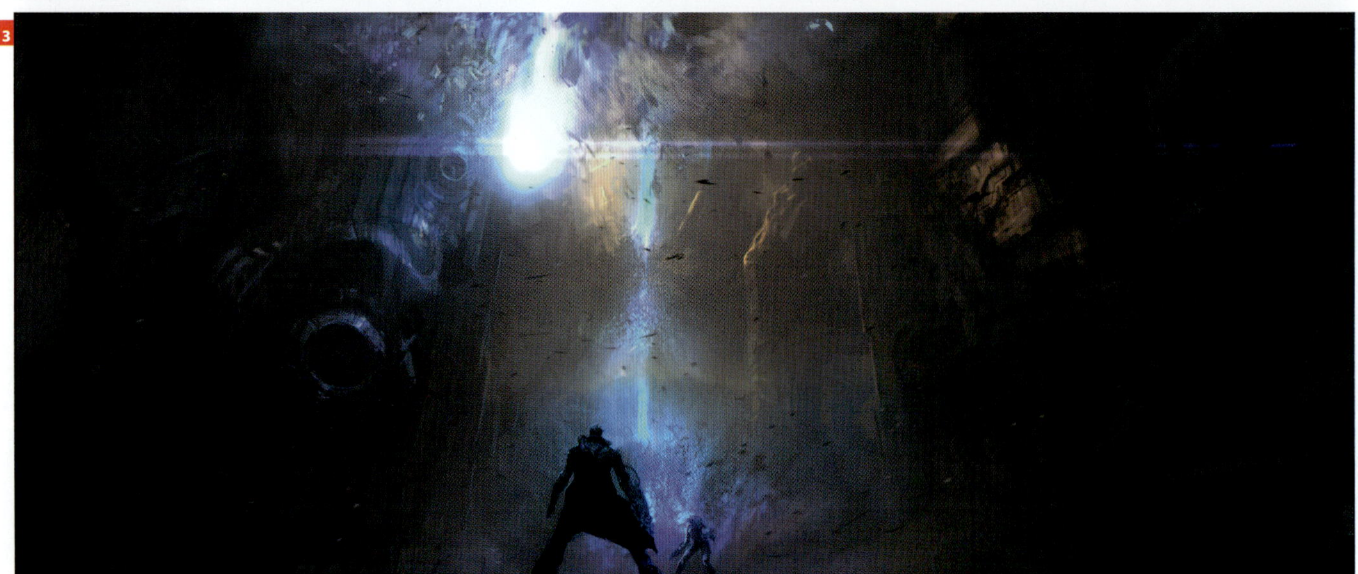

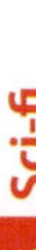

Annihilator Entry by Mark Yang [1]
Modo 501, Photoshop CS6 | © Mark Yang

Gate 54 by Neil Maccormack [2]
LightWave 11, Photoshop CS5 | © Neil Maccormack

Lamar Attack by Maxim Revin [3]
Photoshop CS4 | © Maxim Revin

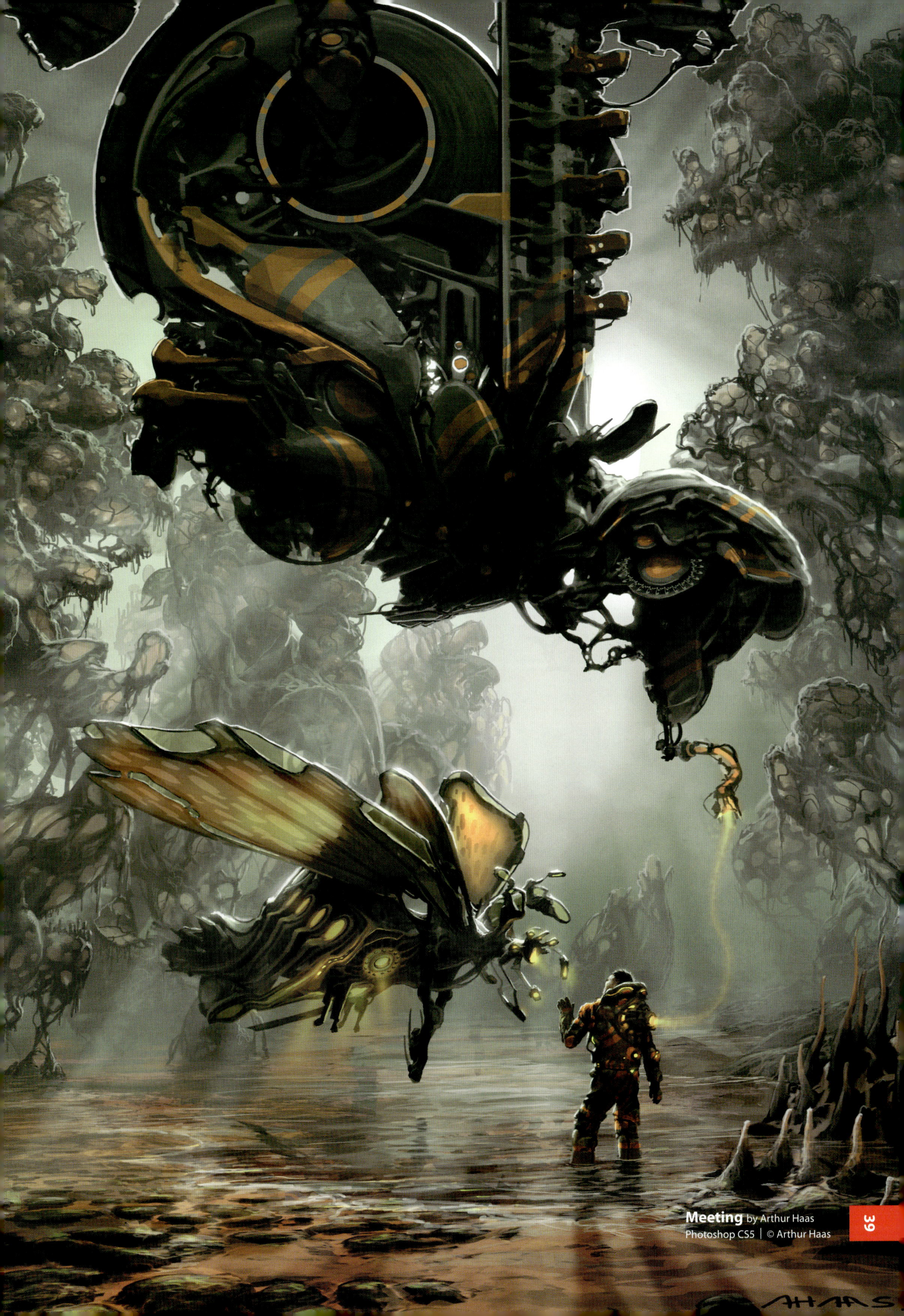

Meeting by Arthur Haas
Photoshop CS5 | © Arthur Haas

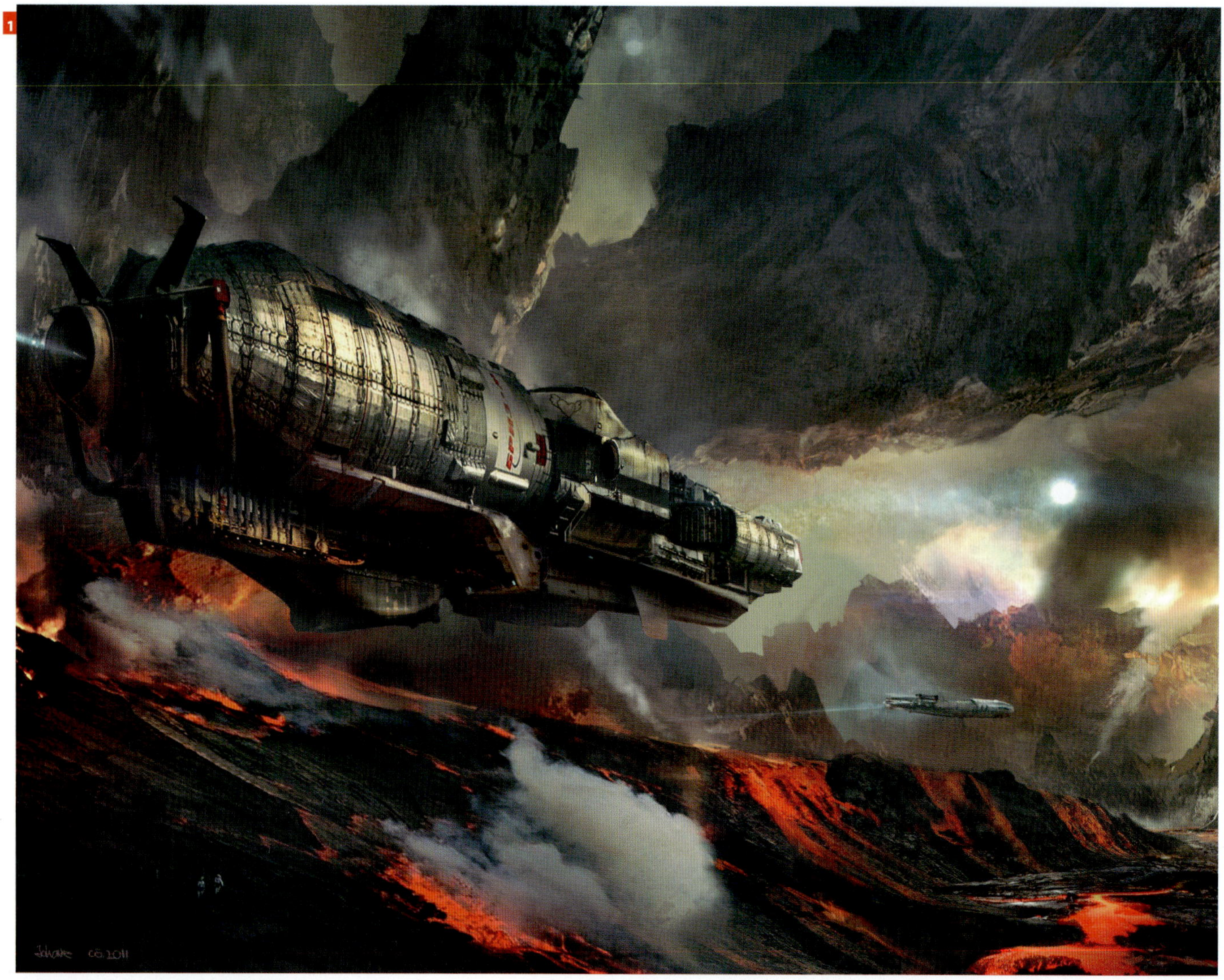

1

2

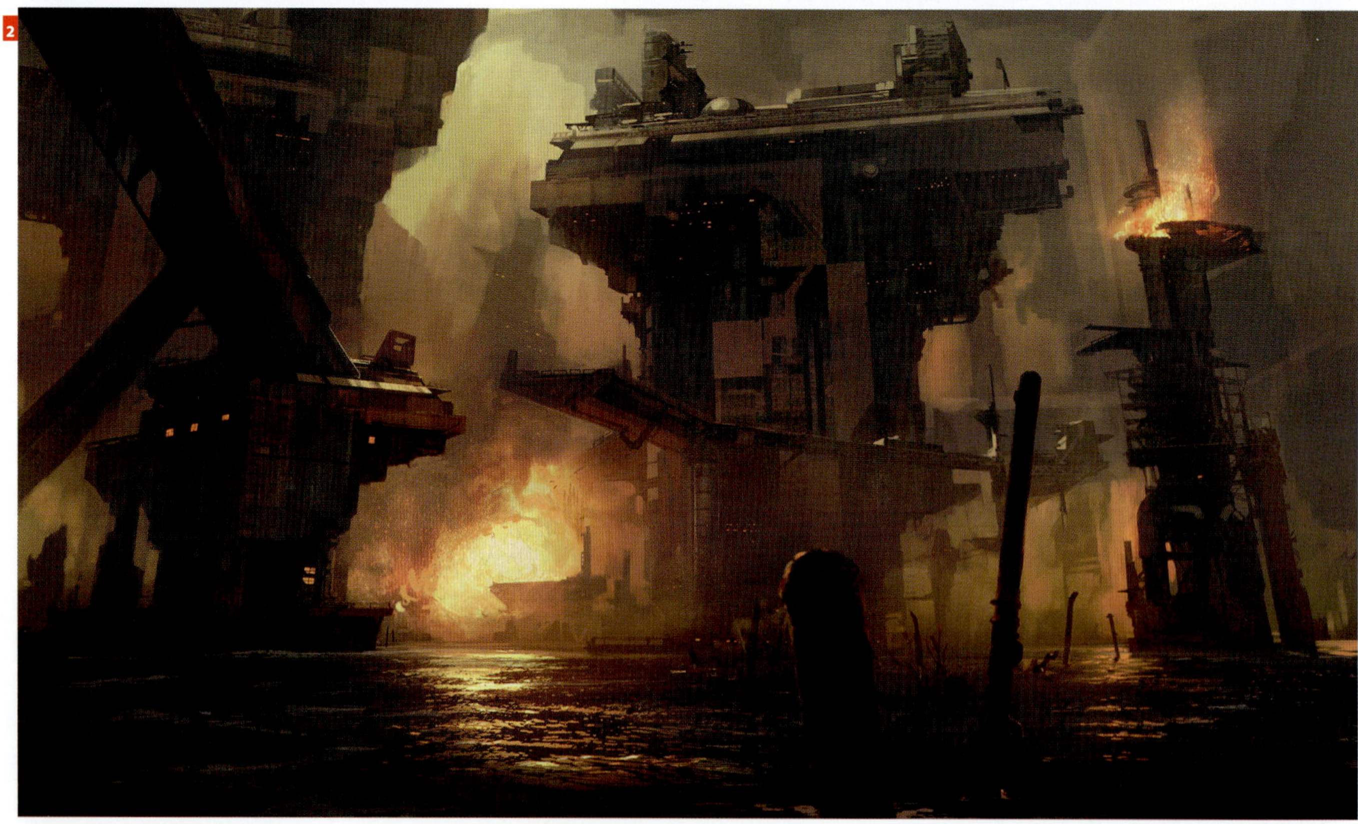

Refuel by Ioan Dumitrescu [1]
Photoshop CS5 | © Ioan Dumitrescu

Elements 2666 A.D by Tuomas Korpi [2]
Photoshop CS3 | © Tuomas Korpi

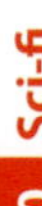

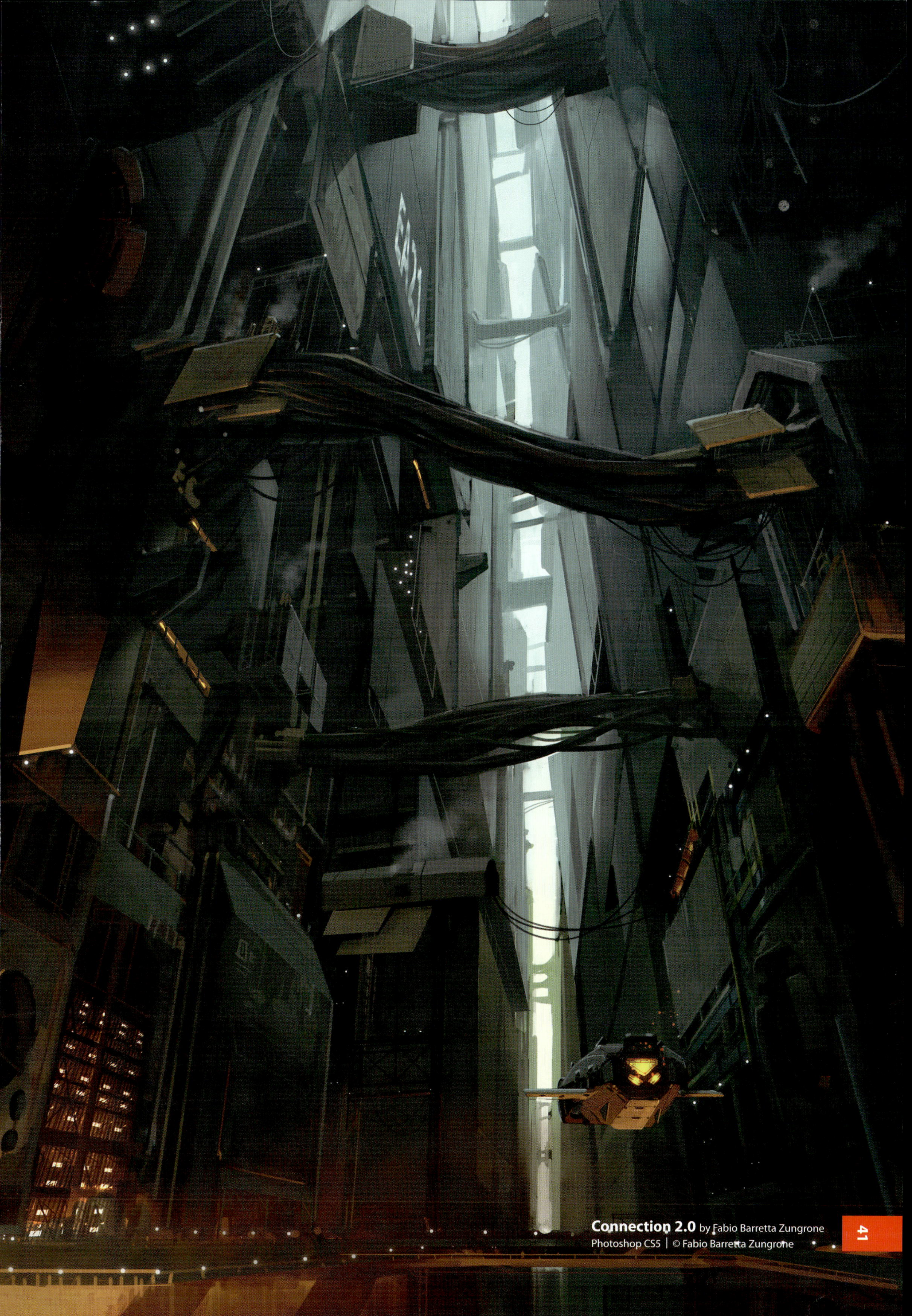

Connection 2.0 by Fabio Barretta Zungrone
Photoshop CS5 | © Fabio Barretta Zungrone

1

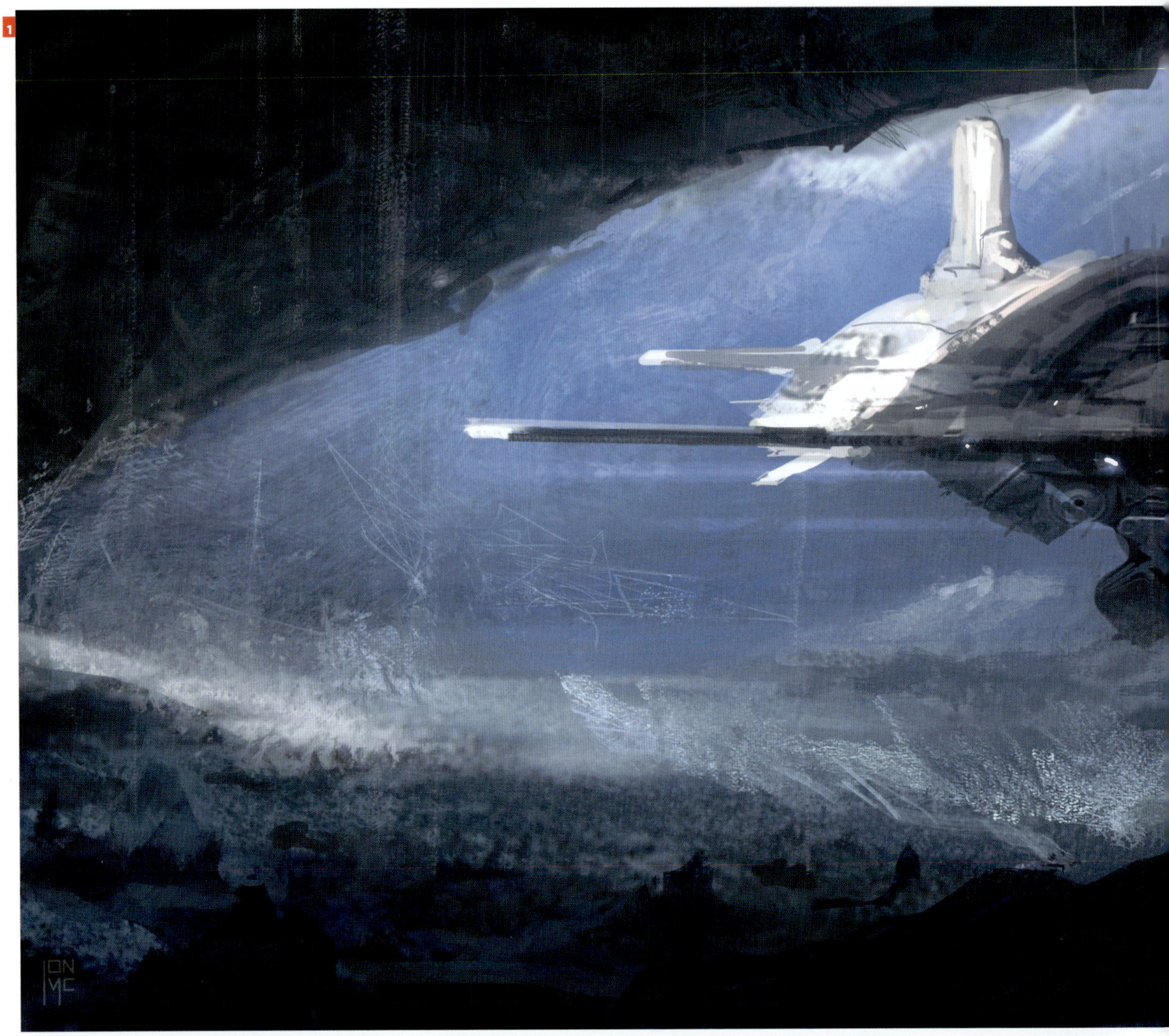

2

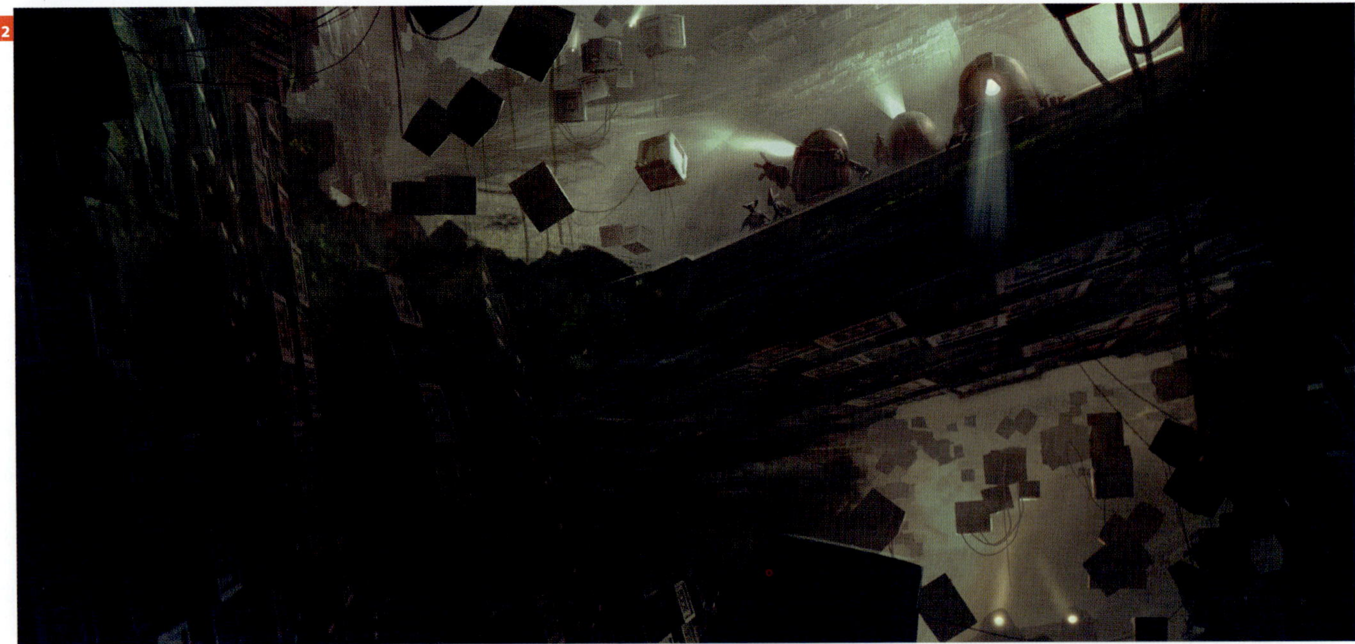

DarkSci 02 by Jon McCoy [1]
Photoshop CS5 | © Jon McCoy

Asura Cave – *Guild Wars 2* by Levi Hopkins [2]
Photoshop CS5 | © All *Guild Wars* materials are property of ArenaNet/NCSoft and are used with permission

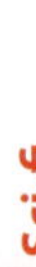

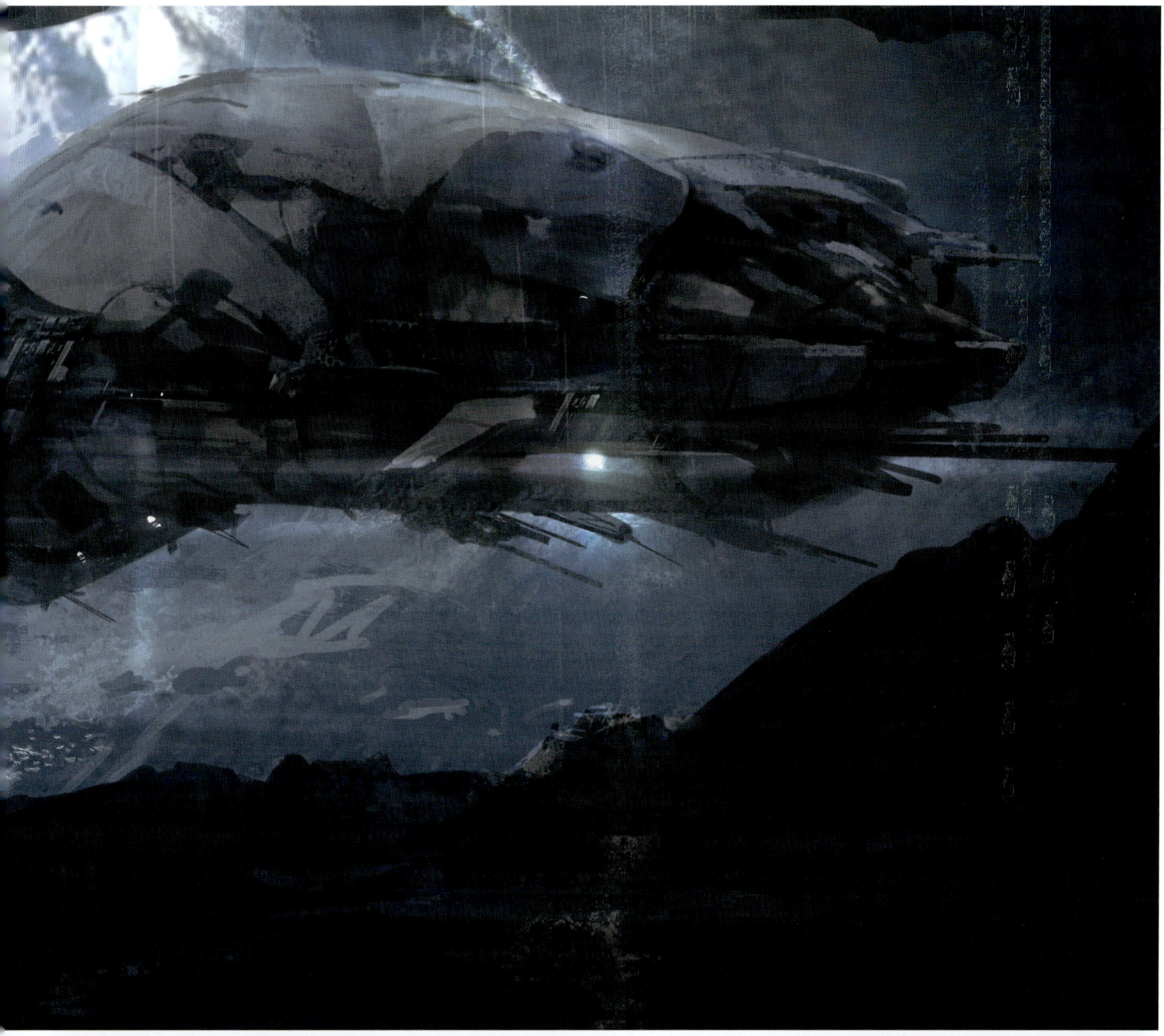

3

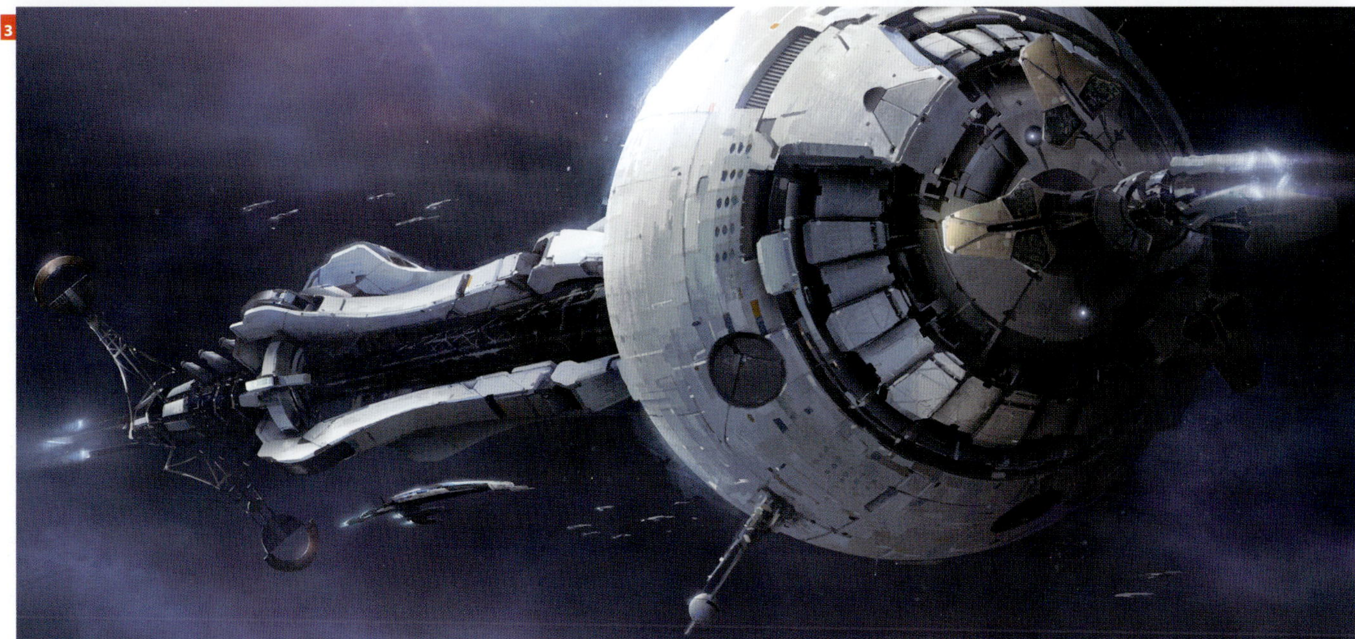

The Crucible by Brian Sum [3]

Photoshop CS3 | © 2012 EA International (Studio and Publishing) Ltd. *Mass Effect*, the *Mass Effect* logo, BioWare and the BioWare logo are trademarks of EA International (Studio and Publishing) Ltd. EA and the EA logo are trademarks of Electronic Arts Inc. All other trademarks are the property of their respective owners.

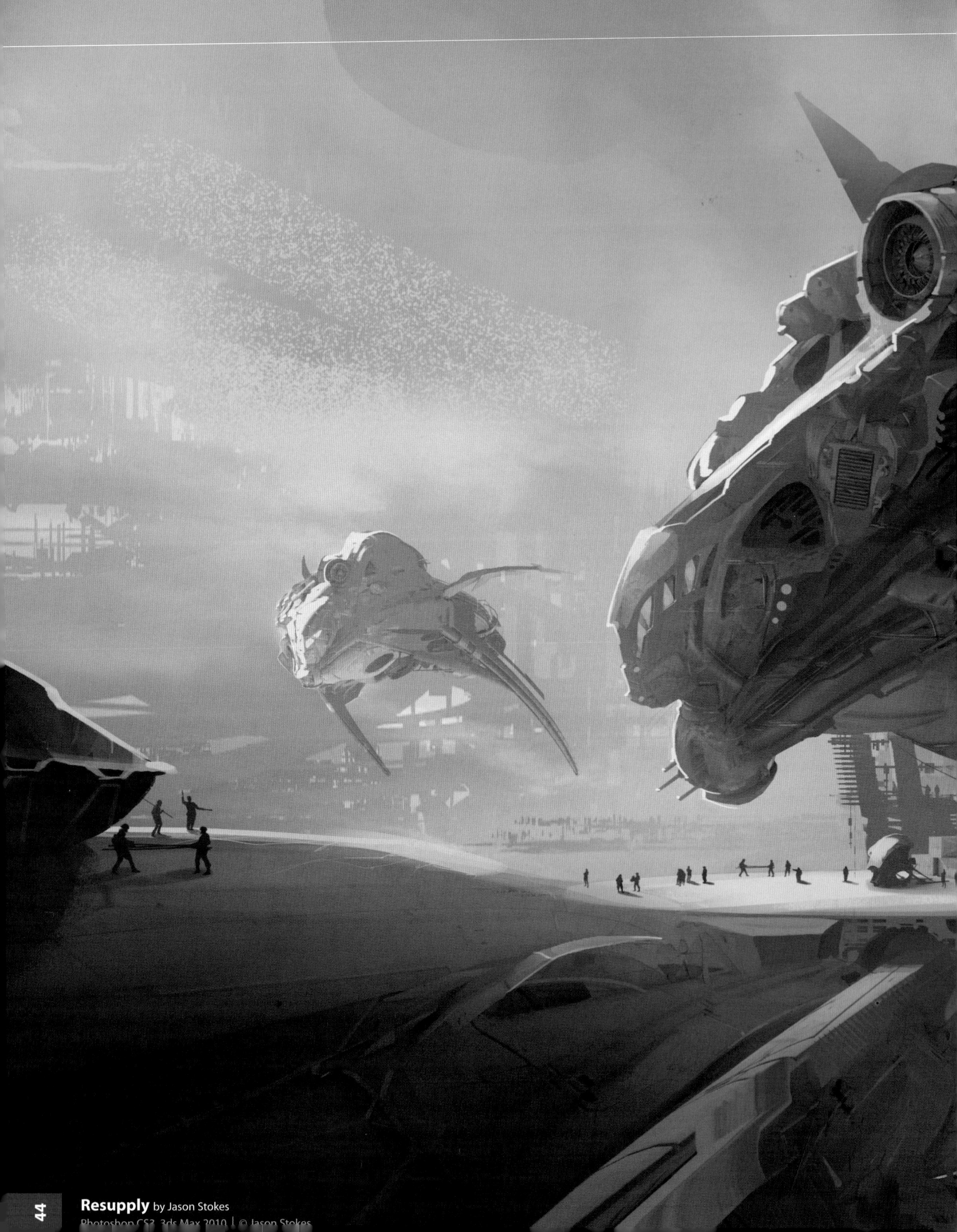

Resupply by Jason Stokes
Photoshop CS3, 3ds Max 2010 | © Jason Stokes

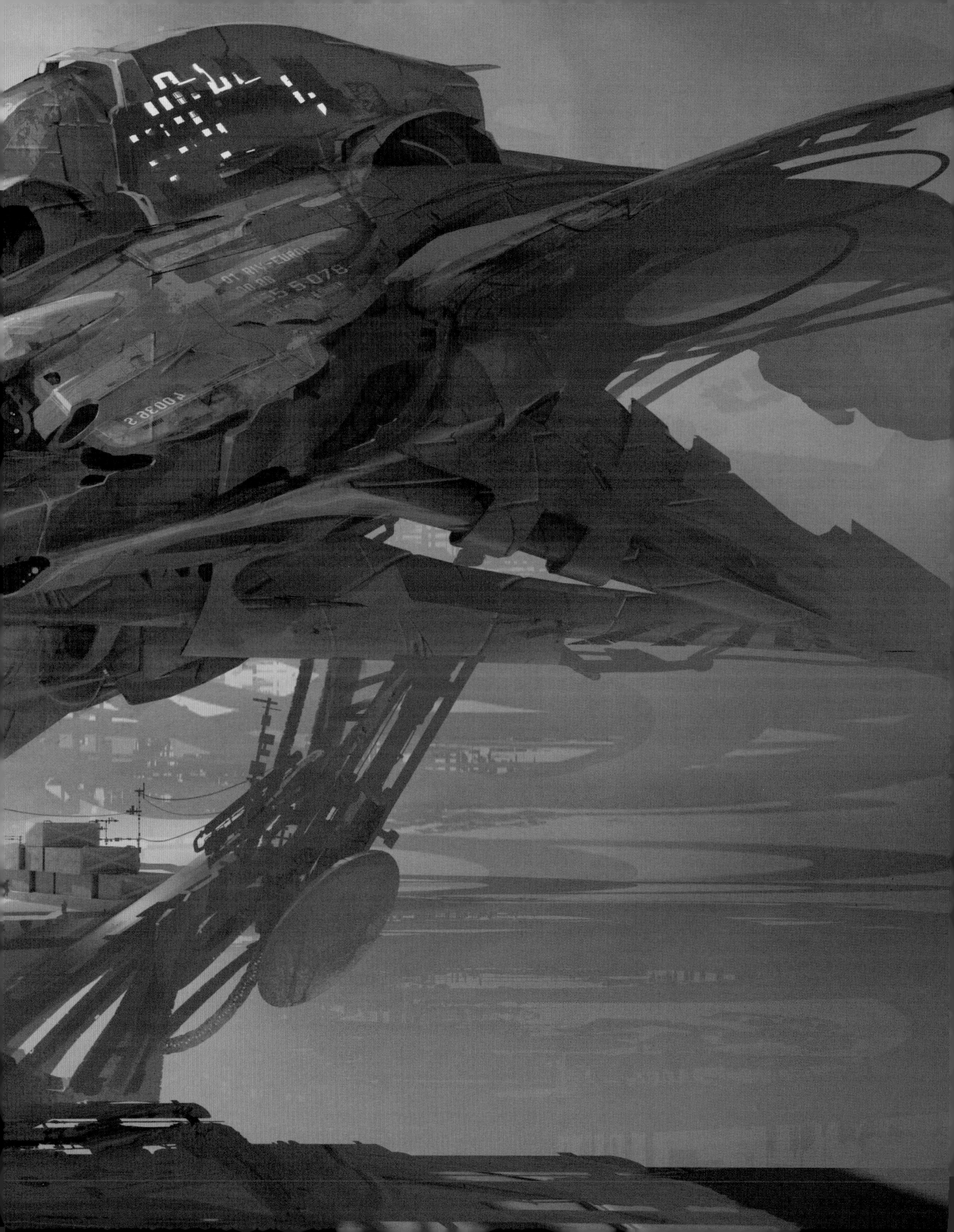

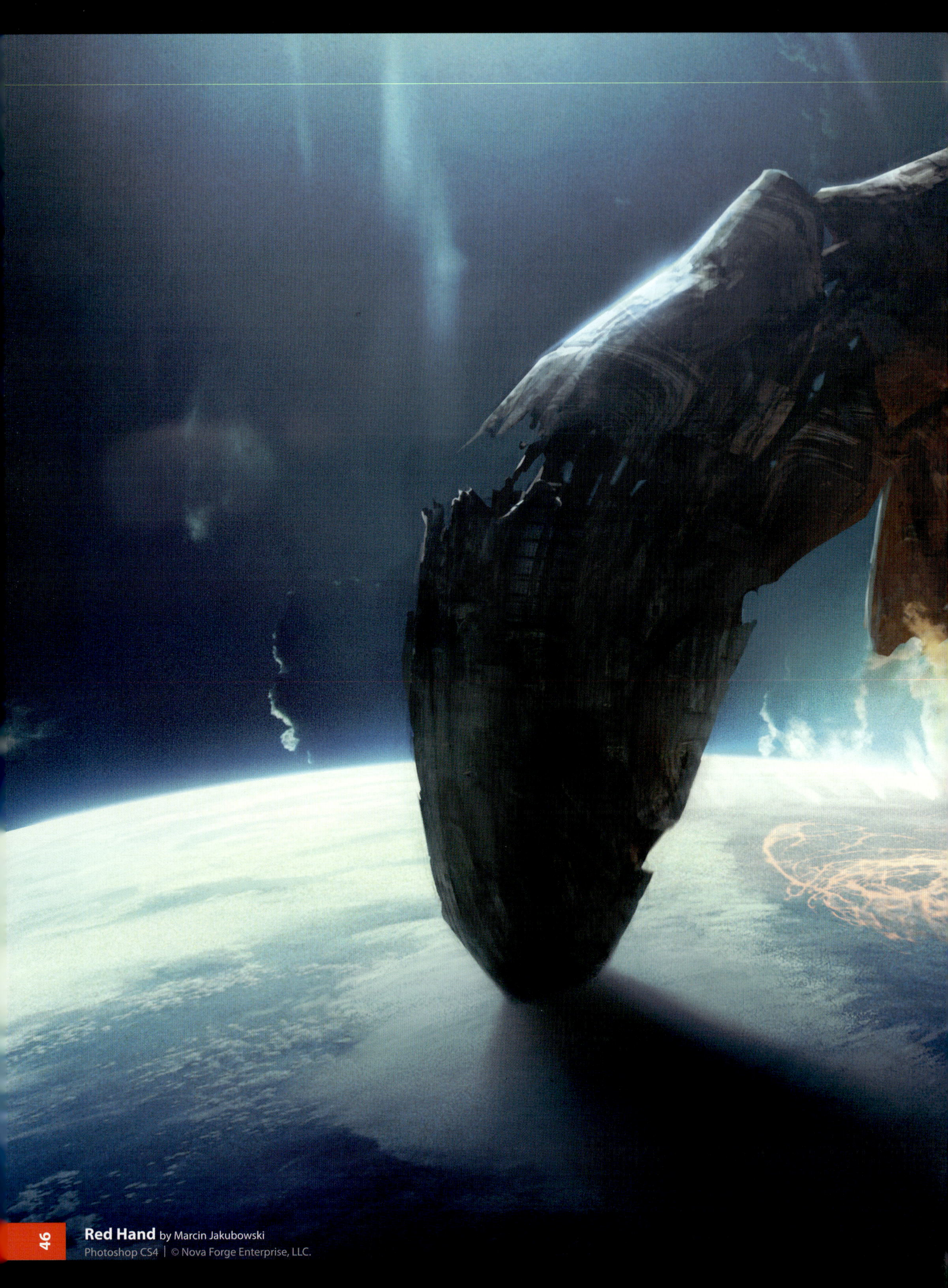

Red Hand by Marcin Jakubowski
Photoshop CS4 |

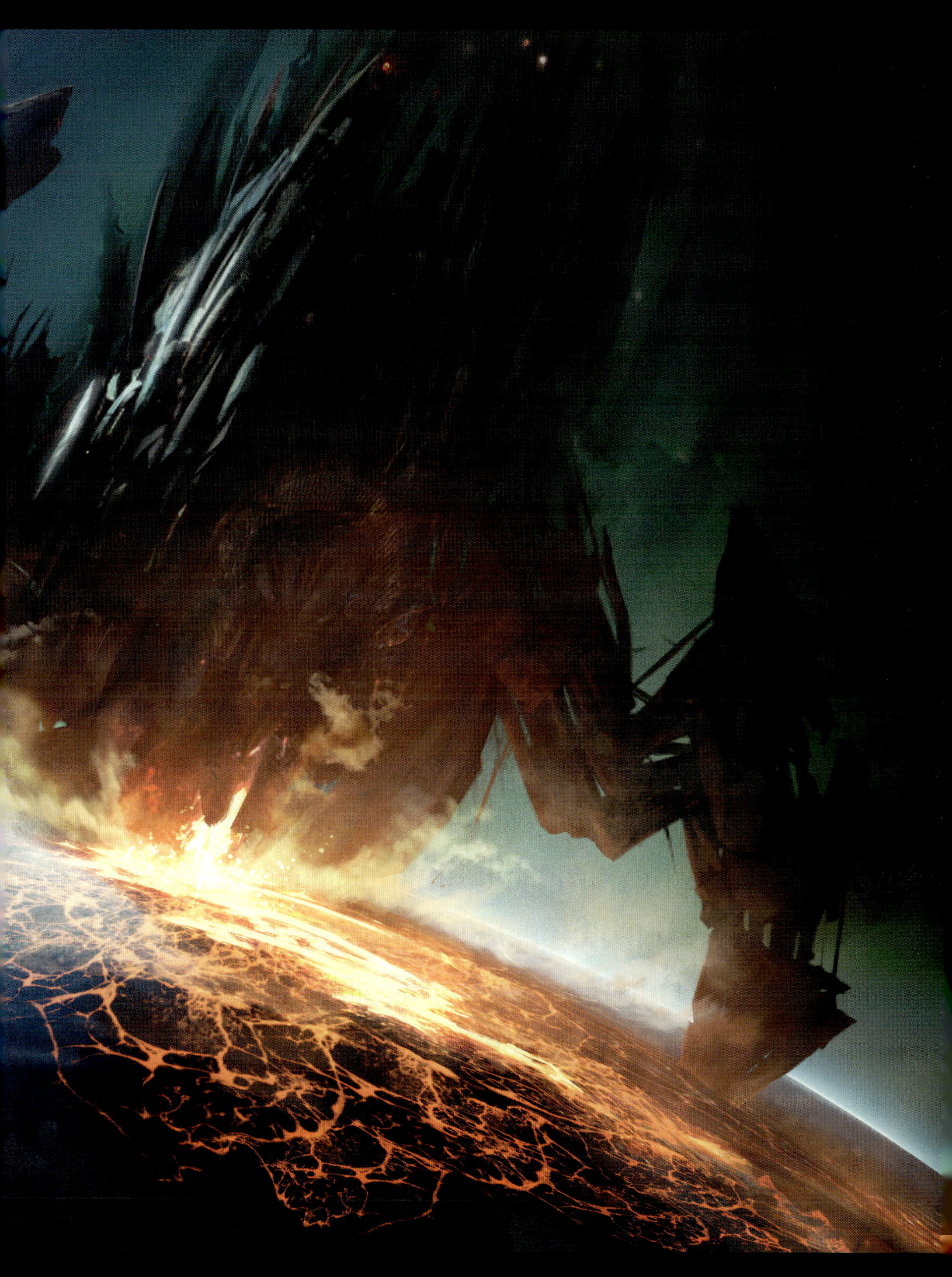

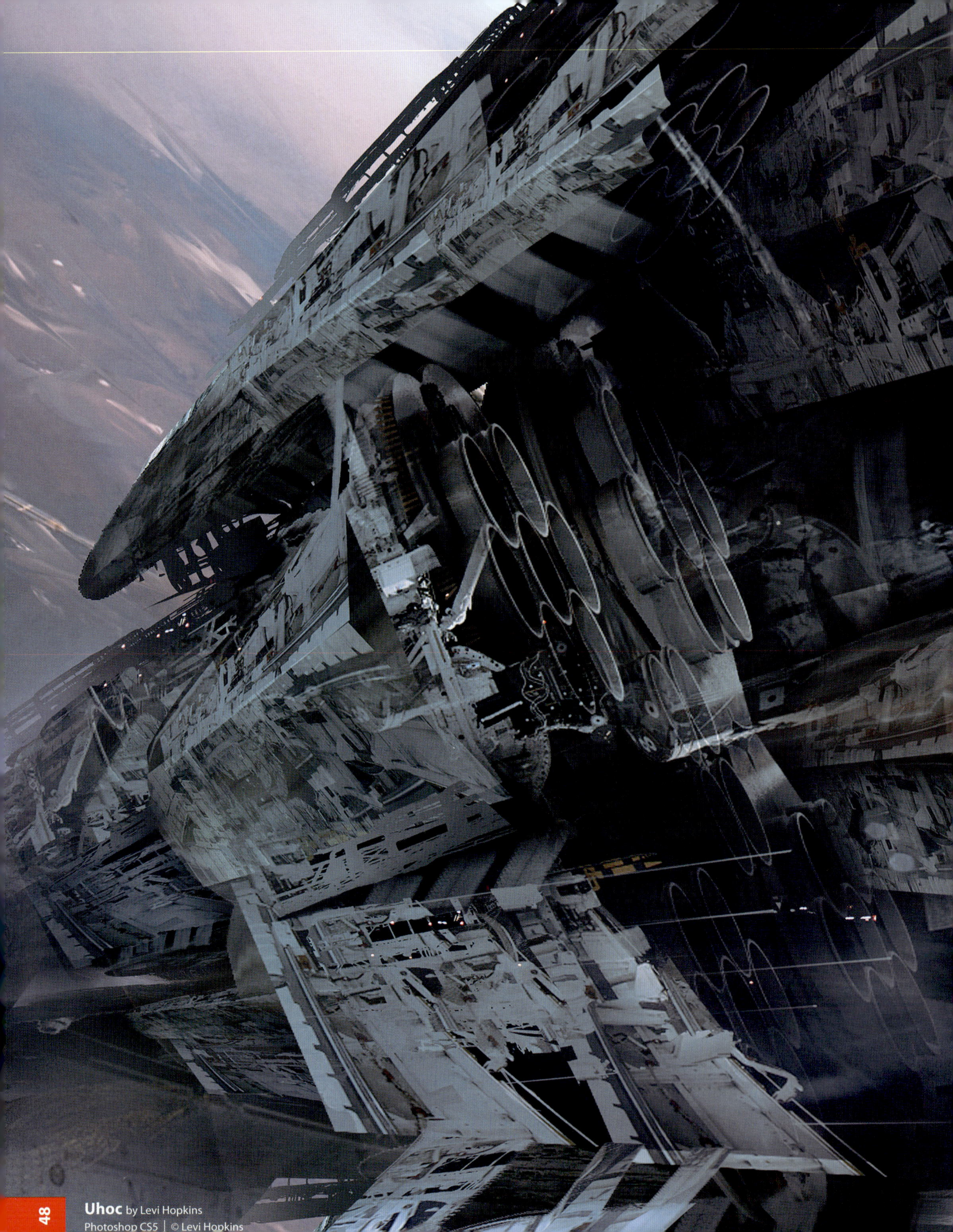

Uhoc by Levi Hopkins
Photoshop CS5 | © Levi Hopkins

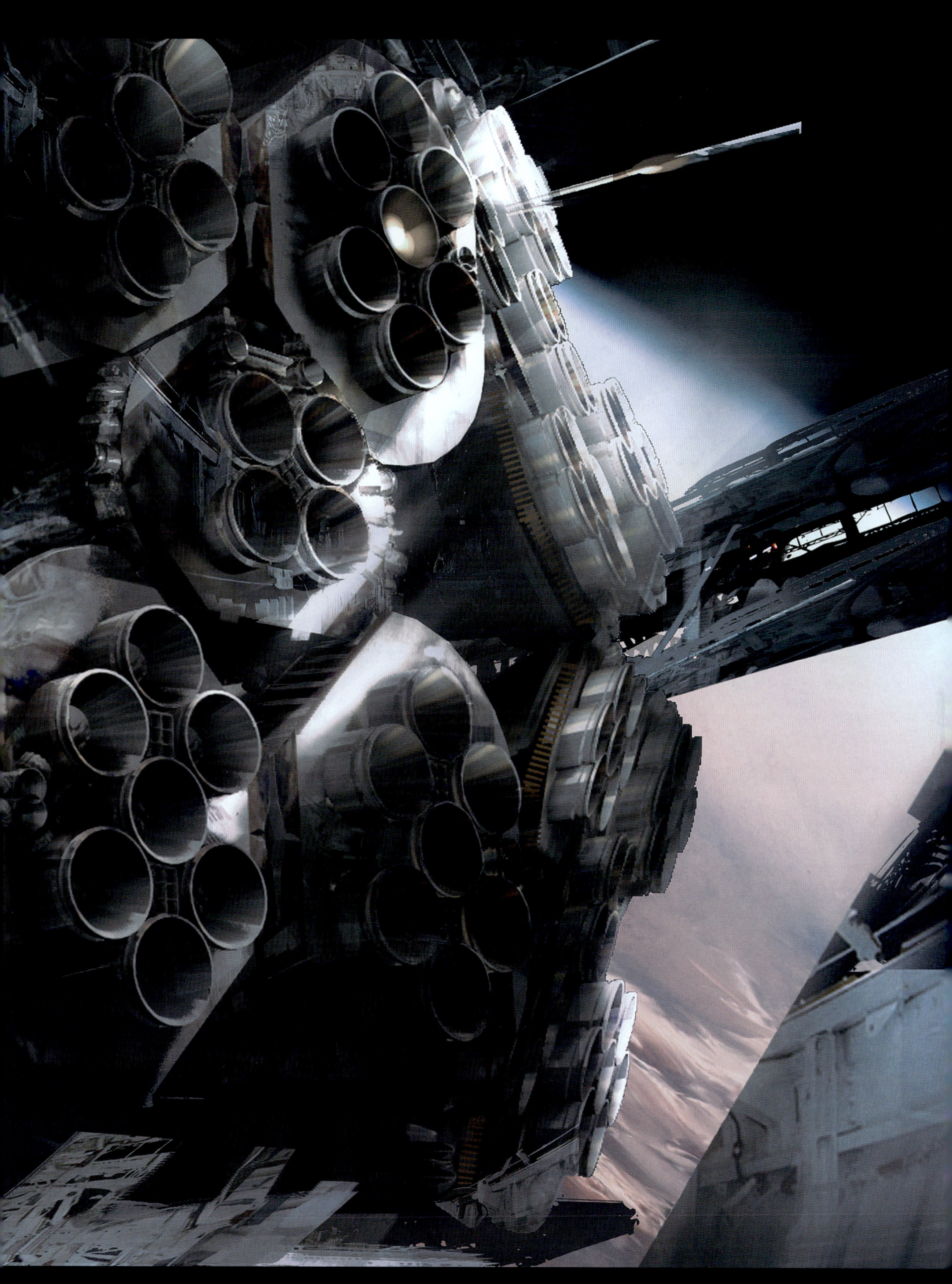

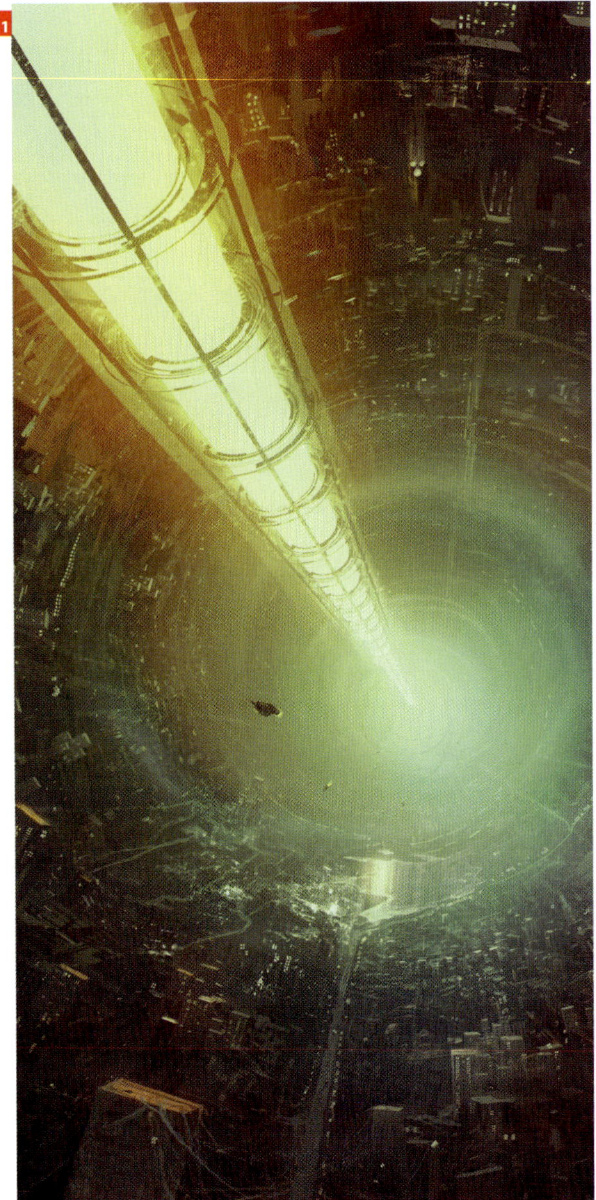

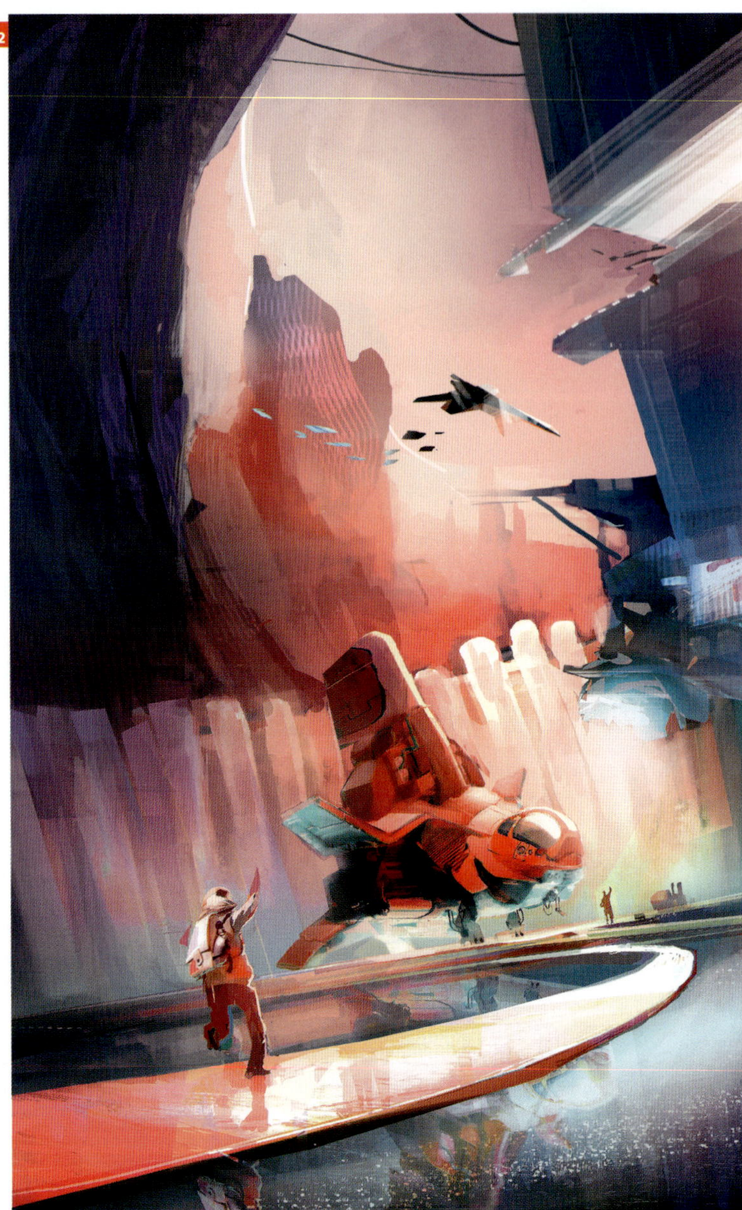

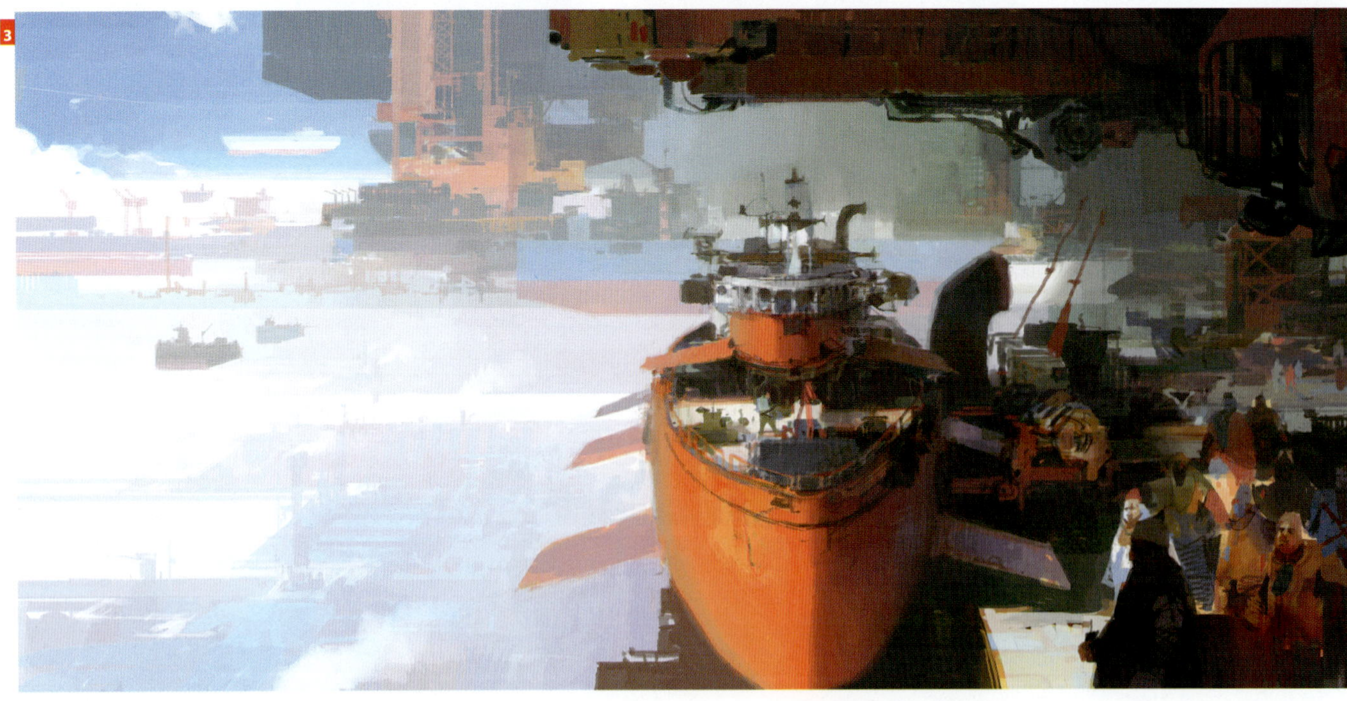

Amalthea by Viktor Titov [1]
Photoshop CS3 | © Viktor Titov

Shipping Nemo by Xavier Etchepare [2]
Photoshop CS3 | © xavieretchepare

Red Tug by Theo Prins [3]
Photoshop CS3 | © Theo Prins

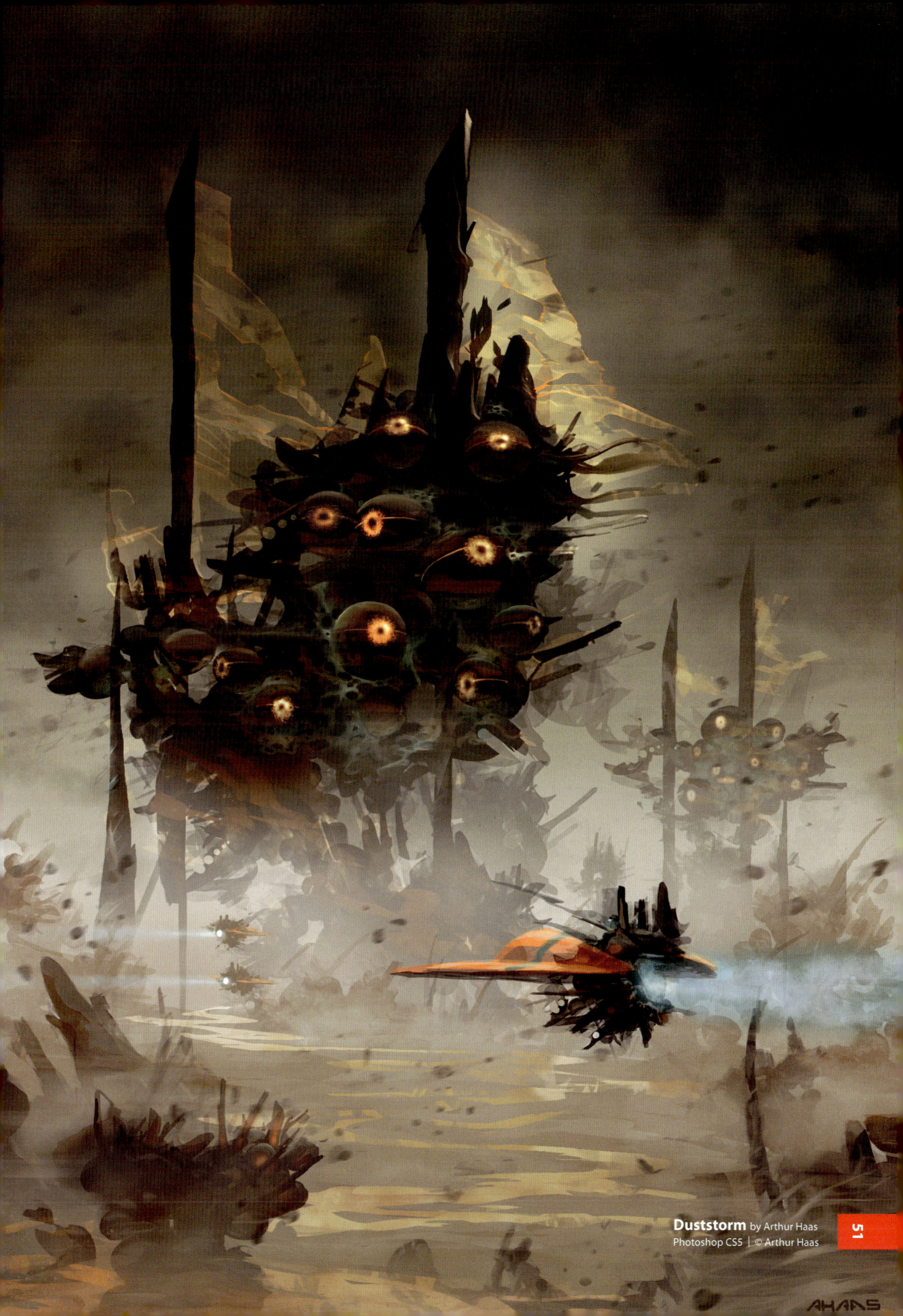

Duststorm by Arthur Haas
Photoshop CS5 | © Arthur Haas

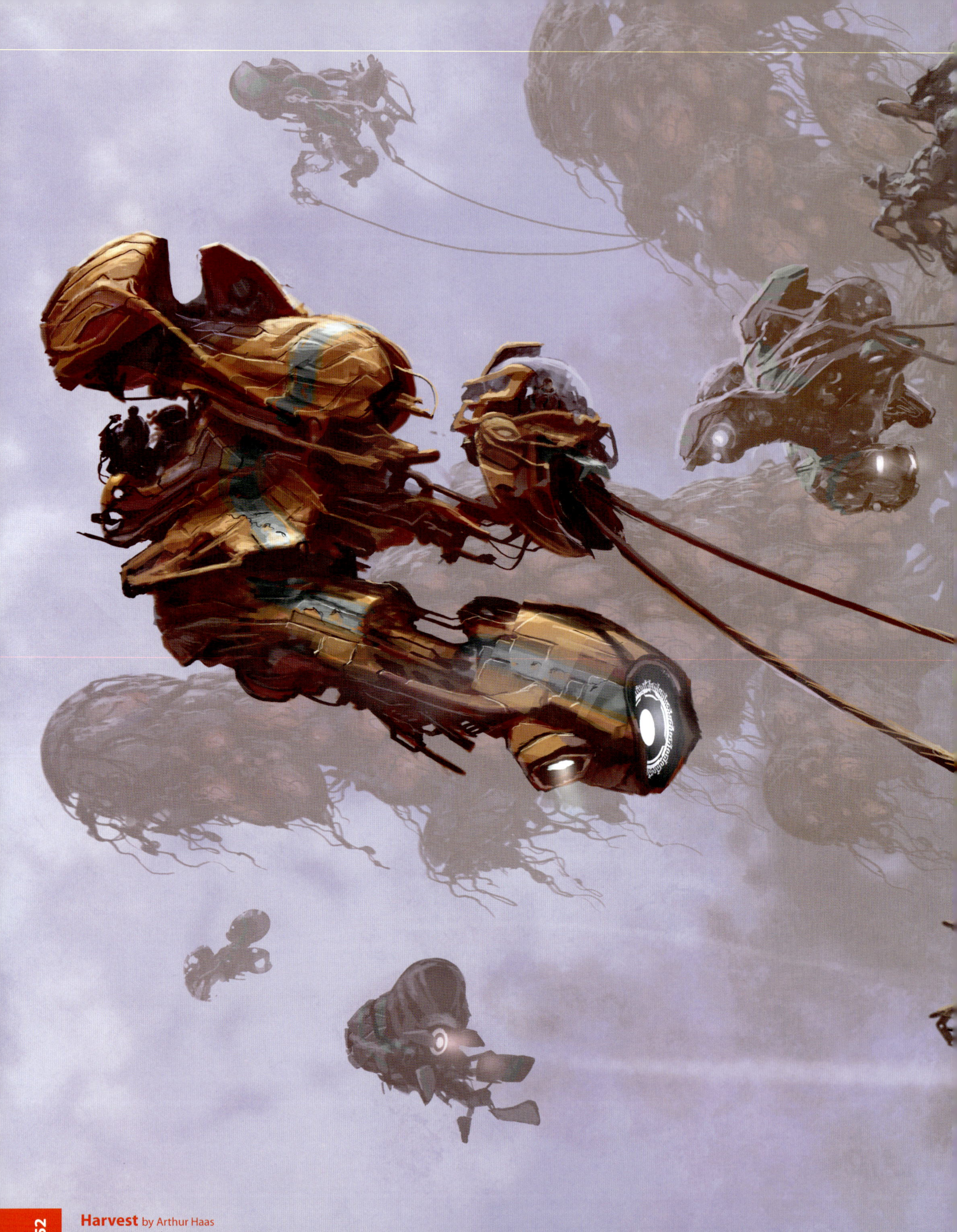

Harvest by Arthur Haas
Photoshop CS5 | © Arthur Haas

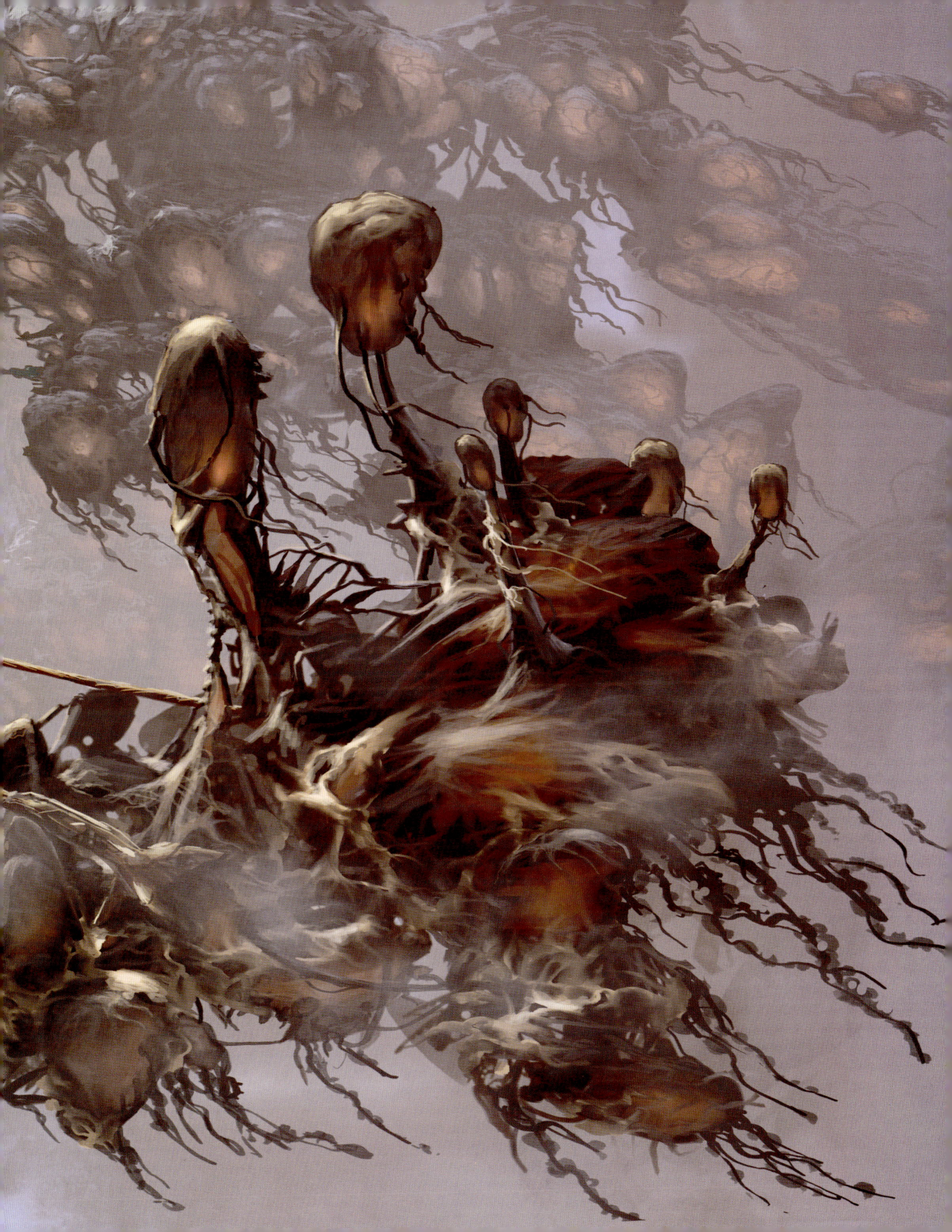

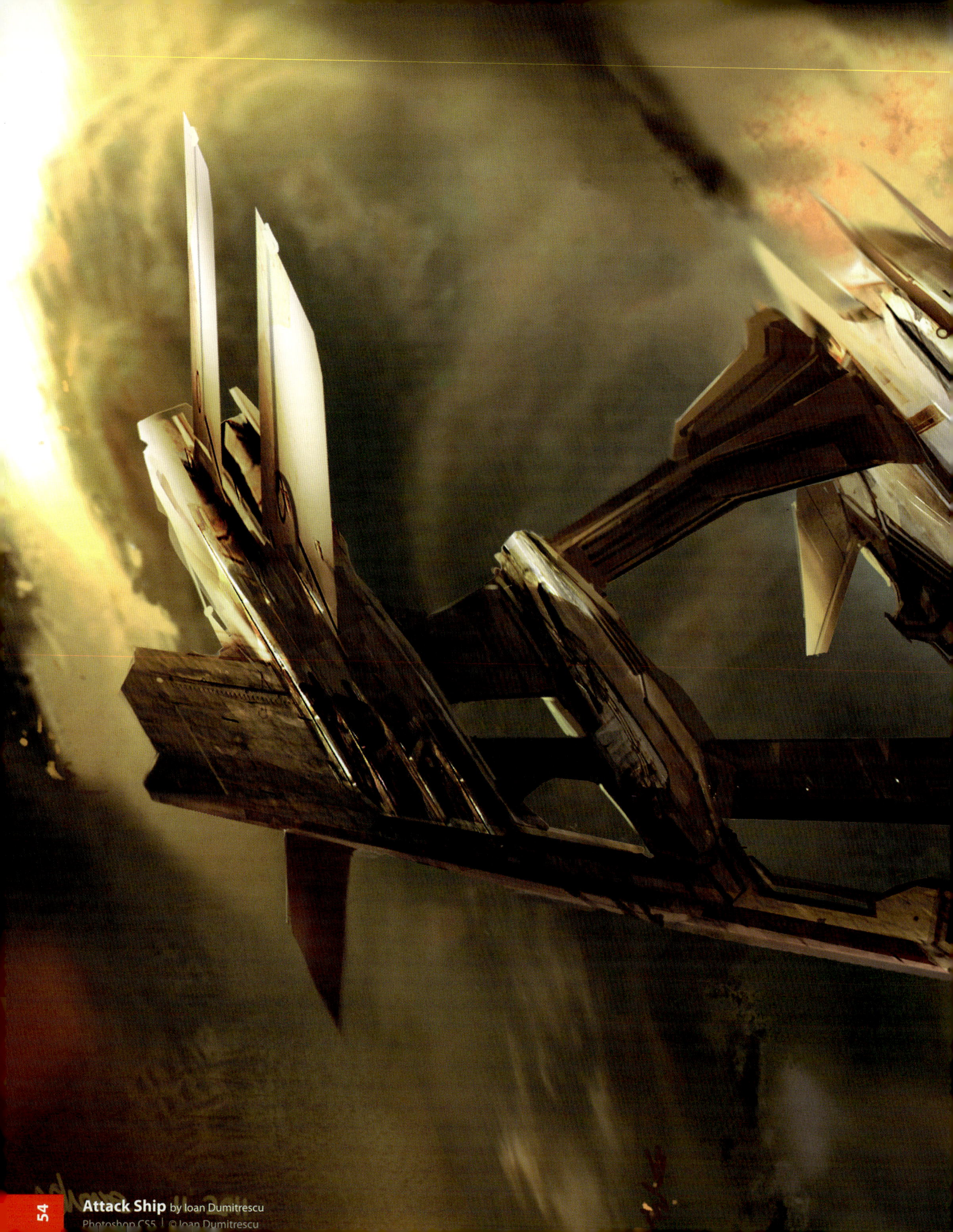

Attack Ship by Ioan Dumitrescu
Photoshop CS5 |

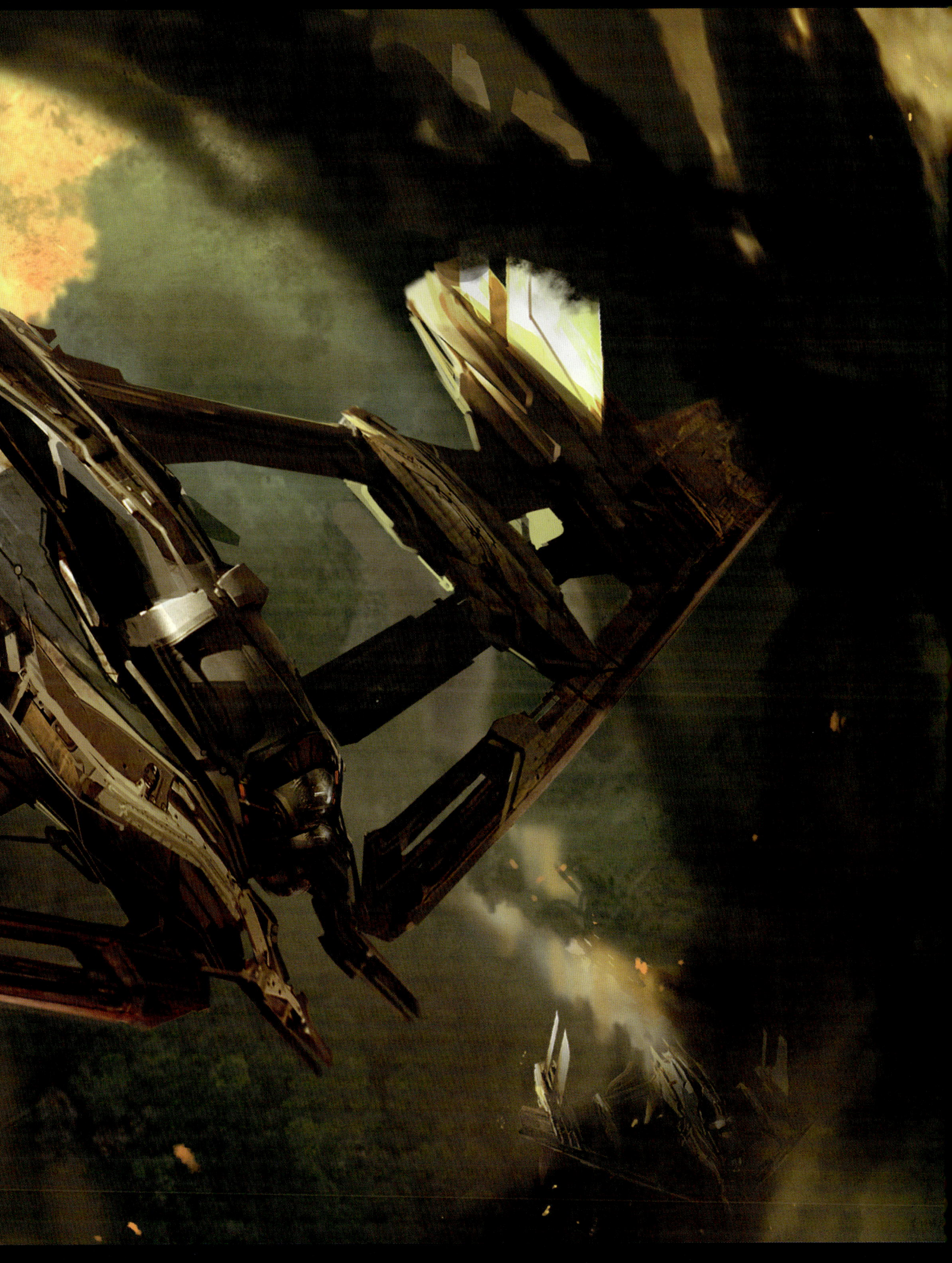

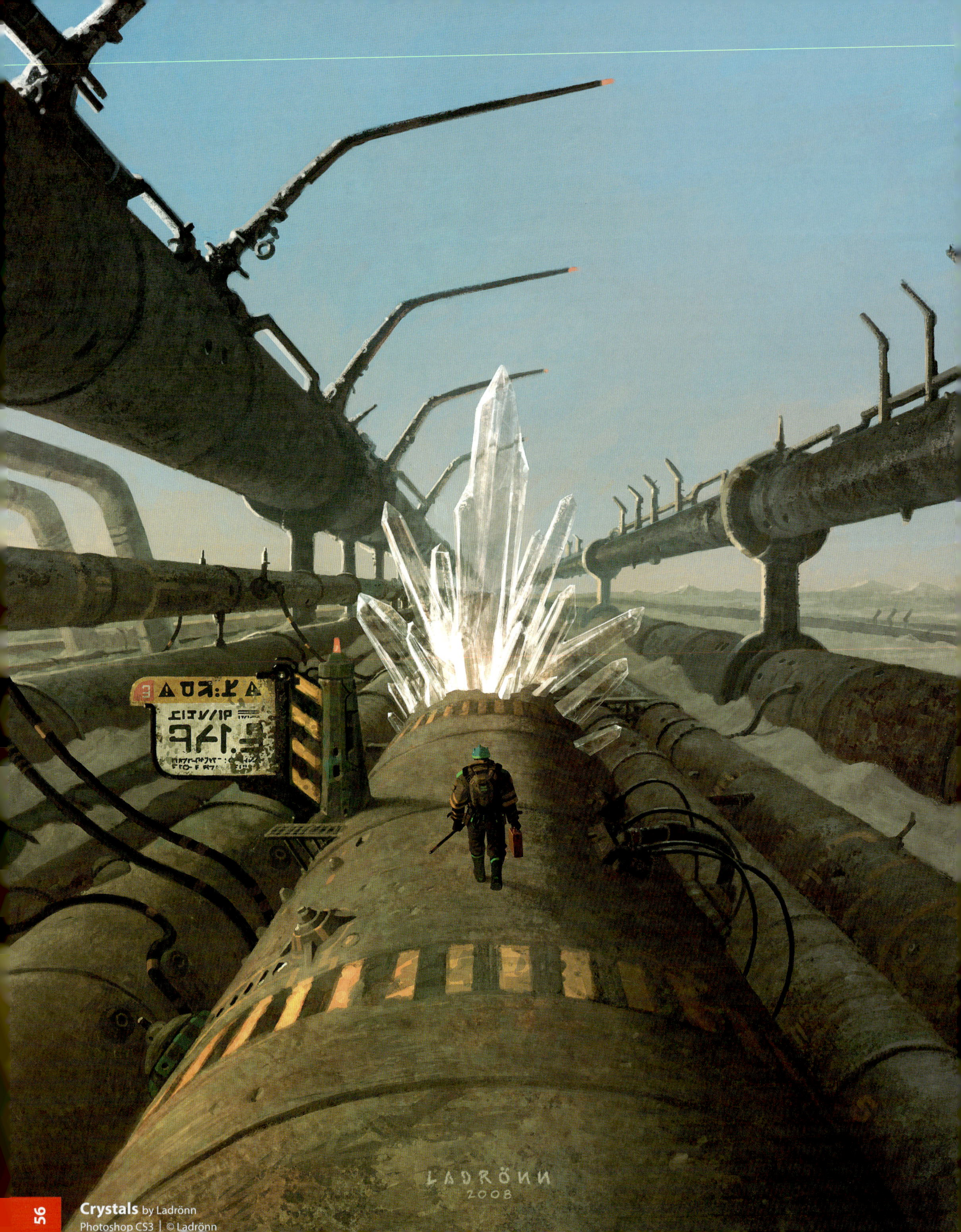

Crystals by Ladrönn
Photoshop CS3 | © Ladrönn

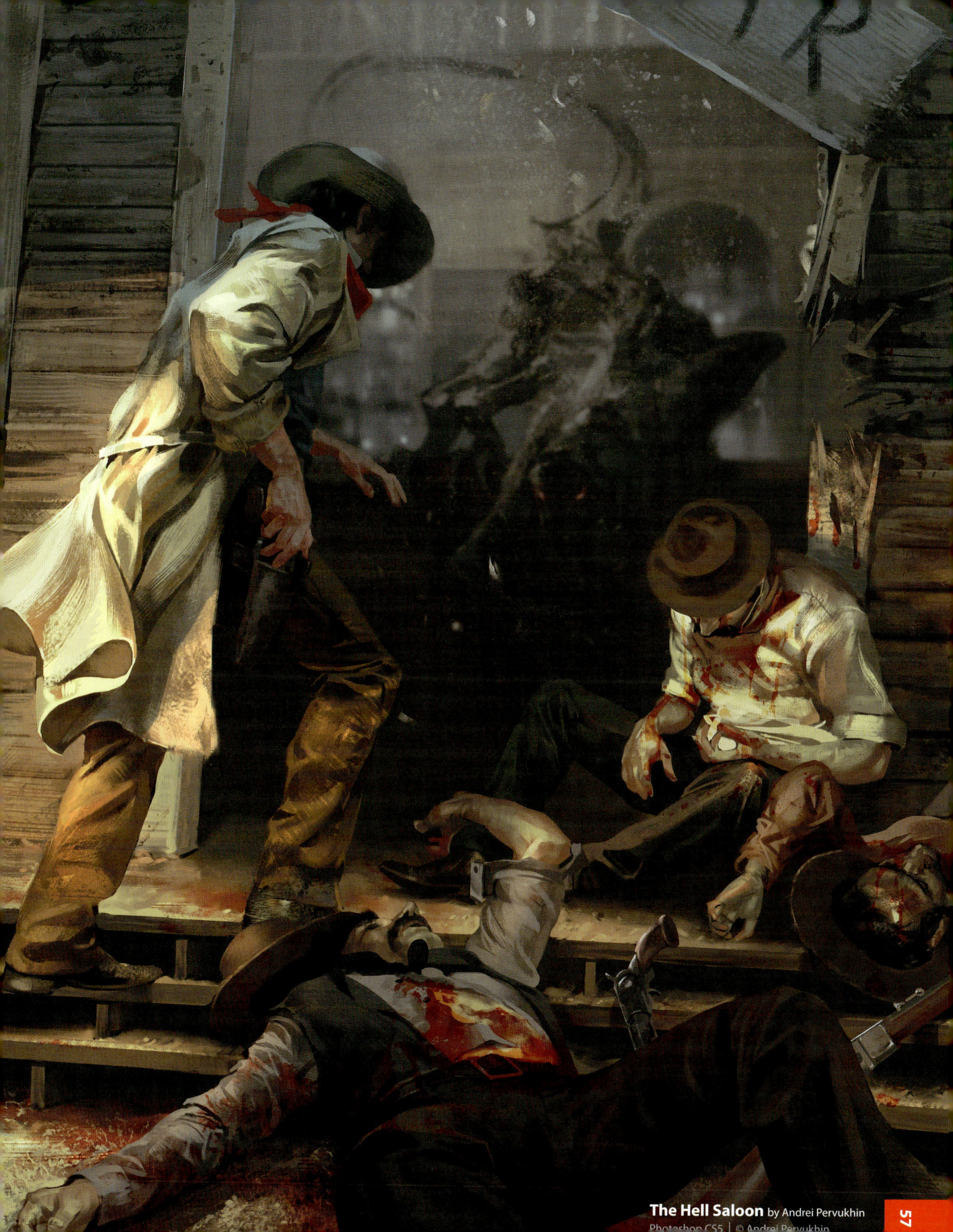

The Hell Saloon by Andrei Pervukhin
Photoshop CS5 |

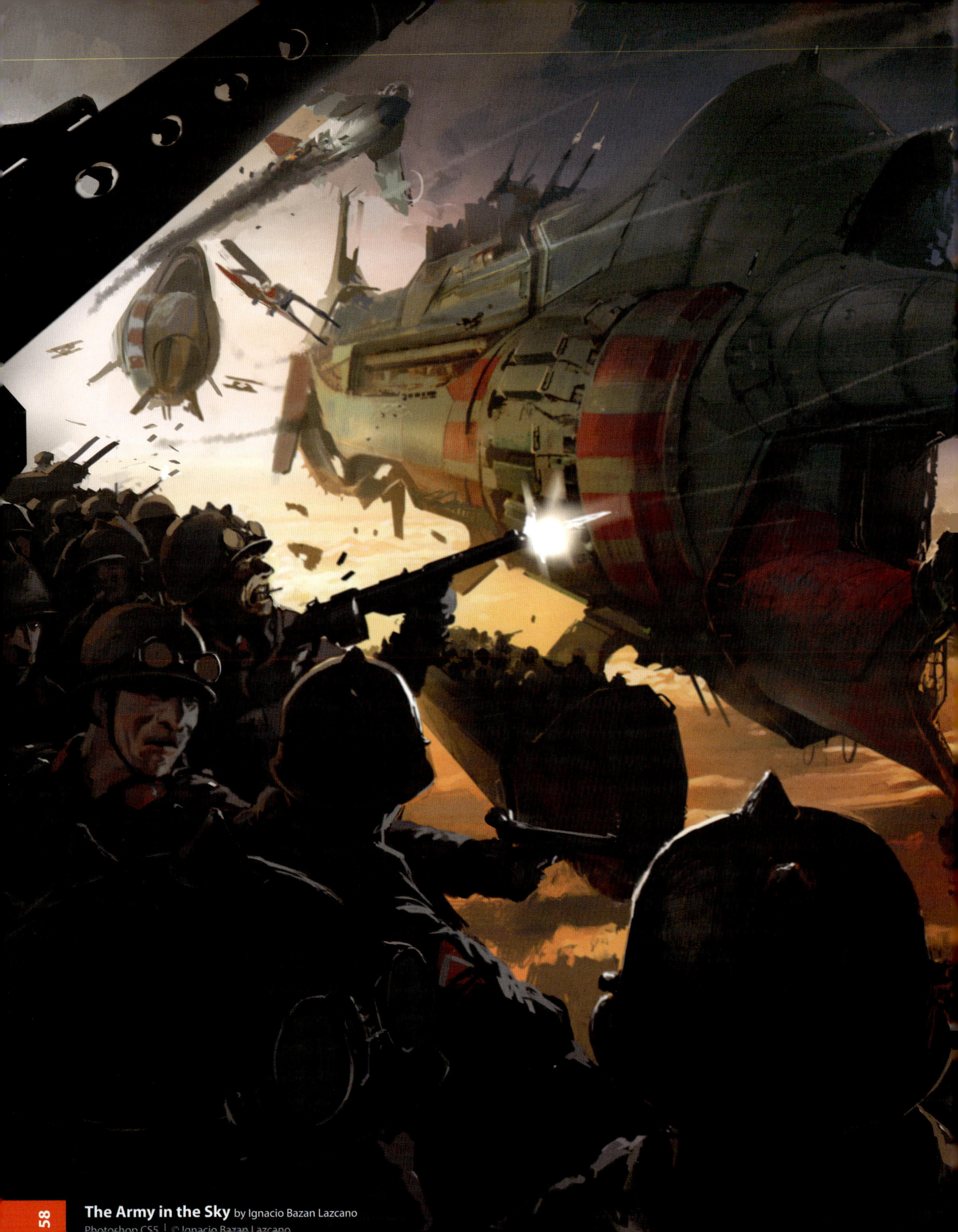

The Army in the Sky by Ignacio Bazan Lazcano

Photoshop CS5 |

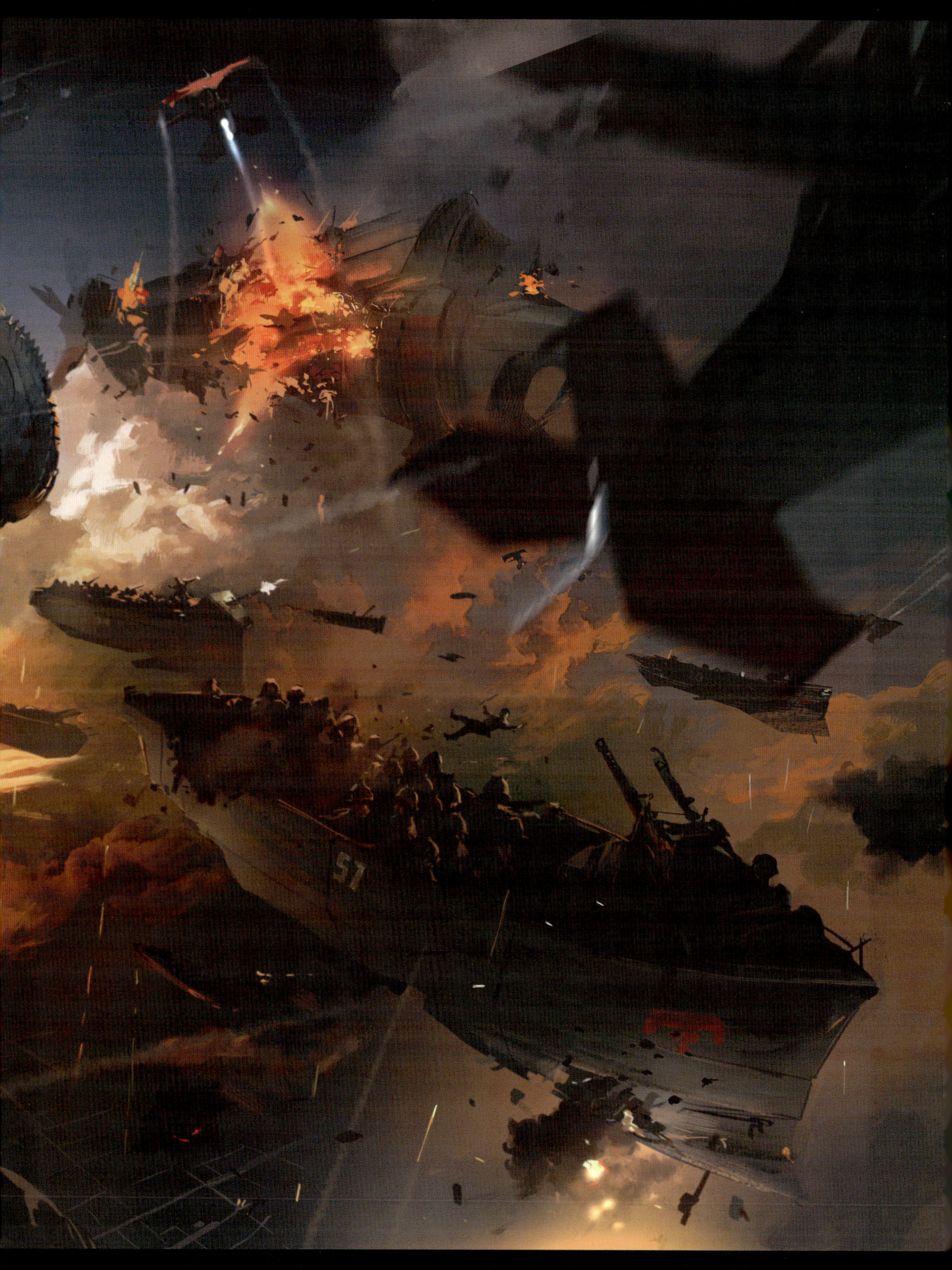

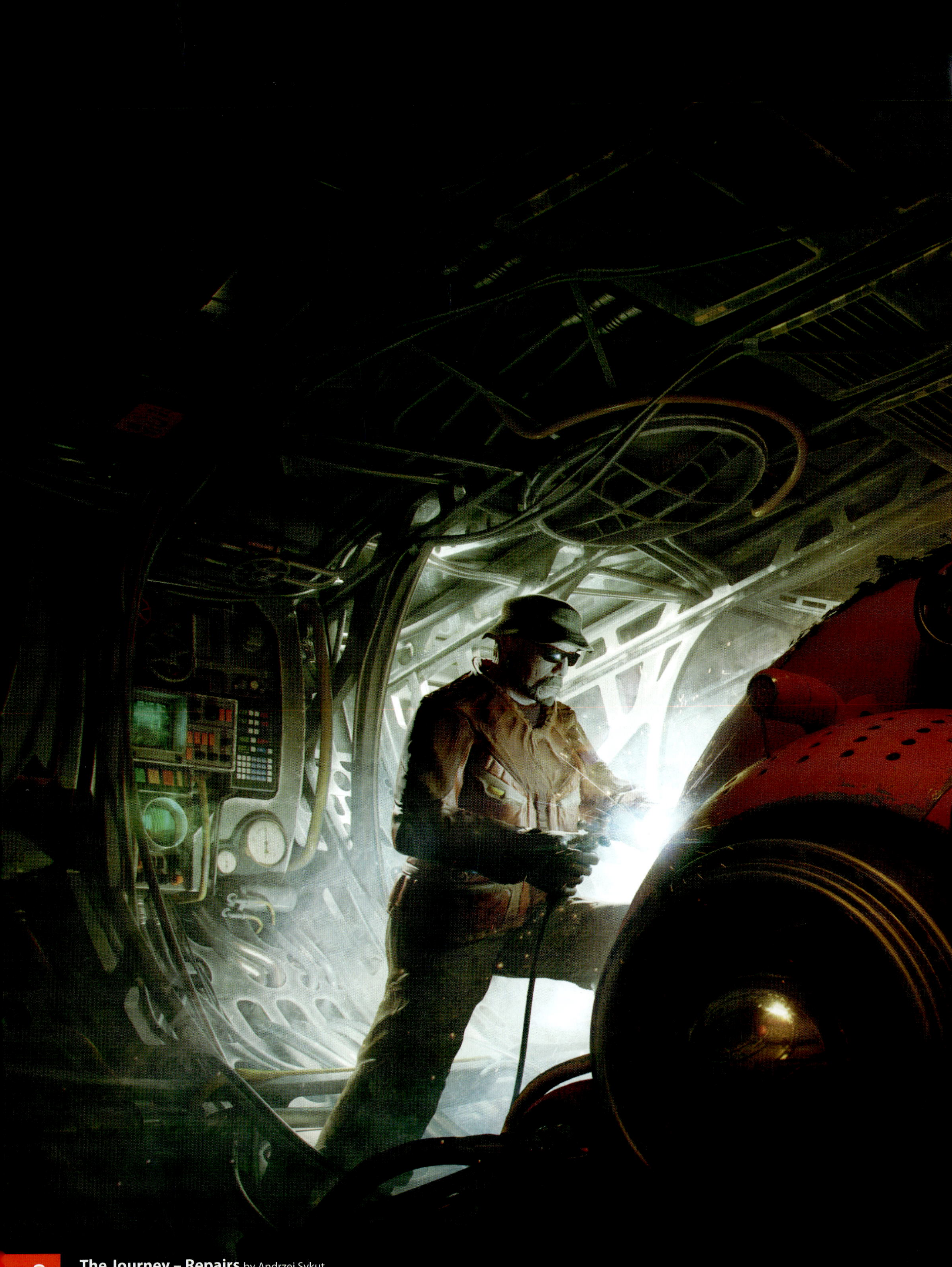

The Journey – Repairs by Andrzej Sykut
3ds Max 2011, ZBrush 4R3 | © Andrzej Sykut

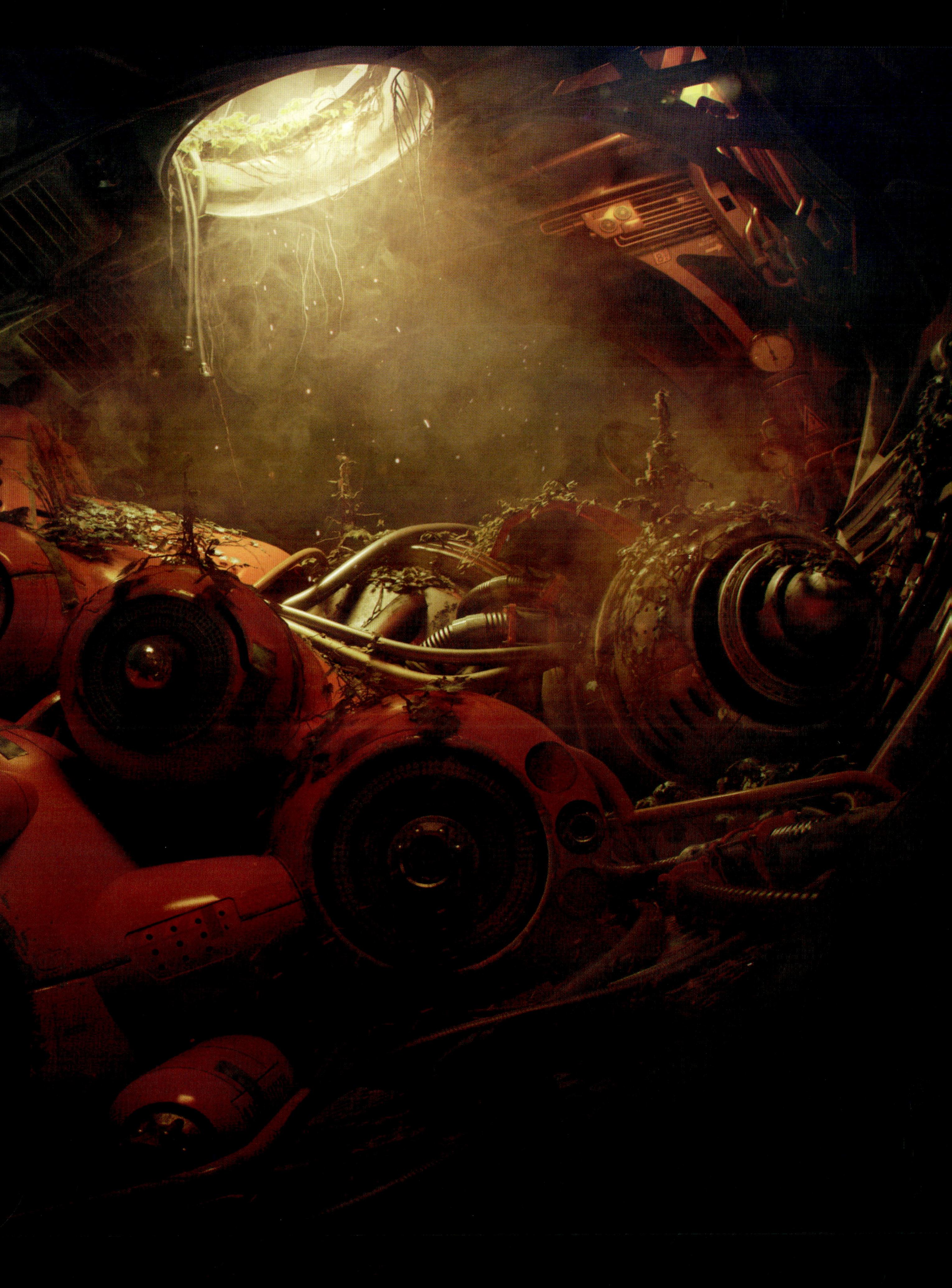

1

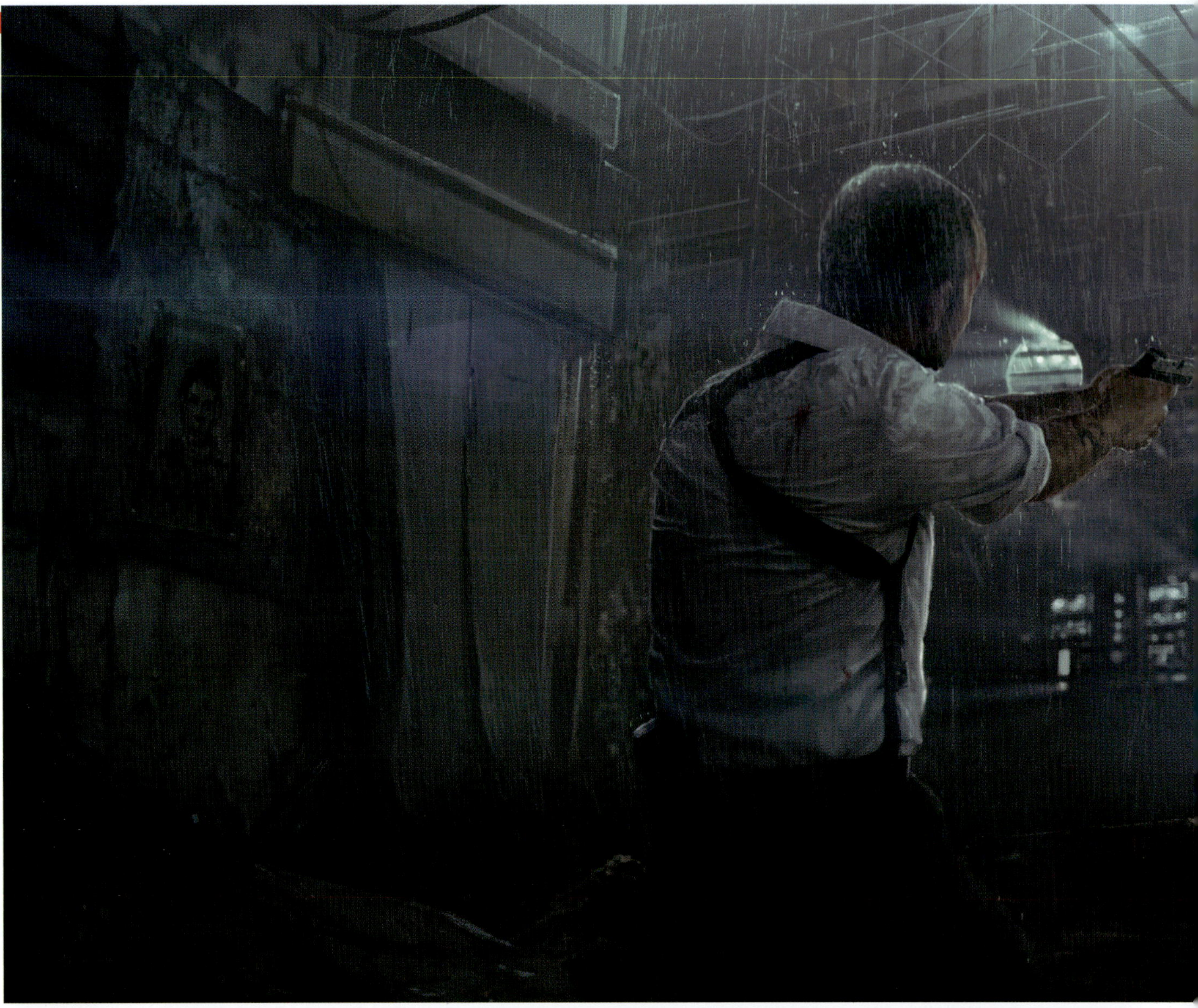

2

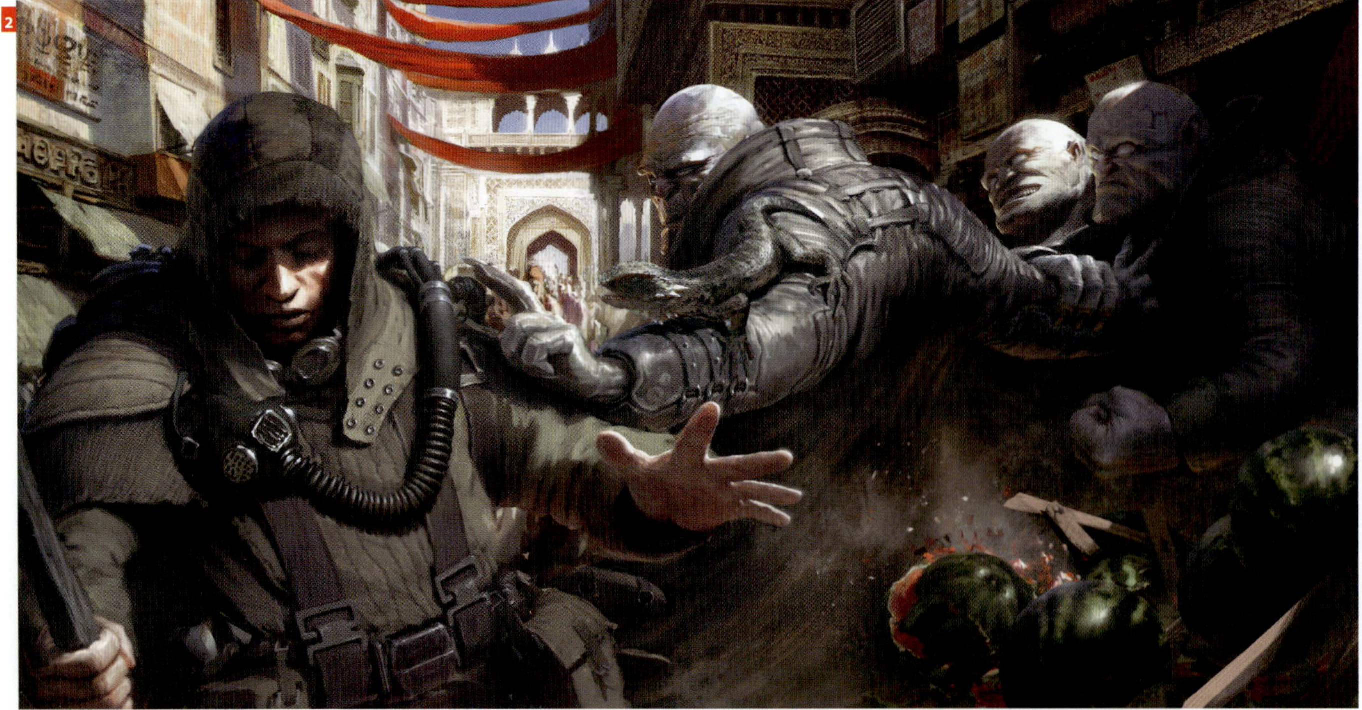

Leave Him by Simon Weaner [1]
Photoshop CS2 | © Simon Weaner

Stranger by Marcin Jakubowski [2]
Photoshop CS4 | © Marcin Jakubowski

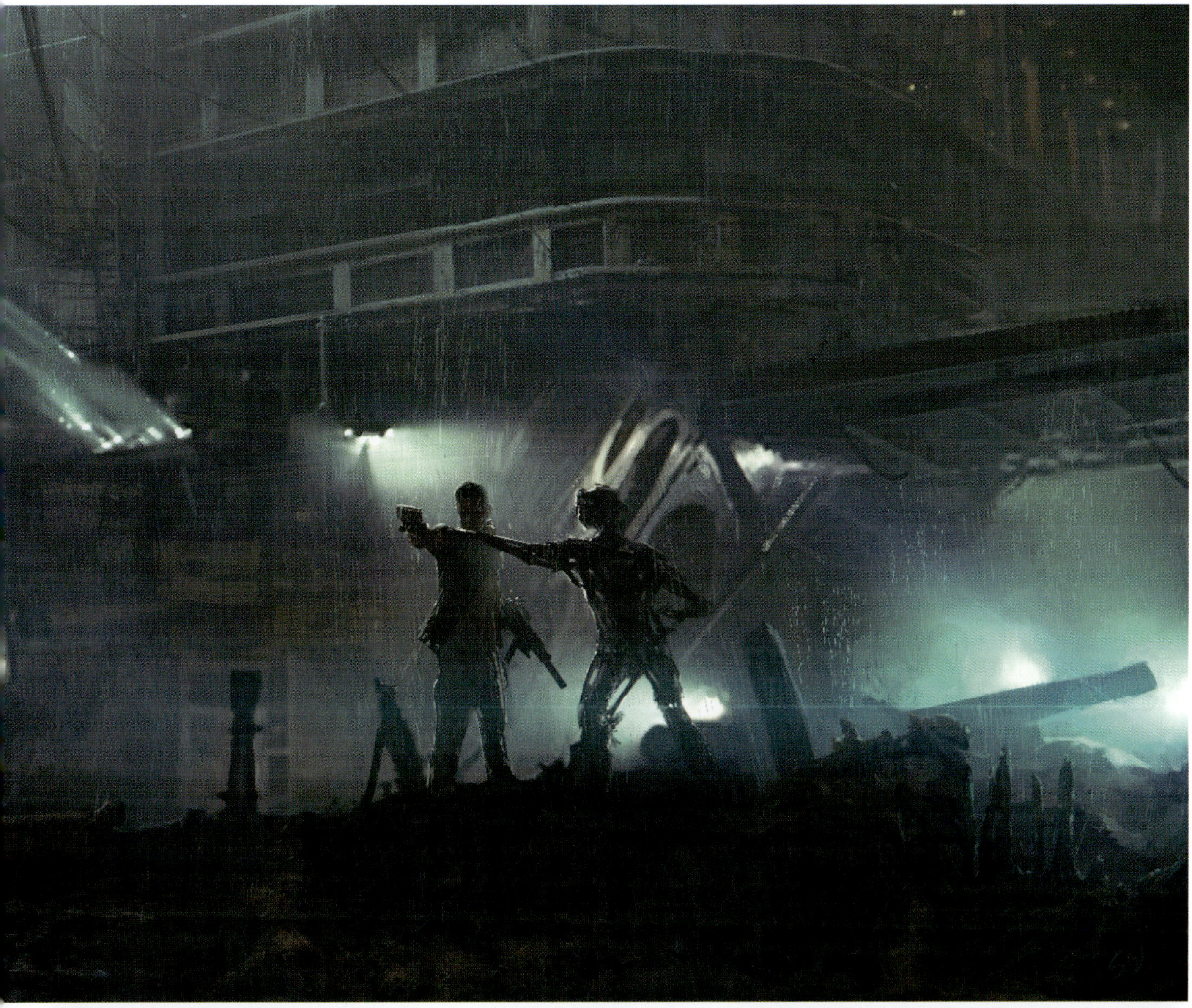

3

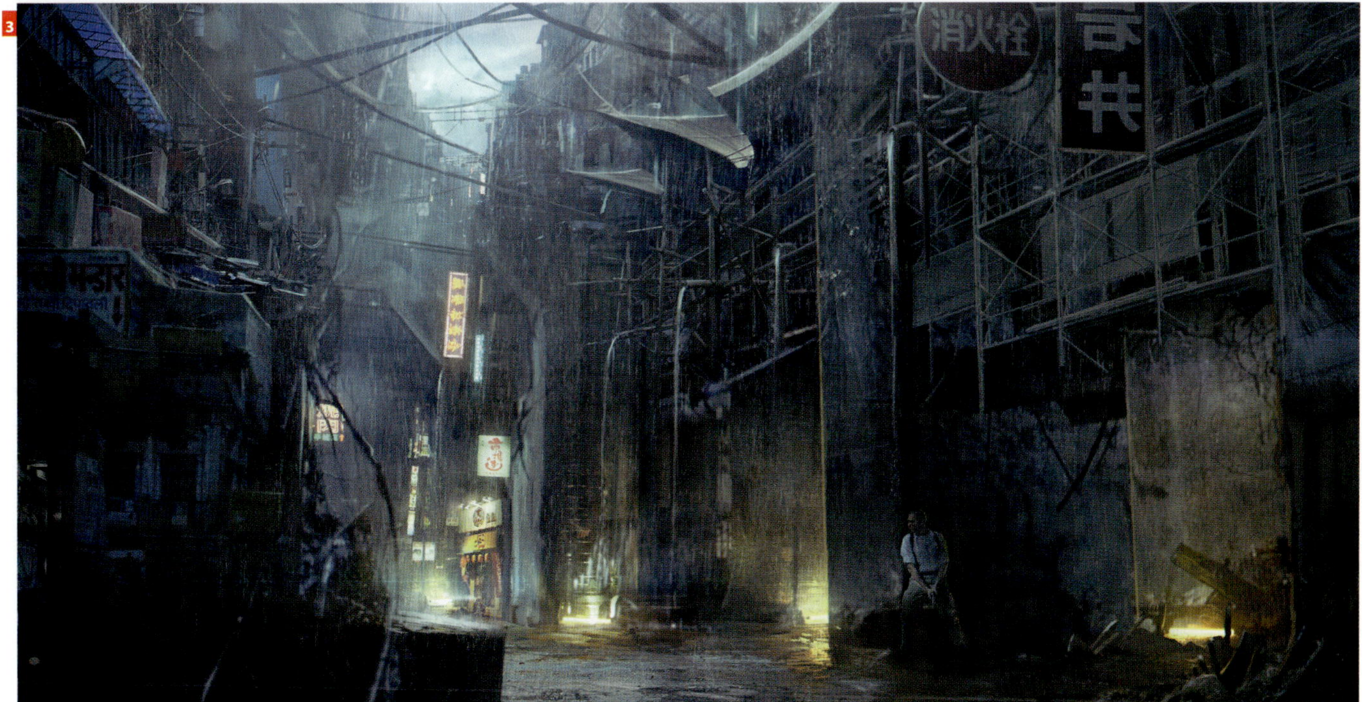

The Alley by Simon Weaner [1]
Photoshop CS2 | © Simon Weaner

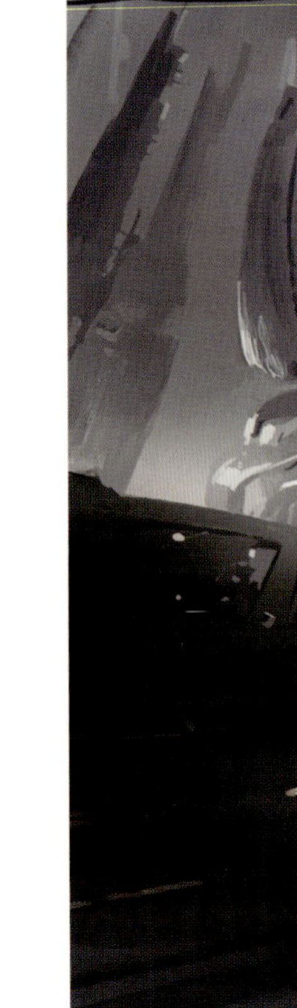

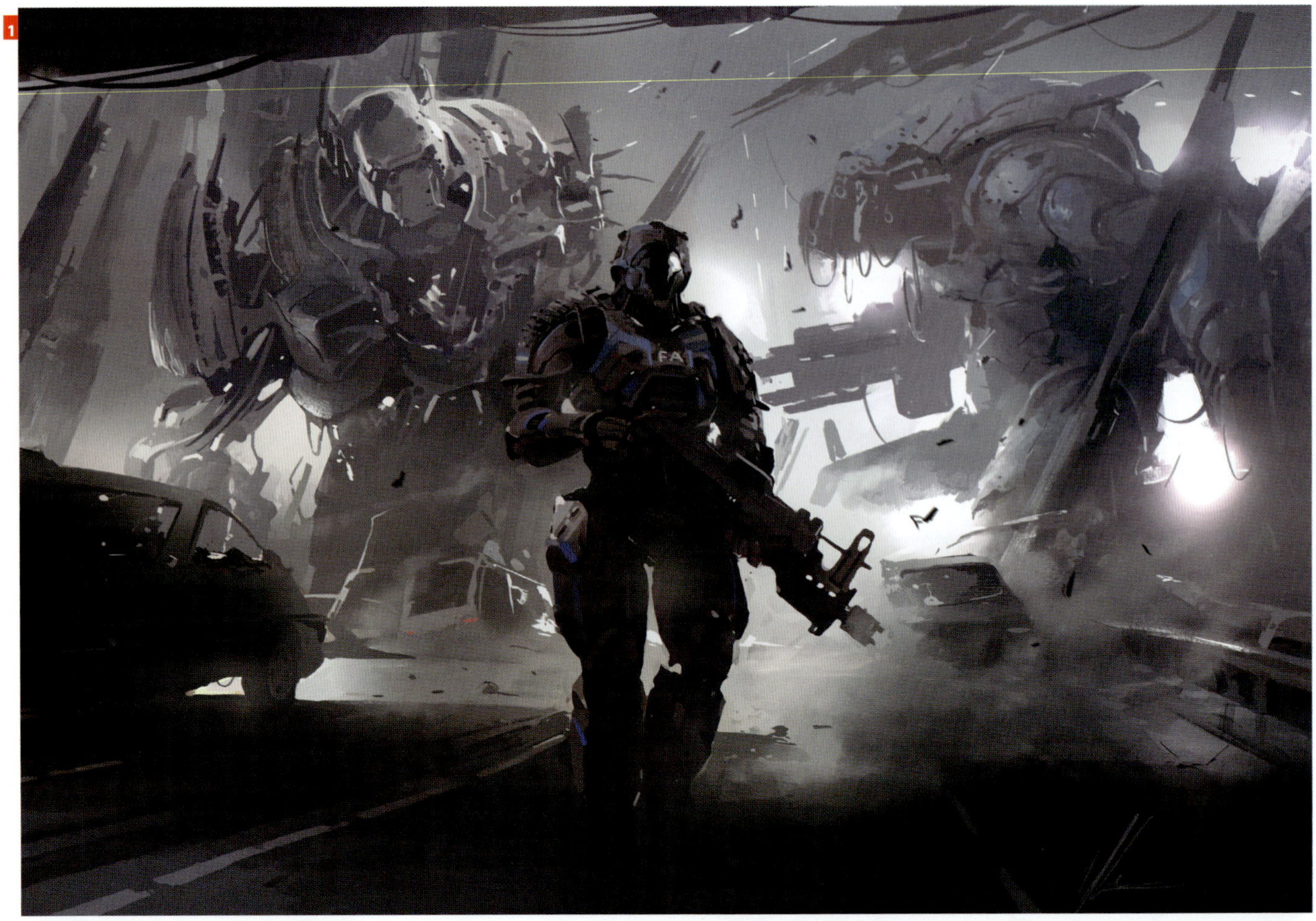

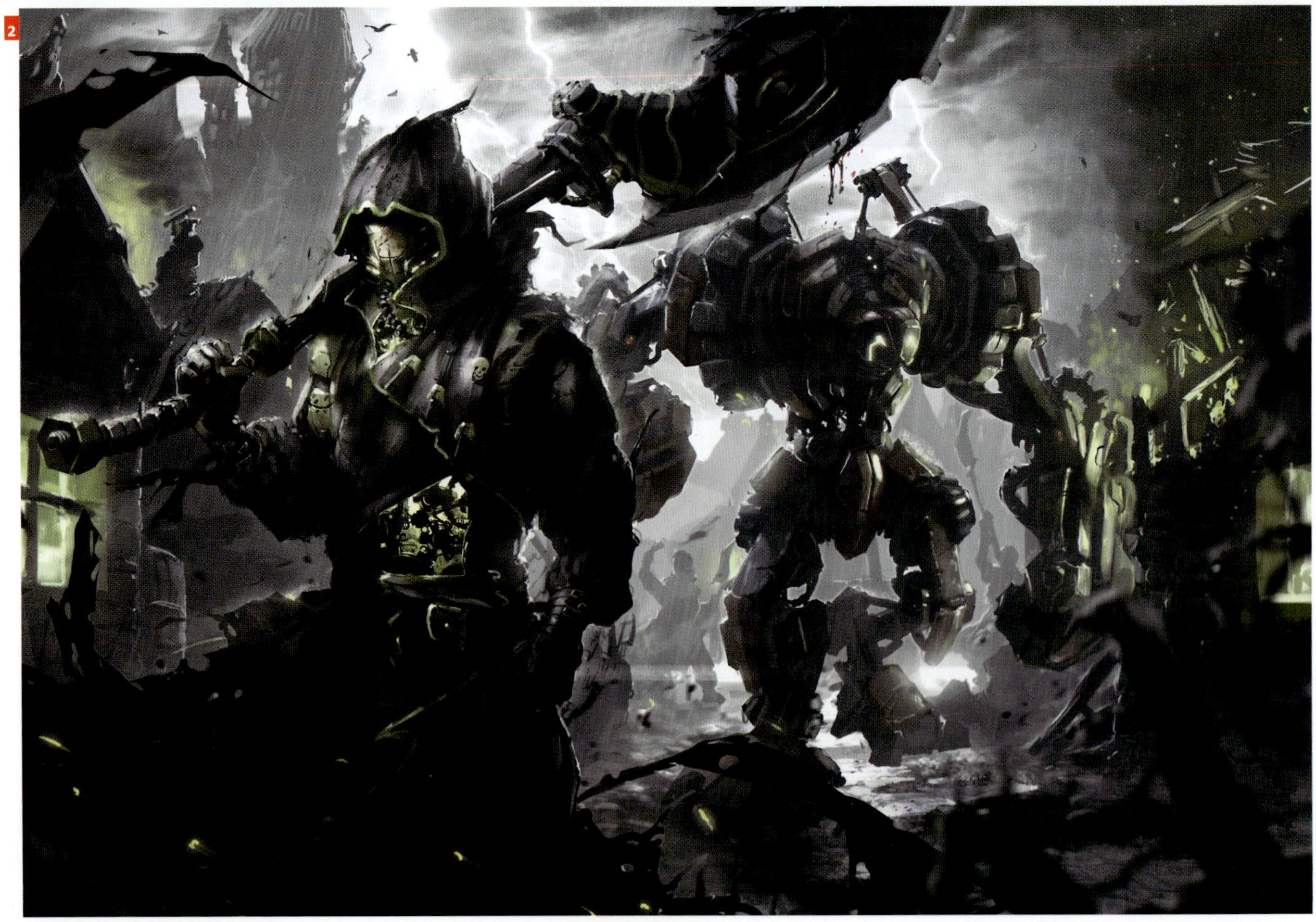

1

2

Sci-fi Character Design by Ignacio Bazan Lazcano [1]
Photoshop CS3 | © Ignacio Bazan Lazcano

Mecamage by Lefevre Vincent [2]
Photoshop CS3 | © Lefevre Vincent

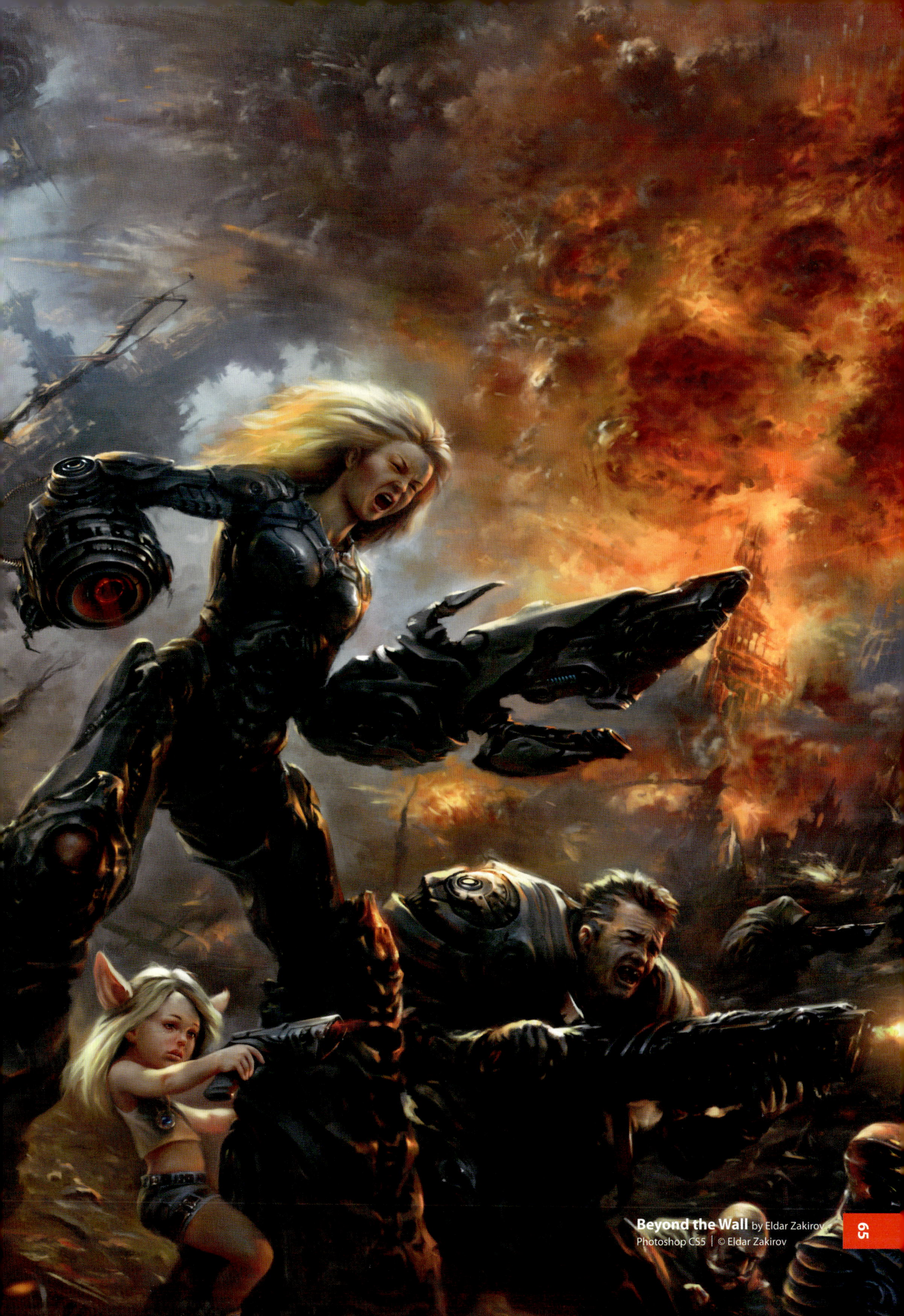

Beyond the Wall by Eldar Zakirov
Photoshop CS5 | © Eldar Zakirov

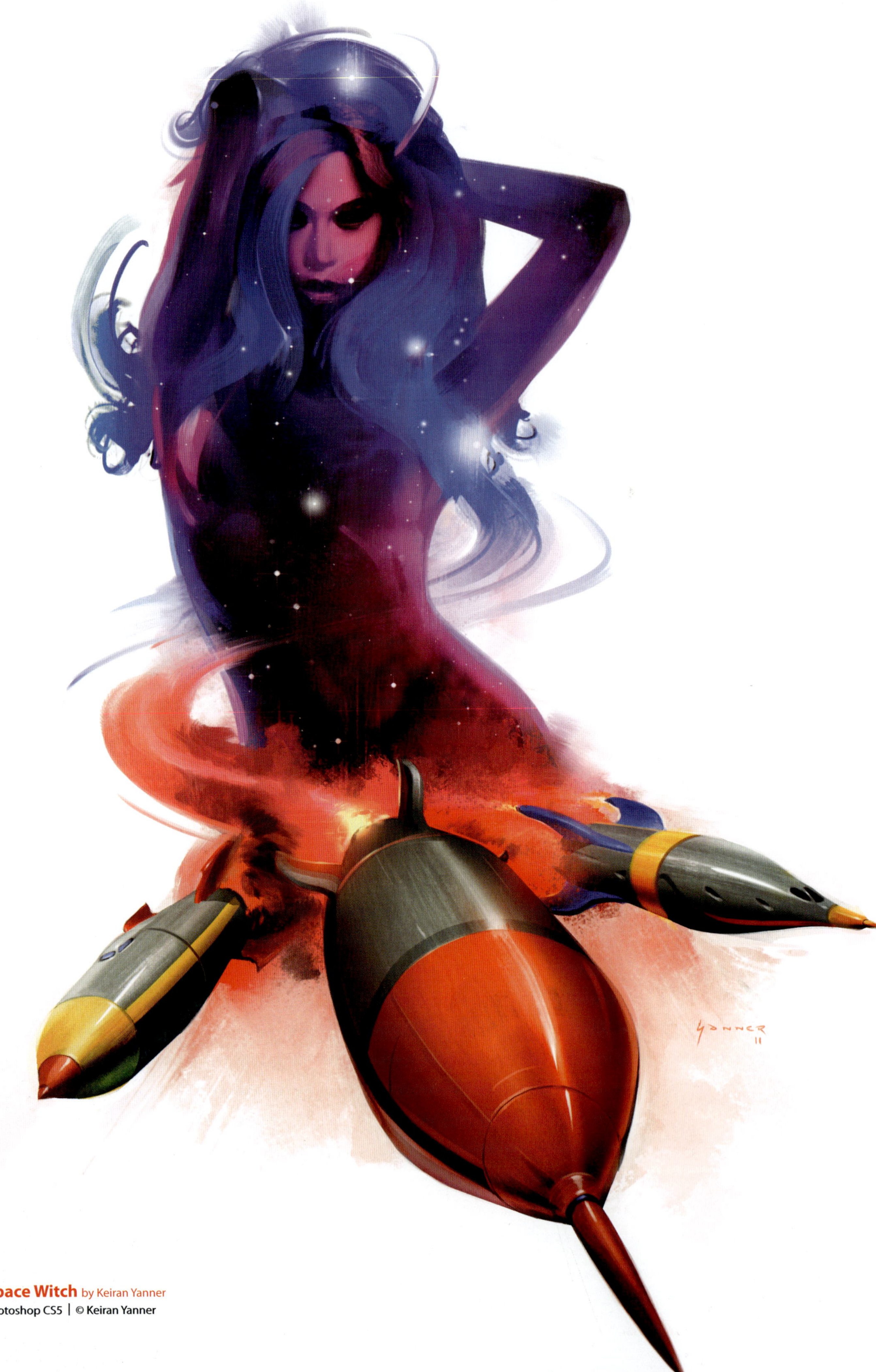

Space Witch by Keiran Yanner
Photoshop CS5 | © Keiran Yanner

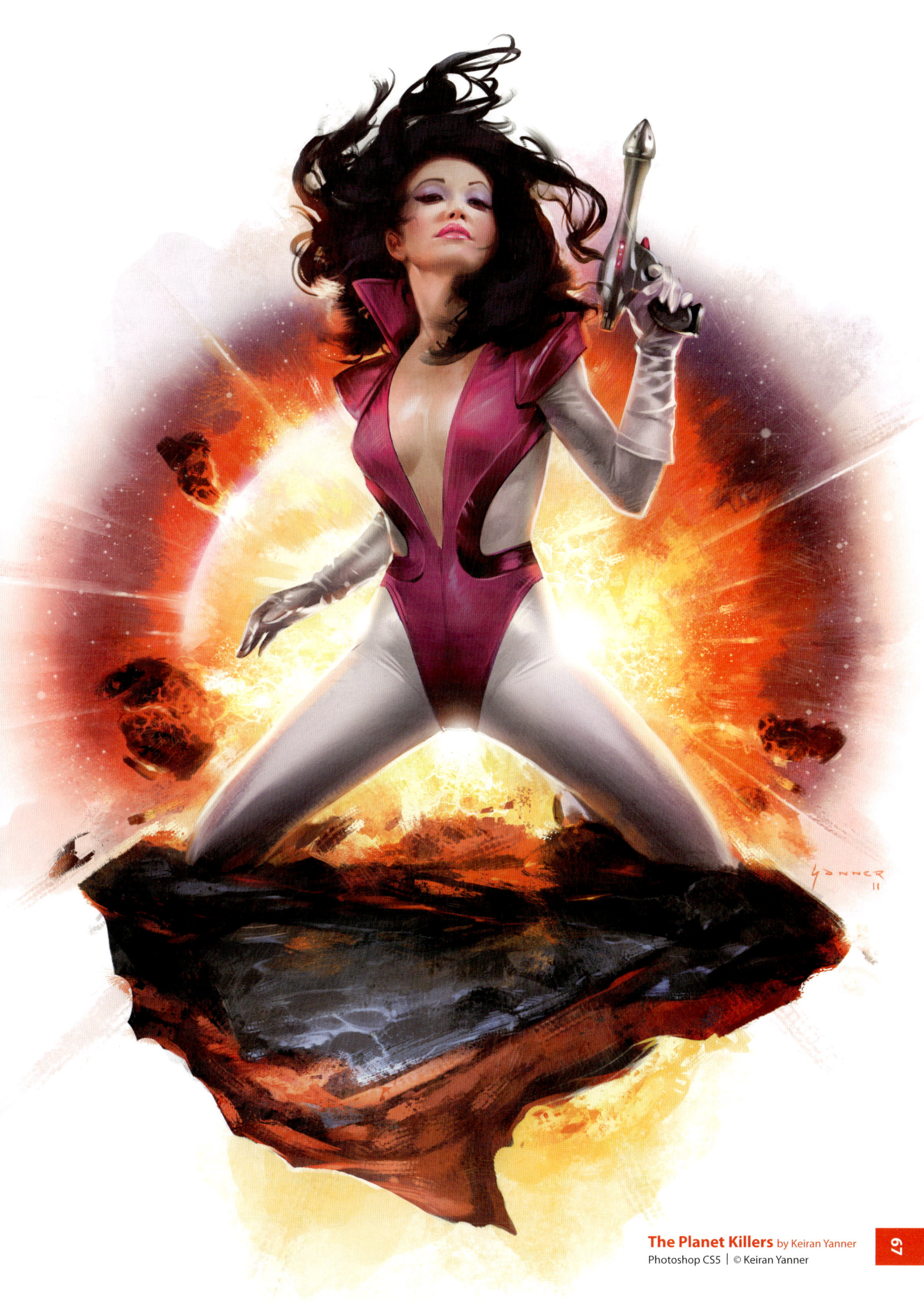

The Planet Killers by Keiran Yanner
Photoshop CS5 | © Keiran Yanner

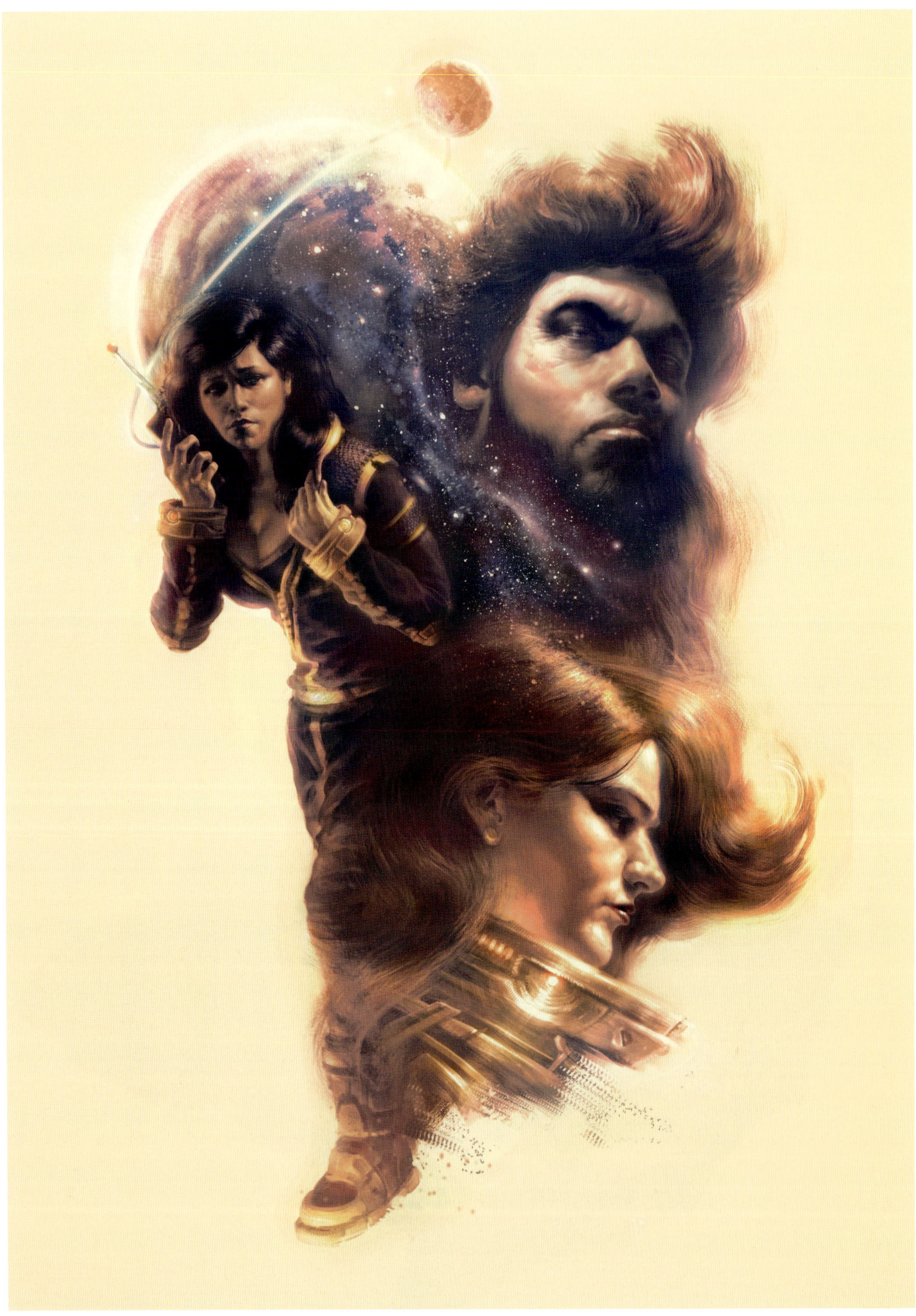

Lies of Convenience by Irvin Rodriguez
Photoshop CS5 | © Irvin Rodriguez

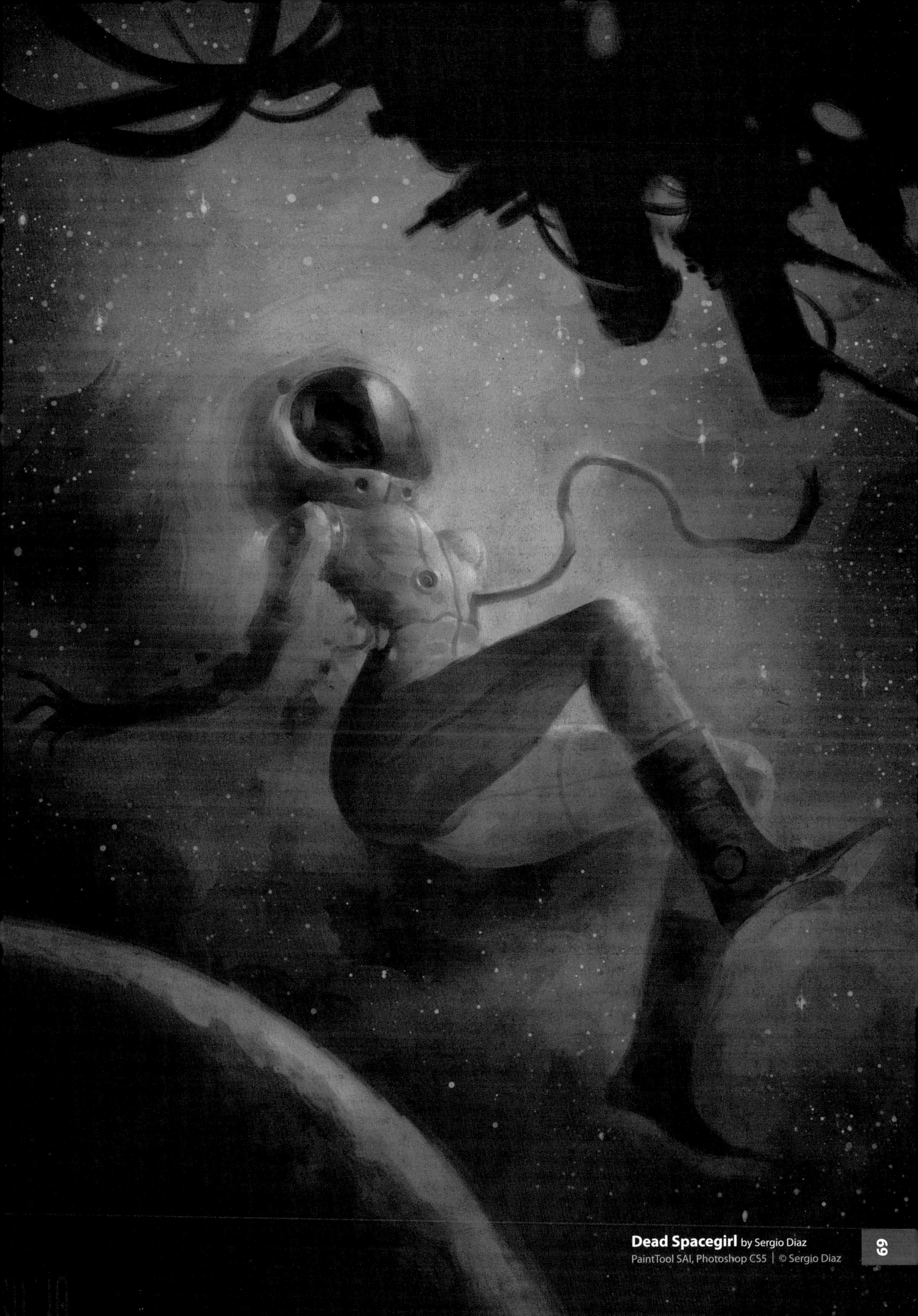

Dead Spacegirl by Sergio Diaz
PaintTool SAI, Photoshop CS5 |

1

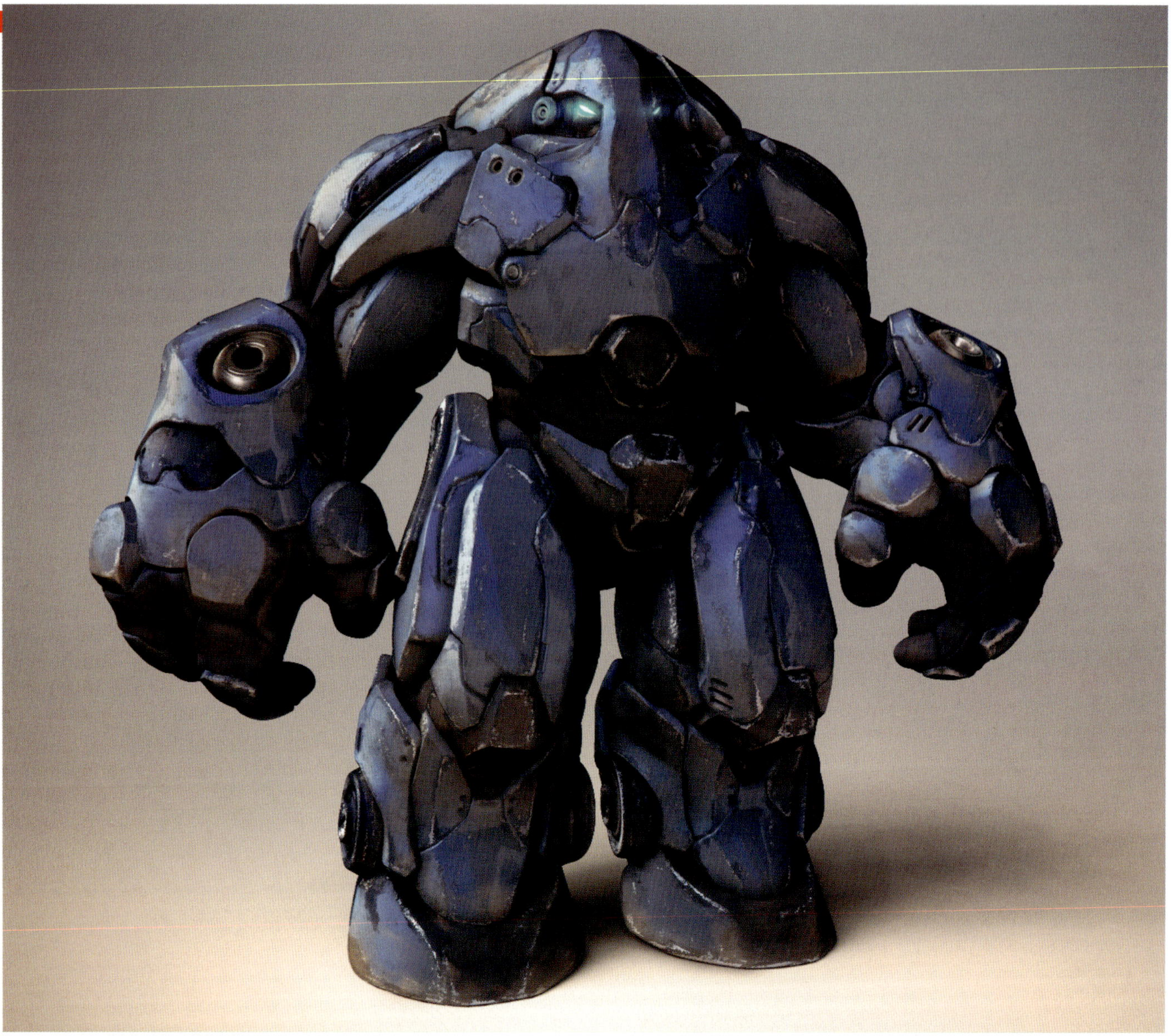

2

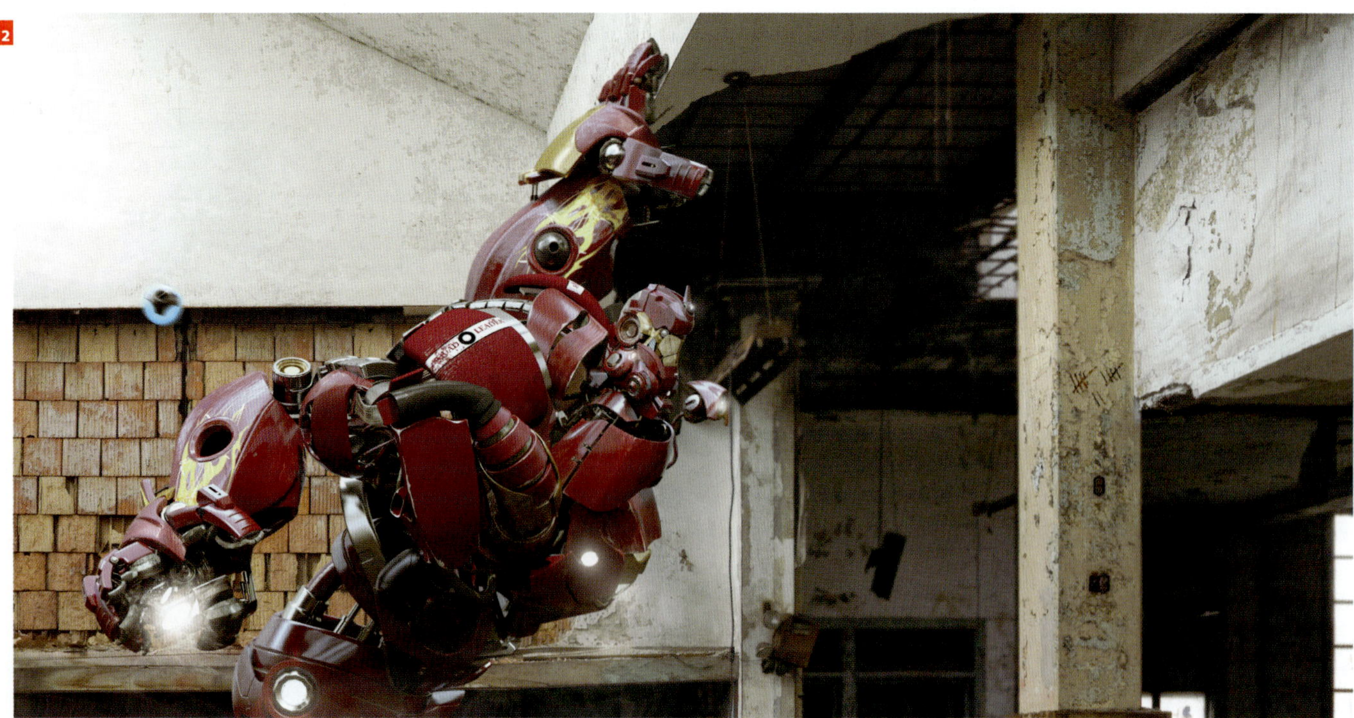

Pix-beta by Mike Jensen [1]
ZBrush 4R2 | © Mike Jensen

The Hunt by Tarik Ali [2]
3ds Max 2009, V-Ray 1.5 | © Tarik Ali

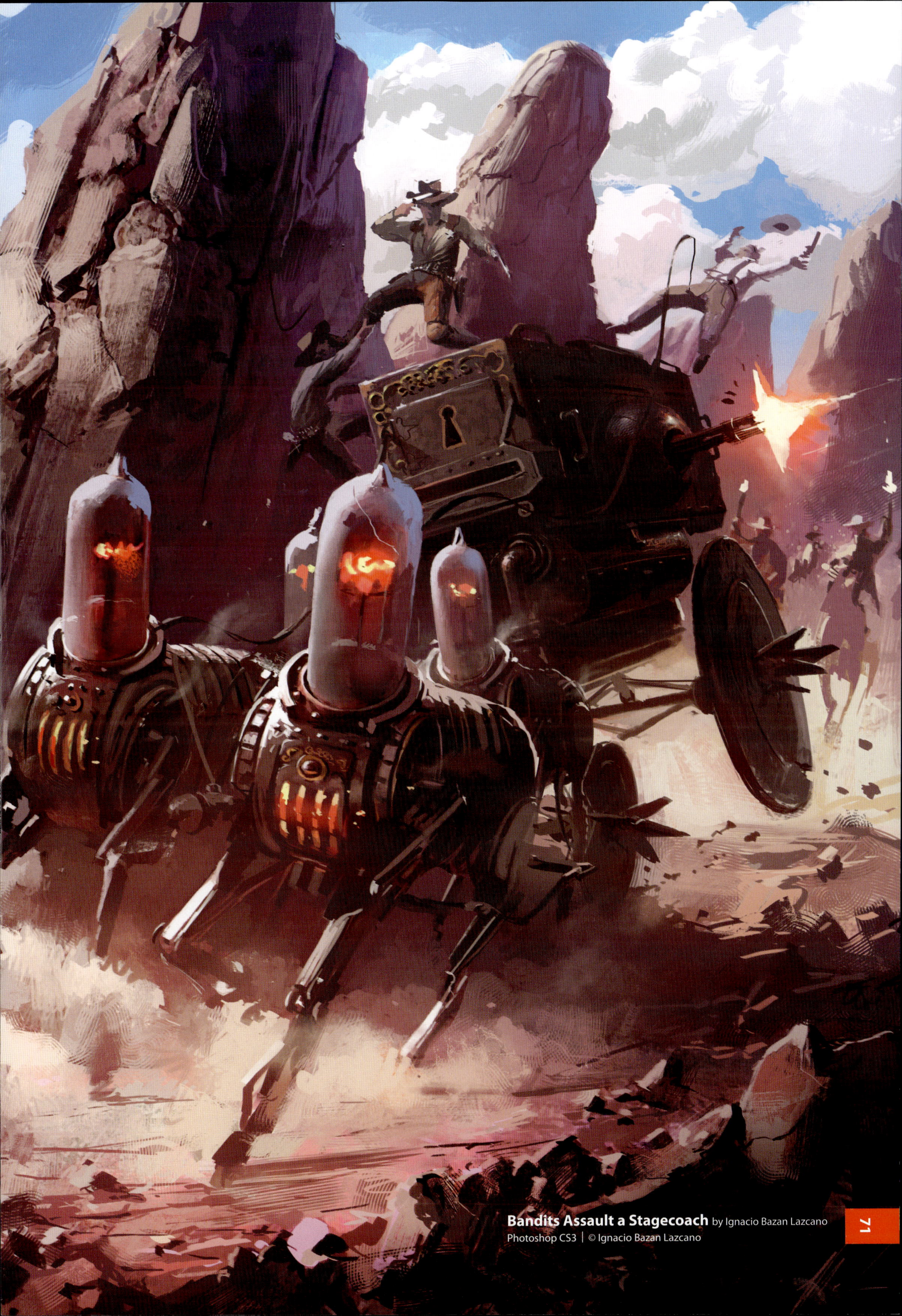

Bandits Assault a Stagecoach by Ignacio Bazan Lazcano
Photoshop CS3 | © Ignacio Bazan Lazcano

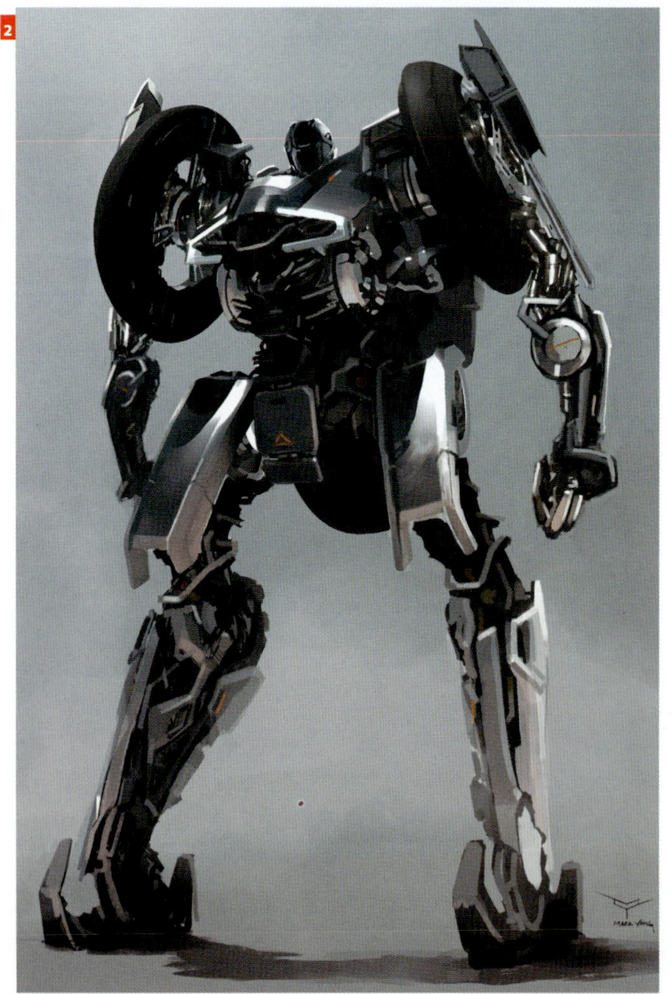

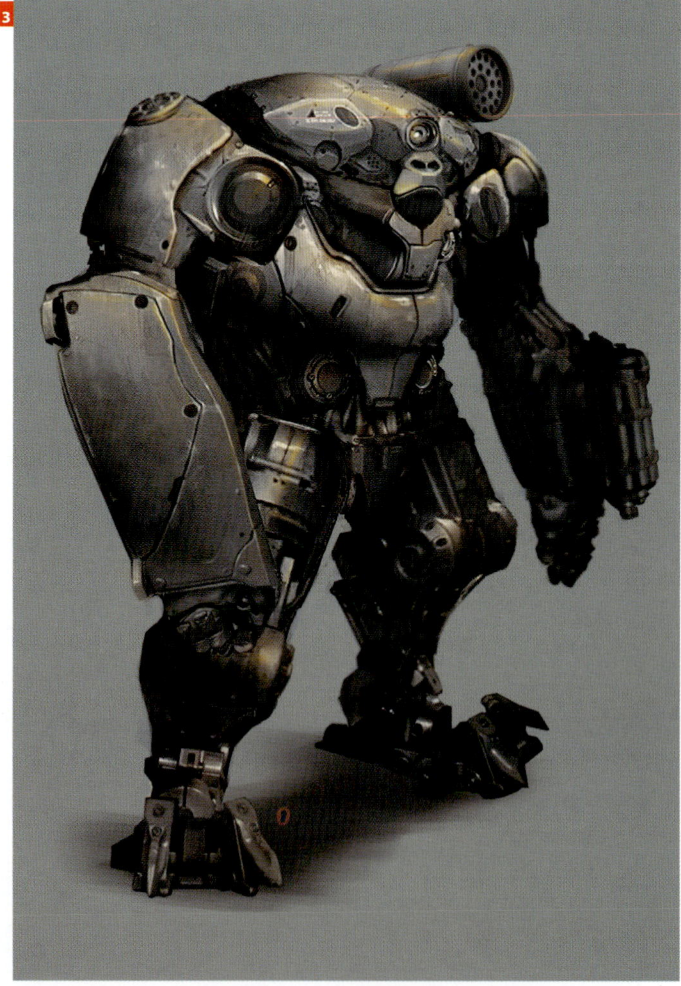

Illuminate My Soul by Facundo Diaz [1]
Photoshop CS3 | © Facundo Diaz

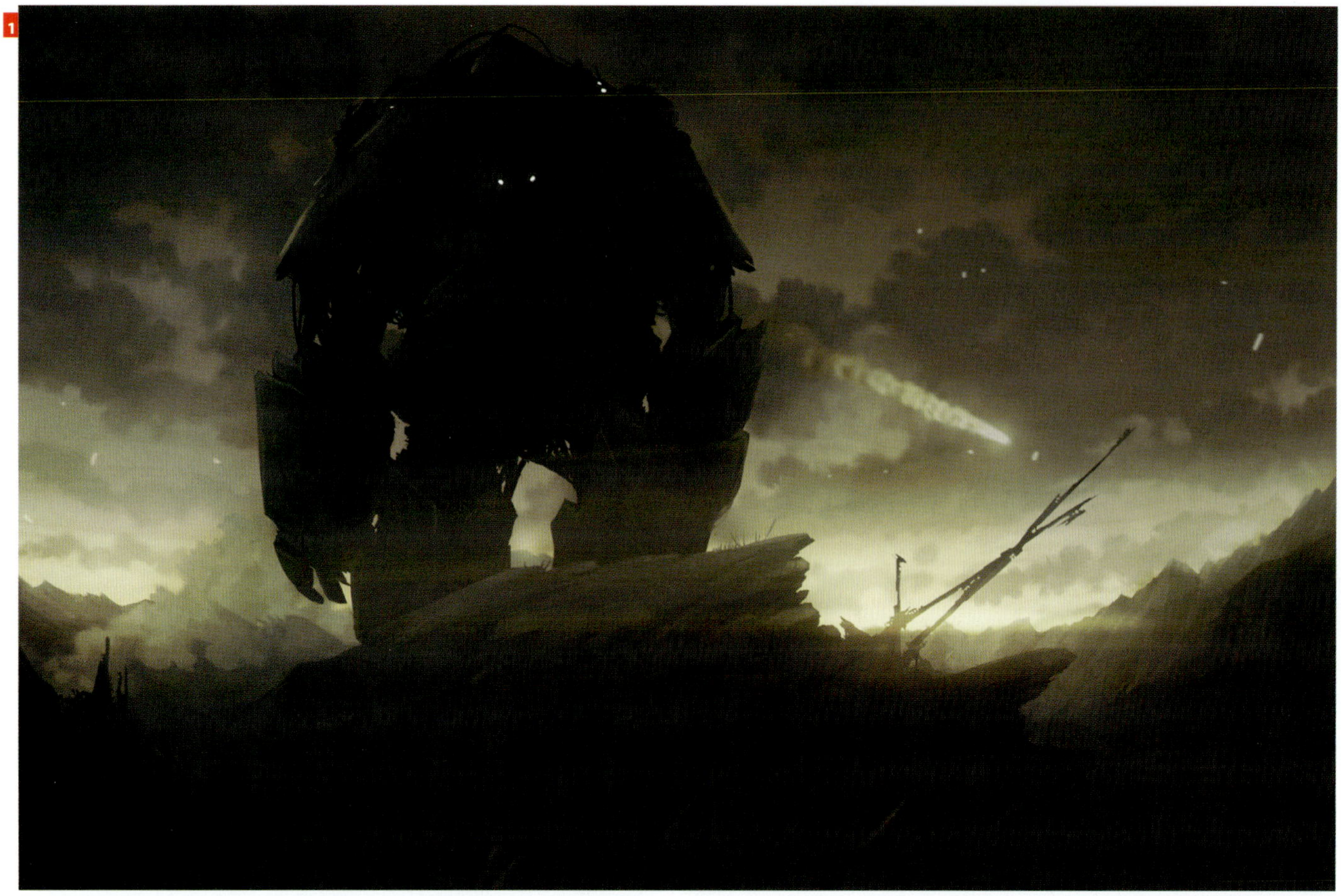

Annihilator Motorsuit Mode by Mark Yang [2]
Photoshop CS6, modo 501 | © Mark Yang

Roboape by Justin Adams [1]
Photoshop CS5 | © Zdonk Entertainment 2012

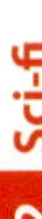

4

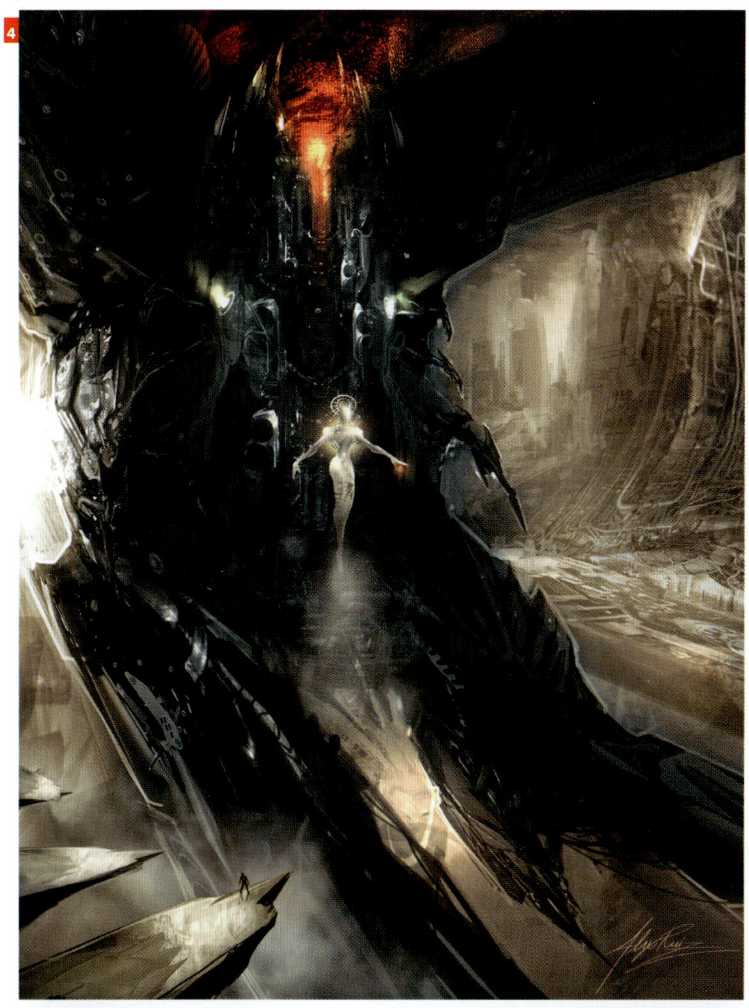

5

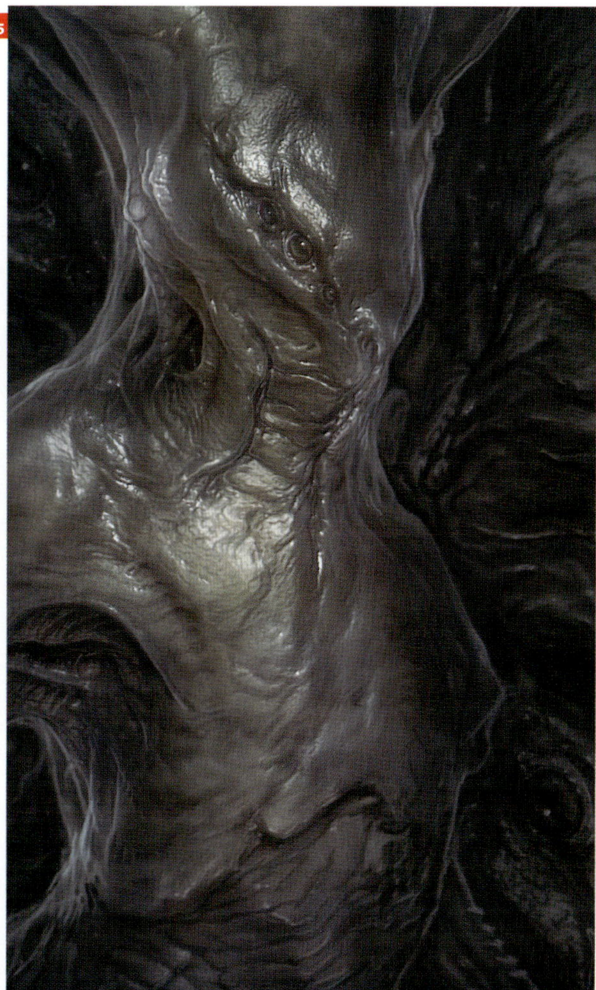

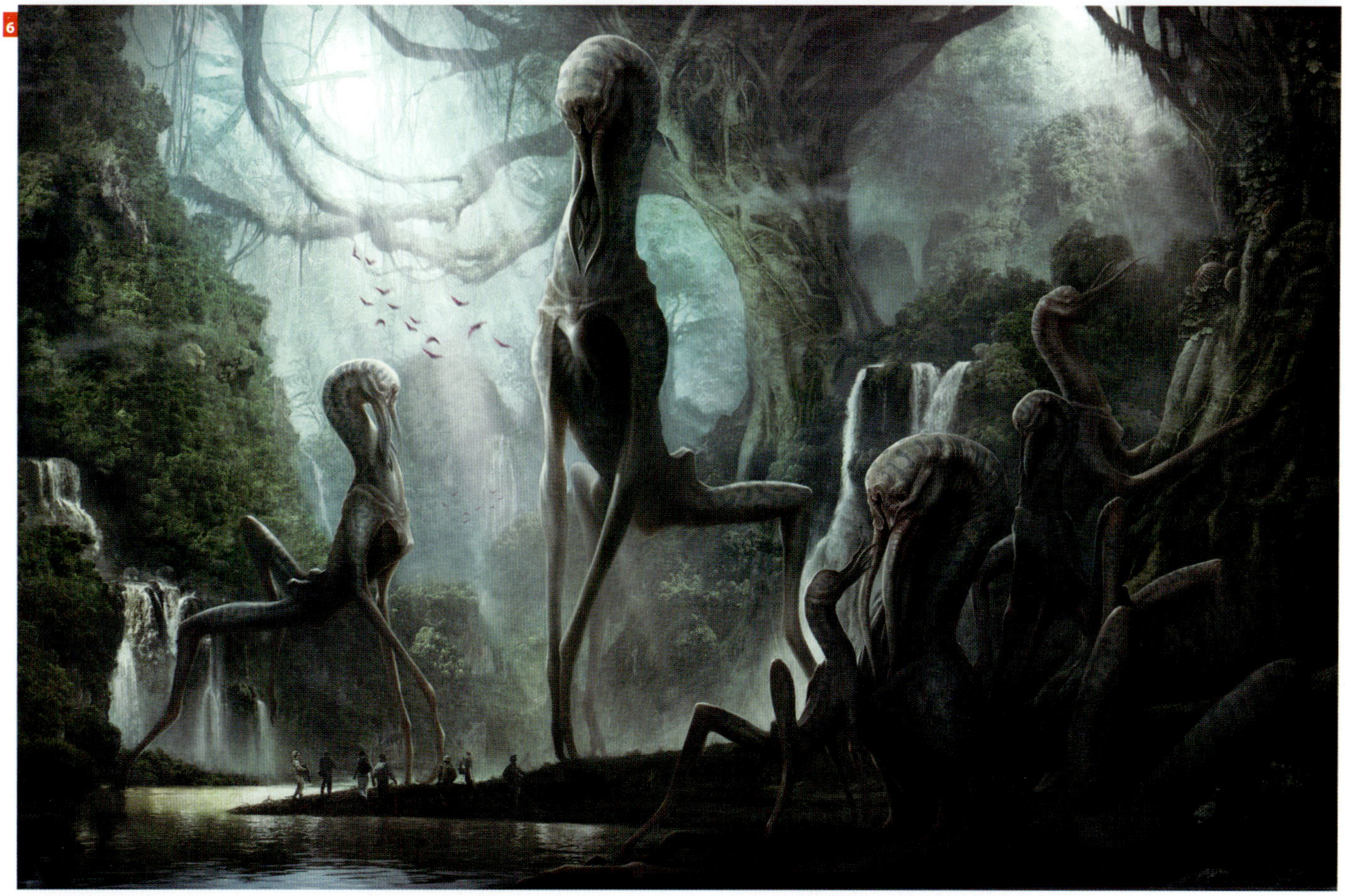

6

The Queen by Alex Ruiz [4]
Photoshop CS3 | © Alex Ruiz

Alien Forming by Andrew Baker [5]
ZBrush 4R2 | © Andrew Baker

New World by Ken Barthelmey [6]
Photoshop CS4 | © Ken Barthelmey

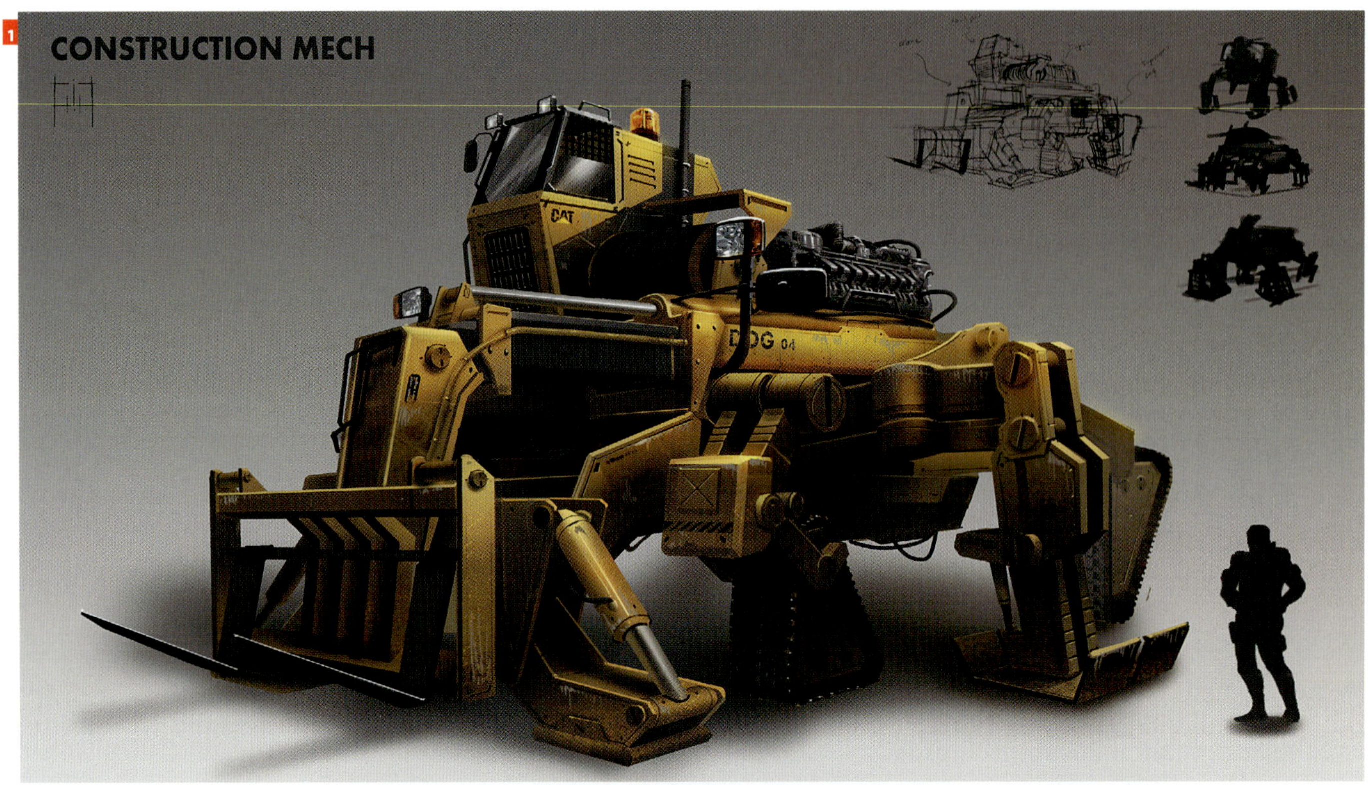

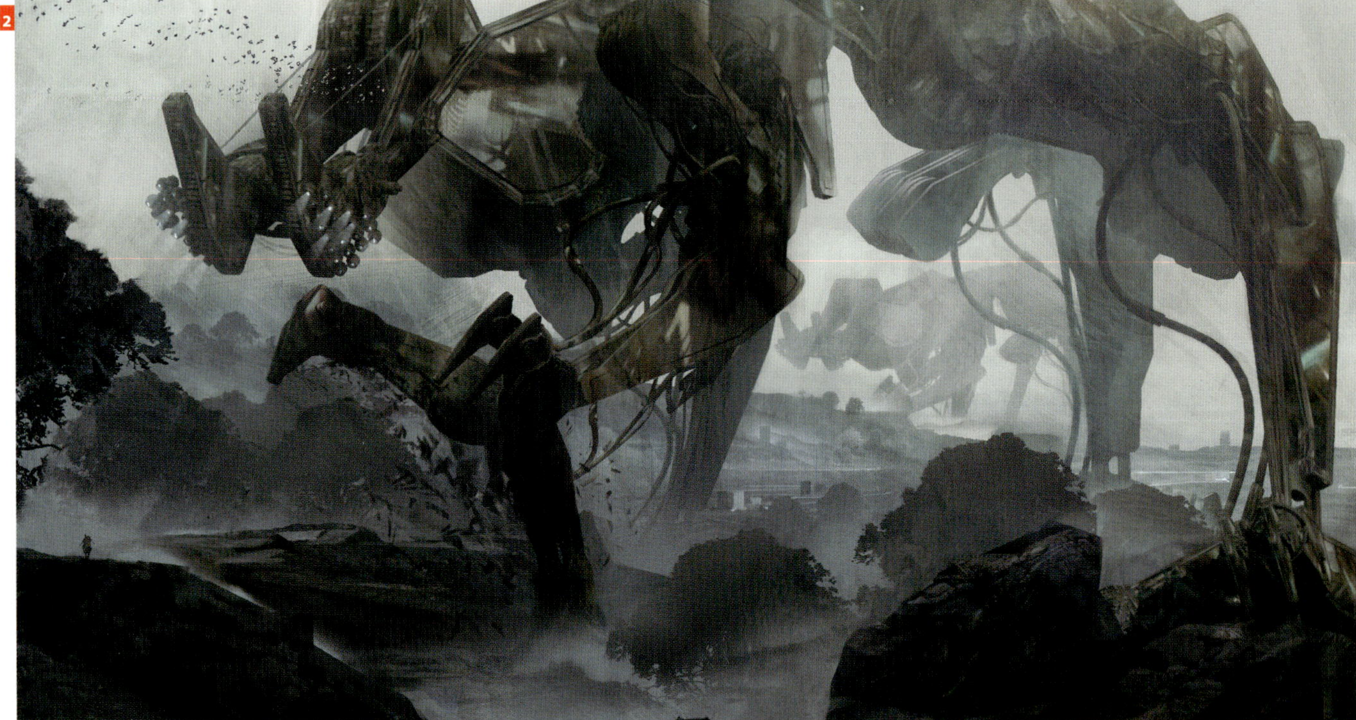

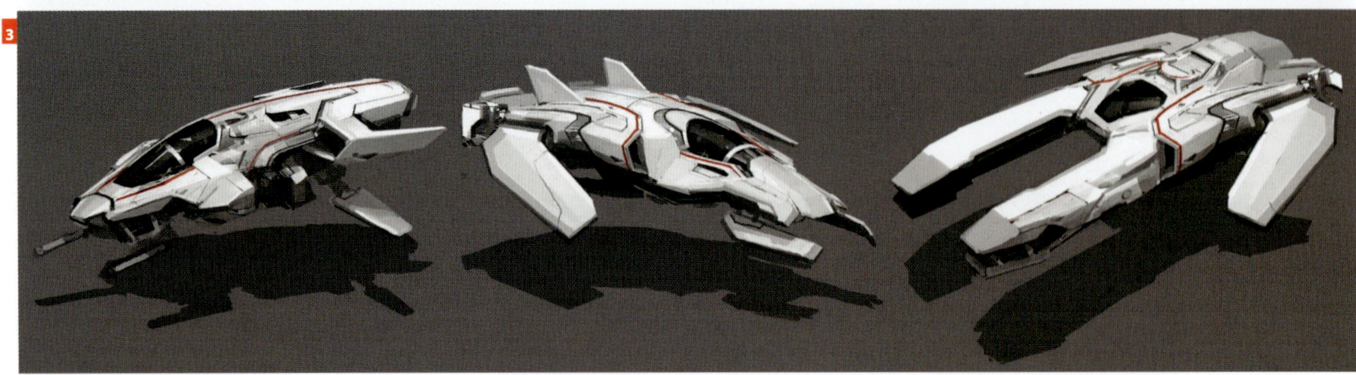

Construction Mech by Gia Nguyen Hoang [1]
Photoshop CS5 | © GiaNguyen

HH Mech by Levi Hopkins [2]
Photoshop CS5 | © Levi Hopkins

Sci-fi Ships by Sam Brown [3]
Photoshop CS2 | © Sam Brown

4

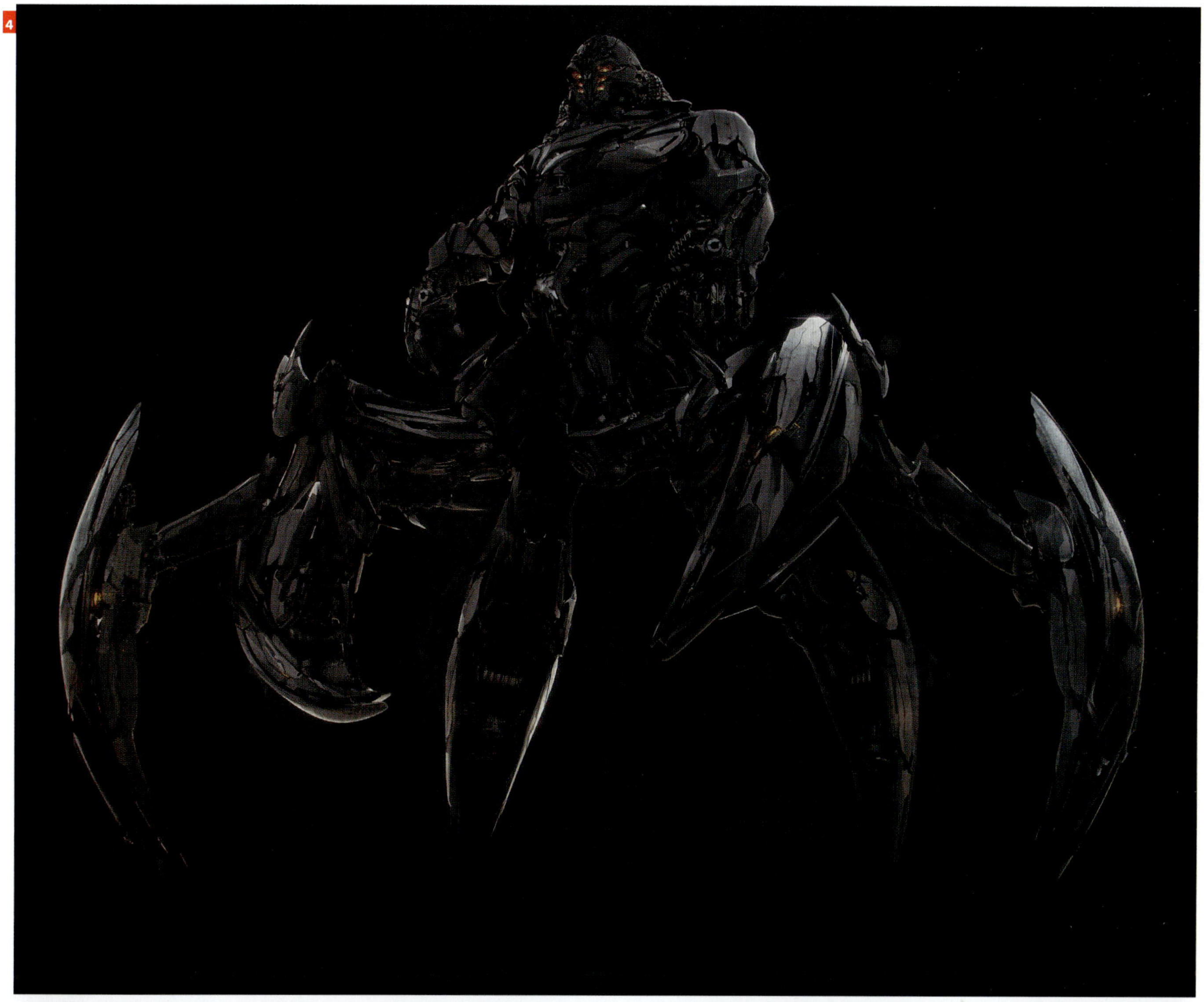

5

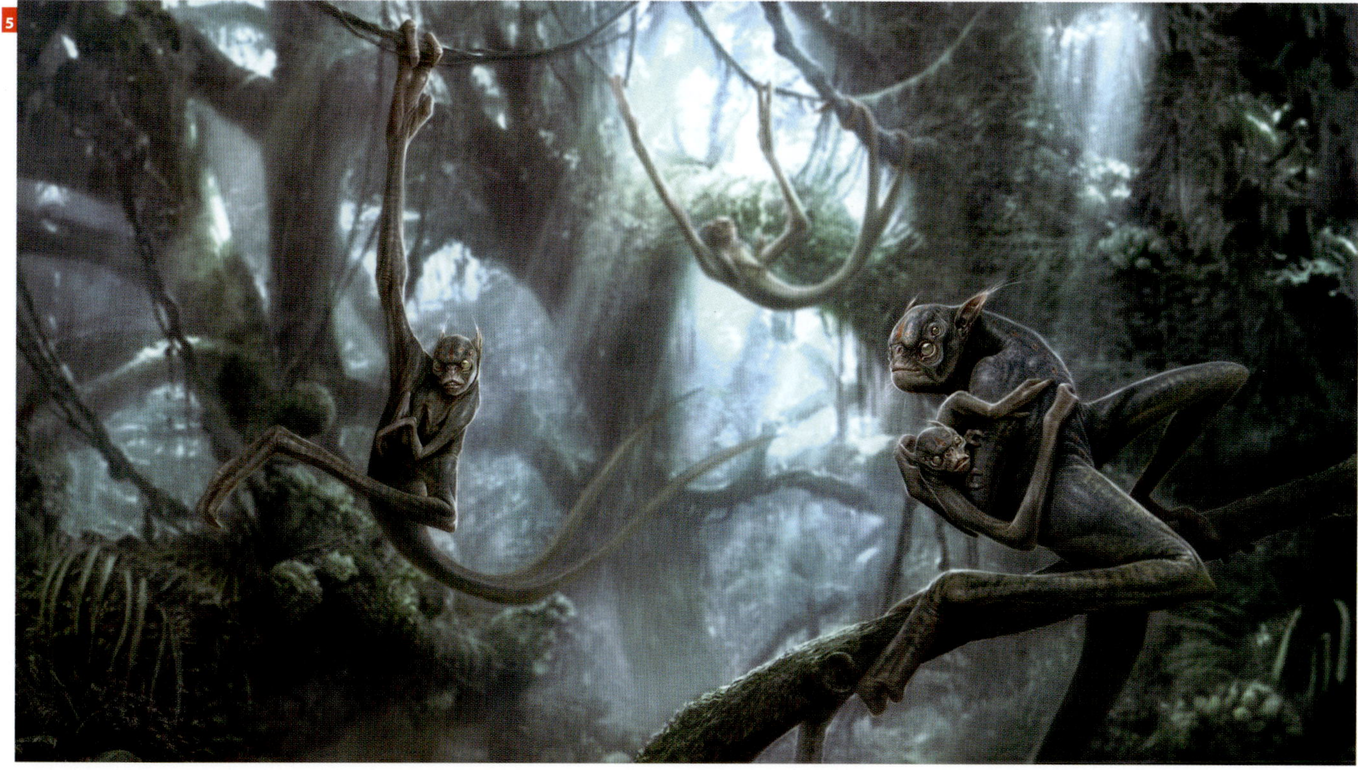

Warrior by Renato Nicolas Gonzalez Aguilante [4]
Photoshop CS5, ZBrush 4R3 | © Renato Nicolas Gonzalez Aguilante

Alien-Apes by Ken Barthelmey [5]
Photoshop CS4 | © Ken Barthelmey

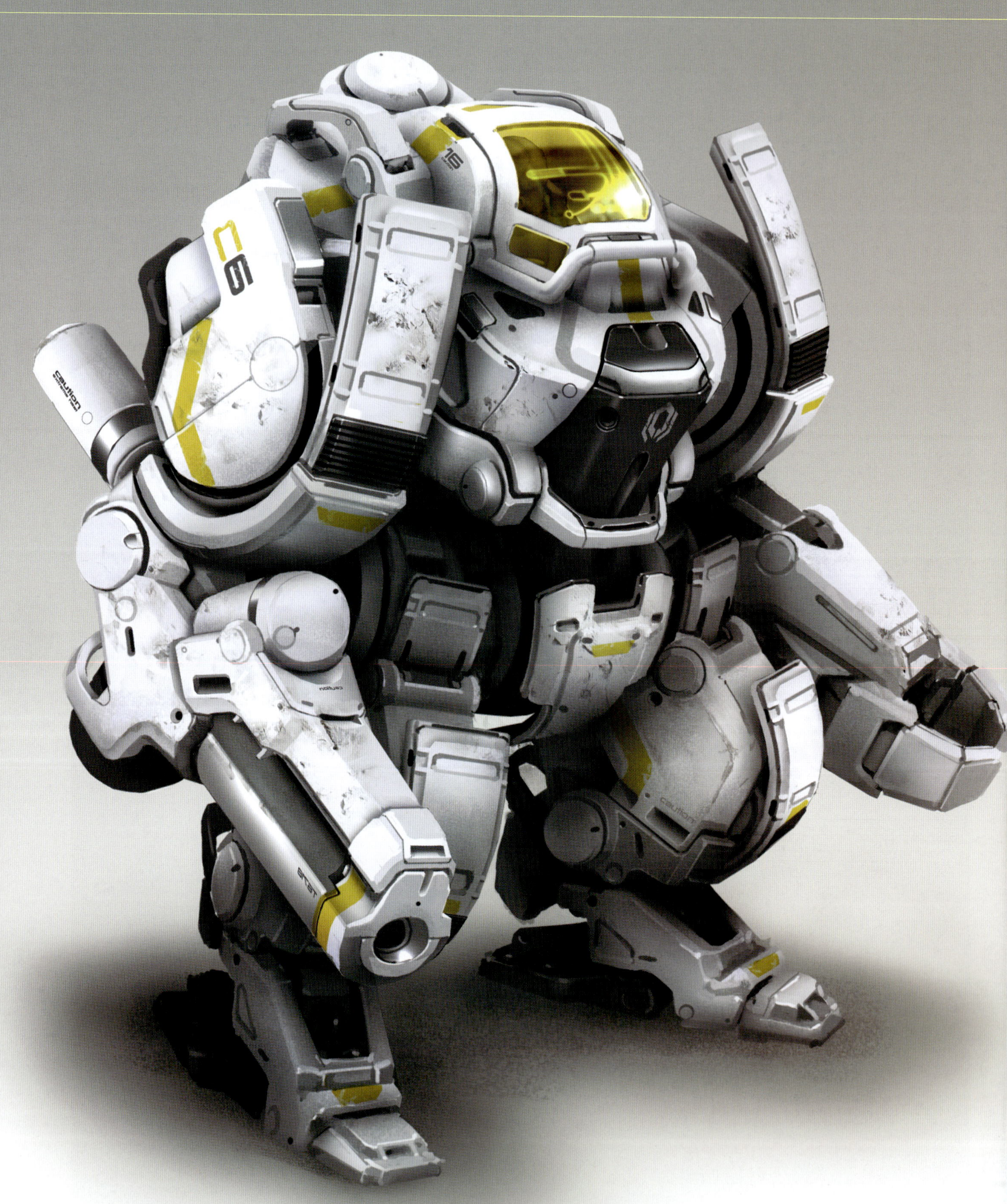

Cerberus Atlas by Brian Sum

Photoshop CS3 |

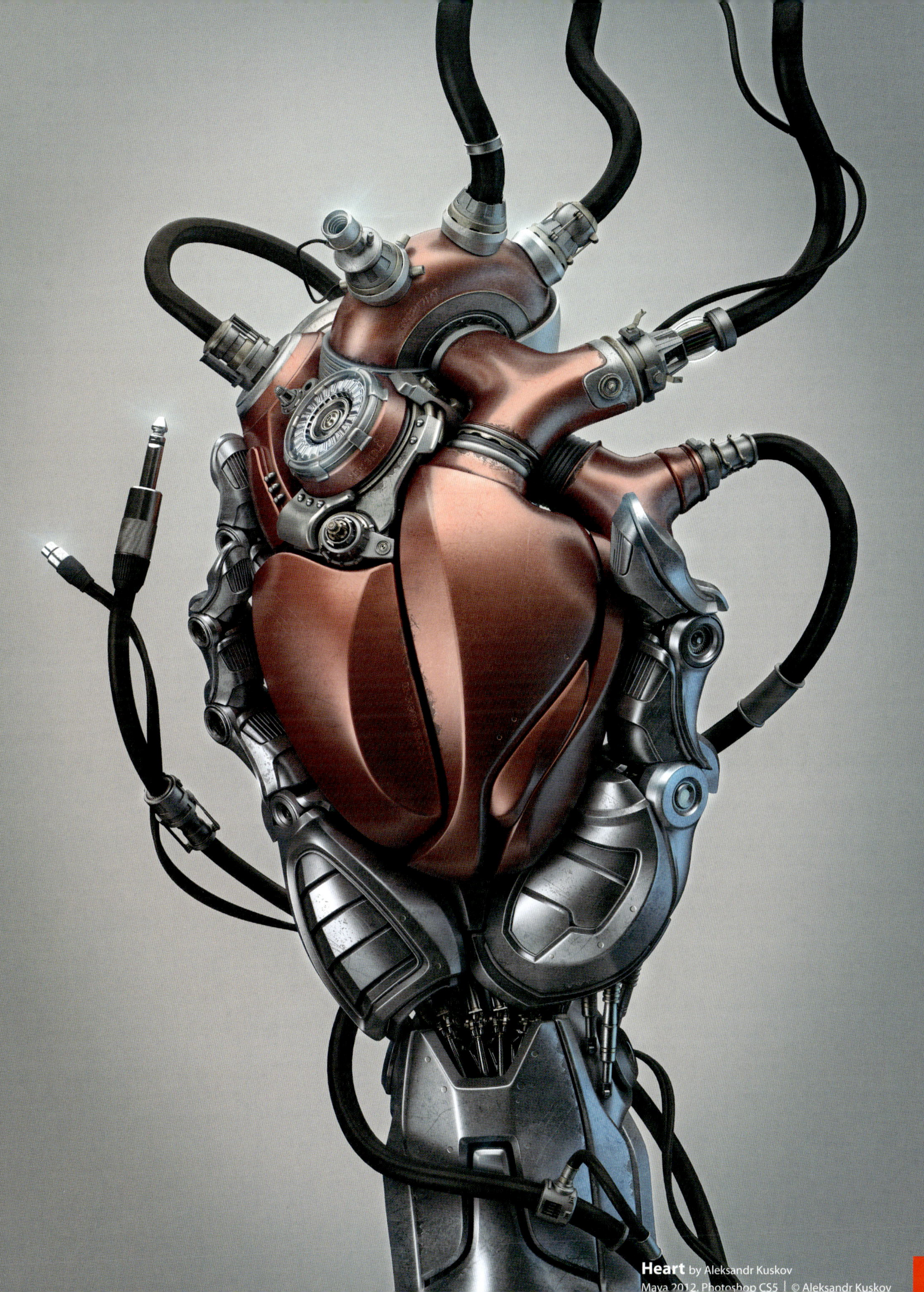

Heart by Aleksandr Kuskov
Maya 2012, Photoshop CS5 | © Aleksandr Kuskov

Artist **Index**

Aleksandr **Kuskov**
natikks@gmail.com
http://revision.ru/a/AleksCG

Alex **Ruiz**
conceptmonster@gmail.com
http://conceptmonster.net

Andrée **Wallin**
andree.wallin@gmail.com
http://andreewallin.com

Andrei **Pervukhin**
earfirst@gmail.com
http://pervandr.deviantart.com

Andrew **Baker**
androo.baker@gmail.com
http://andbakerdesigns.blogspot.co.uk

Andrzej **Sykut**
eltazaar@gmail.com
http://azazel.carbonmade.com

Arthur **Haas**
erahaas@yahoo.com
http://www.ahaas.nl

Brian **Sum**
brian@briansum.com
http://briansum.com

Dan **Ghiordanescu**
dghiordanescu@yahoo.com
http://www.danoid.com

Eldar **Zakirov**
eldar-sky-fi@inbox.ru
http://dartheldarious.deviantart.com

Fabio Barretta **Zungrone**
f_barretta@hotmail.com
http://www.fabiobarretta.com

Facundo **Diaz**
facu_kw@hotmail.com
http://www.fdportfolio.com.ar

François **Baranger**
francois@francois-baranger.com
http://www.francois-baranger.com

Gia Nguyen **Hoang**
gia.nguyenhoang@gmail.com
http://gia-nguyen.net

Ignacio Bazan **Lazcano**
i.bazanlazcano@gmail.com
http://neisbeis.deviantart.com

Ioan **Dumitrescu**
jononespo@yahoo.com
http://jonone.cghub.com

Irvin **Rodriguez**
hola@irvin-rodriguez.com
http://irvin-rodriguez.com

Jason **Stokes**
jason@futurepoly.com
http://www.futurepoly.com

Jon **McCoy**
jonmccoydesigns@gmail.com
http://www.jonmccoyart.com

Joon Hyung **Ahn**
joon5245@hotmail.com
http://cargocollective.com/joonahn

Justin **Adams**
variastudios@gmail.com
http://variastudios.carbonmade.com

Keiran **Yanner**
kieran.yanner@me.com
http://www.kieranyanner.com

Ken **Barthelmey**
info@theartofken.com
http://theartofken.com

Kentaro **Kanamoto**
korbox2@yahoo.com
http://www.kentarokanamoto.com

Ladrönn
ladronn@ladronn.com
http://www.ladronn.com

Lefevre **Vincent**
vptit_vinc@hotmail.com
http://ptitvinc.deviantart.com

Levi **Hopkins**
levimhopkins@hotmail.com
http://levihopkinsart.blogspot.co.uk

Marcin **Jakubowski**
marcin@balloontree.com
http://www.balloontree.com

Marek **Denko**
marek.denko@gmail.com
http://marekdenko.net

Mark **Yang**
markydesign@gmail.com
http://phantomworks.blogspot.co.uk

3DTotal **Publishing**
Correspondence: publishing@3dtotal.com

Website: http://www.3dtotalpublishing.com

First published in the United Kingdom, 2012, by 3DTotal Publishing.

Softcover ISBN: 978-0-9568171-4-3

Printing & Binding: Everbest Printing (China)
http://www.everbest.com

Design and Layout: Christopher Perrins

If you need to contact us, the details are:
publishing@3dtotal.com

Maxim **Revin**
maxrevin@mail.ru
http://maximrevin.blogspot.co.uk

Mike **Jensen**
mikered@gmail.com
http://mikejensen.daportfolio.com

Neil **Maccormack**
neil@bearfootfilms.com
http://www.bearfootfilms.com

Ray **Jin**
307754406@qq.com
http://blog.sina.com.cn/dumpling8679

Renato **Gonzalez**
pehato@hotmail.com
http://pehato.cgsociety.org/gallery

Rudolf **Herczog**
rudy@rochr.com
http://www.rochr.com

Sam **Brown**
sambrown36@gmail.com
http://sambrown36.blogspot.com

Sergio **Diaz**
diaz.sergio@live.com
http://www.sergiodiaz.com.ar

Simon **Weaner**
simonweaner@gmail.com
http://www.simonweaner.daportfolio.com

Tarik **Ali**
tarik3d@googlemail.com
http://www.tarik-ali.com

Tarik **Keskin**
tarikkeskin89@gmail.com
http://siamon89.deviantart.com

Theo **Prins**
theo.w.prins@gmail.com
http://www.theoprins.com

Tuomas **Korpi**
tuomas.korpi@gmail.com
http://www.tuomaskorpi.com

Victor **Mosquera**
victorconcept@yahoo.com
http://www.victormosquera.com

Viktor **Titov**
work@grafitart.ru
http://grafitart.com

Vukasin **Bagic**
vbagilla@gmail.com
http://vbagi.deviantart.com

Xavier **Etchepare**
xavier.etchepare@gmail.com
http://xetchepare.cgsociety.org/gallery

The Art of Daarken
Elysium

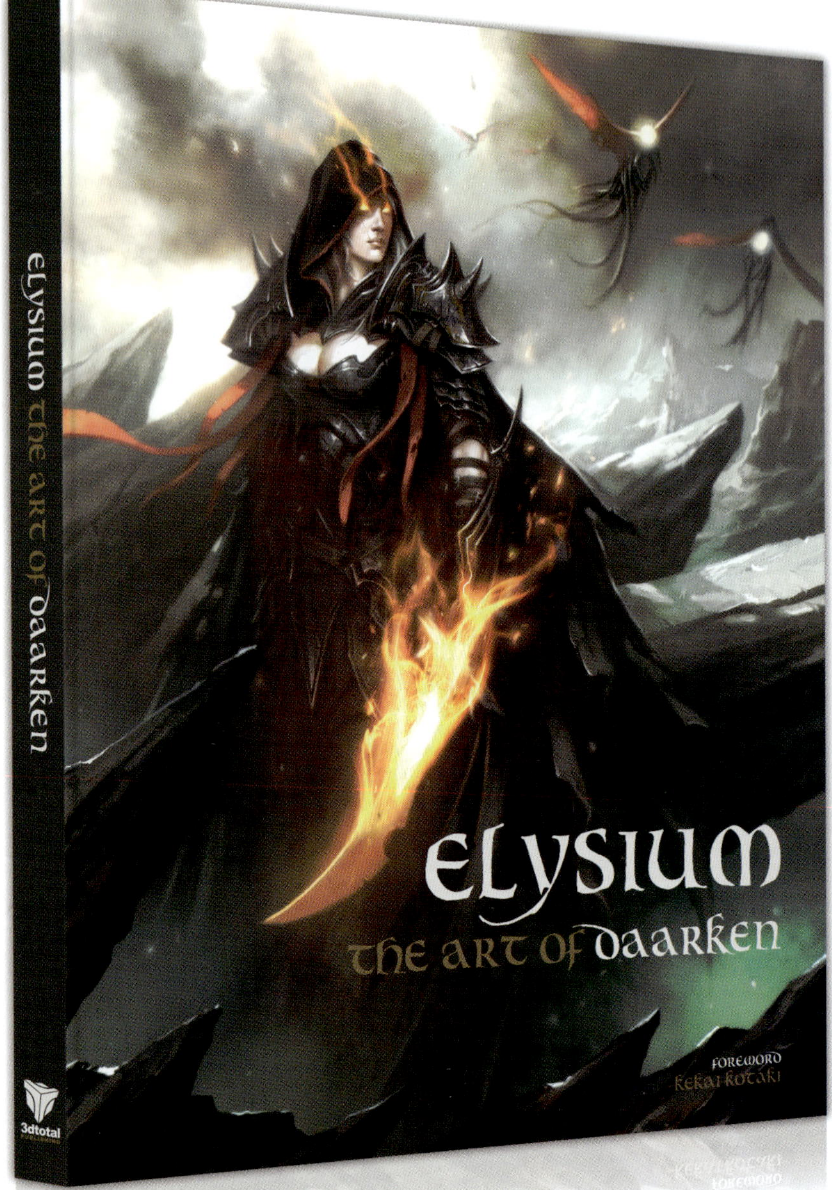

"Daarken's art is always awesome and his style has always stood out to me as totally his own; I could spot it anywhere. Not only that, but you can say the name Daarken and any artist will know exactly who you're talking about. That's very powerful in this industry and I've always admired that."
Dave Rapoza | Illustrator
http://daverapoza.blogspot.co.uk

Take a trip through Daarken's mind as you travel from epic fantasy to contemporary beauty in *Elysium – The Art of Daarken*, the culmination of the past four years of this freelance artist's work in the gaming industry.

This exciting journey begins with a tour through a selection of Daarken's personal illustrations and private commissions, ranging from CD covers to charity art, accompanied by his thoughts regarding the illustration and concept art industry. This is followed by an exclusive look at previously unseen pieces for world-famous franchises such as *Magic: The Gathering* (Wizards of the Coast) and *World of Warcraft* (Blizzard), before culminating in an in-depth tutorial covering how Daarken created the cover illustration in Photoshop.

If you are a fan of fantasy and sci-fi art, then *Elysium – The Art of Daarken* will suit your every need and leave you longing to see more work by this talented artist.

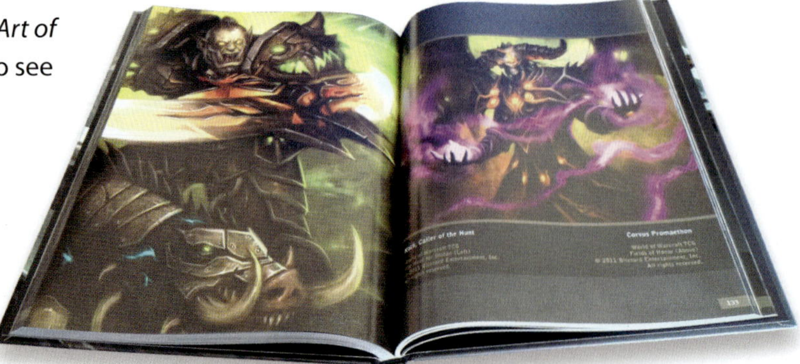

22 x 28 cm I 200 pages
ISBN: 978-0-9568171-3-6